"THEIR BOND, AS WELL AS THE REALITY OF CONFLICT IN VIETNAM, IS RECOUNTED SO SIMPLY AND SO ARTLESSLY THAT IT HAS AN ENORMOUS EMOTIONAL IMPACT. . . . FEW BOOKS ON VIETNAM, OR ON WAR ITSELF, ARE SO EVOCATIVE IN HUMAN TERMS. IT IS *THE RED BADGE OF COURAGE* AGAIN." —*Chicago Tribune*

MY FATHER, MY SON
Admiral Elmo Zumwalt, Jr.
and Lieutenant Elmo Zumwalt III
with John Pekkanen

"IT IS THE WORDS OF BOTH FATHER AND SON THAT GIVE THE STORY ITS POWER. . . . IT IS A TESTAMENT TO WHAT FAMILIES . . . CAN SOMETIMES ACCOMPLISH."
—*The Wall Street Journal*

"WE FEEL AS IF WE HAVE OPENED A FAMILY PHOTO ALBUM AND CAUGHT PEOPLE JUST AS THEY ARE, OR AS THEY WANT TO BE SEEN, NOT FOR THE PUBLIC BUT FOR EACH OTHER." —*Los Angeles Times Book Review*

"HIGHLY MOVING . . . SKILLFUL AND ENGAGING . . . A SOLID, WORTHY ADDITION TO THE GROWING RETROSPECTIVE ON OUR VIETNAM EXPERIENCE."
—*Boston Herald*

"PROVIDES SOME FRESH OBSERVATIONS ON THE ENTIRE VIETNAM EXPERIENCE." —*The Denver Post*

"THEY, PERHAPS MORE THAN ANY OTHER SINGLE AMERICAN FAMILY, ARE A LIVING, STRUGGLING MONUMENT TO THE VIETNAM ERA IN THIS COUNTRY."
—*The Washington Post Book World*

P9-CAL-102

ALSO BY ADMIRAL ELMO ZUMWALT, JR.:

On Watch

My Father, My Son

★

ADMIRAL
ELMO ZUMWALT, JR.

and

LIEUTENANT
ELMO ZUMWALT, III

with

John Pekkanen

A DELL BOOK

Published by
Dell Publishing Co., Inc.
1 Dag Hammarskjold Plaza
New York, New York 10017

Dell ® TM 681510, Dell Publishing Co., Inc.

ISBN: 0-440-15973-3

Reprinted by arrangement with Macmillan Publishing Company

Printed in the United States of America

November 1987

10 9 8 7 6 5 4 3 2 1

KRI

CONTENTS

ACKNOWLEDGMENTS

FROM ELMO R. ZUMWALT III:

I was able to tell this story because of the help and support from a number of people. They were always there when I needed them, and are why I have made it to this point.

Dr. Francis M. Counselman, my late father-in-law, taught me many things, especially never to take heated debate too seriously. I also want to single out Jim and Betty Caldwell, my second parents, who have helped me in every way possible for as long as I can remember. Others who understood what we went through and stood by us are: Robert and Sandy Quinn; Whiting and Denise Shuford; Bob Barrett; Kitty Ostrom; Betty McDonald; Donald and Kathryn McCoy; Lynda Miller; Michael Coppola, M.D.; Walter Anderson; Dona Weakley; Lynn Pekkanen; Butch Barton; Lucy and Kelly Ray; Melissa Mendoza; Jennifer Morrell; Sister Cele Gorman; the McCoy, Weaver, Wiggins, Cleveland, and Raper law firm; and the therapists who helped Russell at Children's Orthopedic Hospital in Seattle, Washington.

Finally, I want to thank the outstanding and caring medical people who constantly battled for me: Drs. Doug Henley, Paul Bunn, John Nanfro, Bimal Ghosh, Donnall Thomas, Rainer Storb, Fred Appelbaum, Ann Williams, Steve Petersdorf; and nurses Maria Poblet, Becky Puffenbarger, Sherrie Shiota, Julie McDonald, Diane Doles, Andrea York, Chris Zenner, Rick Taber, and Dee Johnson.

FROM ADMIRAL ELMO R. ZUMWALT, JR.:

We received tremendous support in a host of ways from many friends, some of whom we had not met until they stepped forward to help. Included among them are those acknowledged by my son and co-author, Elmo. In addition, I wish to single out:

The members of my immediate family who among them saw to it that Elmo never took his chemotherapy alone; Rear Admiral Bill Narva for his medical support; Rose Narva and Deborah Szekely for granting Elmo and Kathy interludes of improved quality of life during our travail; Rear Admiral Bill Thompson for easing my grief and paving the way for the Seattle interlude; Lenny Seliger for her love and administrative support to all the Zumwalts during three difficult years; Bob and Sara Bateman, whose friendship and caring attention smoothed our path during our stay in Seattle; Dr. Bob LaGarde of the Washington State Education Department, whose professional judgment established superb special education for my grandson Russell; the law firm of Ferguson and Burdell, whose partners and staff made it possible for me to carry on my work in Seattle; and finally, Dawn Stuchel, who, despite the loss of her husband from cancer, went to the aid of others and was a constant source of support for the Zumwalts in Seattle.

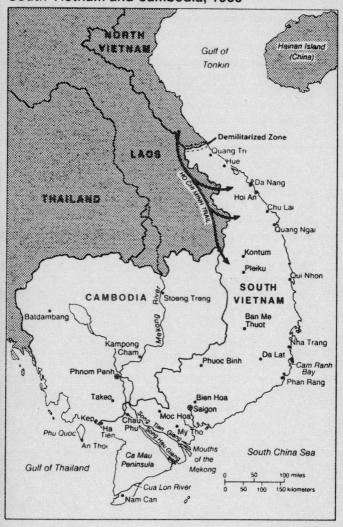

South Vietnam and Cambodia, 1968

PROLOGUE

April 1985. It is almost ten years to the day that Saigon fell, ending a war, but the chapter on its casualties has not been finished.

Elmo Zumwalt III leans forward in his chair as the bright afternoon sun sends its warm rays through the windows of his home. He begins to tell the story of a childhood friend's illness, but his voice catches. He pauses for a moment and tries to continue but he cannot.

His father, Admiral Elmo Zumwalt, Jr., moves his hand to his son's knee and gently squeezes it.

"That memory is still painful for Elmo," he says.

The Admiral picks up his son's story in mid-sentence and completes it.

They always know when the other is in trouble, and they have always been there to help.

When Elmo was younger, he fought in the war in Vietnam. He commanded a swift boat that patrolled the rivers in South Vietnam where the dense, green jungle hid snipers who preyed on the American crews. This jungle was systematically stripped bare by the Agent Orange mists sprayed from American airplanes.

Elmo is now thirty-eight and a lawyer in Fayetteville, North Carolina, and he has two forms of cancer. His eight-year-old son, Elmo Russell Zumwalt IV, whom they call Russell, is plagued by a severe learning disability.

Elmo believes his exposure to Agent Orange is responsible for the cancers and Russell's brain dysfunction. Many other Vietnam veterans and their children suffer similar fates and have come to the same conclusion.

Admiral Zumwalt, whose friends call him Bud, was the commander of the American in-country naval forces in South Vietnam. He was the one who ordered the Agent Orange defoliation to protect his son Elmo and every other man who fought under him in the river war. Bud is a proud and honest man and he accepts responsibility for those orders and their consequences.

Every war exacts a price, and now three generations of Zumwalts are paying an especially heavy one. Linked by more than just blood and name, they are also bound by a deep and abiding father-and-son love. Now more than at any other time in their lives, they are helping each other.

What you are about to read is the story of these two men. It is told in their own words and, at times, with the help of their family, those who served with them in Vietnam, and the people who know and love them.

JOHN PEKKANEN
Bethesda, Maryland

GROWING UP

ONE

──────── ★ ────────

JOHN PEKKANEN:

This is the story of an extraordinary American family named Zumwalt. Four generations of the male members are named Elmo, and I have the pleasure and privilege of knowing three. I have not known the Zumwalts long, but I have grown very close to them. They are a family of honor, candor, humor, and great humanity. These qualities are combined with a tireless and devoted love for one another.

This portion of the family history begins in a small California farming town called Tulare, in the San Joaquin Valley. The first Elmo Zumwalt and his wife Frances were both doctors and raised four children, Saralee, Elmo Junior, Bruce Craig, and Jim.

"After the birth of Bruce Craig," Elmo Junior recalls, "Mom wanted to be at home more so she moved her pediatric practice from the office she shared with Dad into our home to spend more time with us. She was a pretty woman with dark, curly hair and had come from very hard times. When she was a small baby in Vermont both of her French Canadian parents, who were also doctors, died in a smallpox epidemic. She was later adopted by a family that moved to Los Angeles, where Mom grew up. They encouraged her to become a doctor, apparently to follow in the tradition of her parents. A cheerful, outgoing woman, she encouraged me and my siblings to read good books and to aspire. She and Dad had a loving relationship. Every night Dad came home from work they held one another in a long, lingering embrace while we kids pounded on them to get their attention."

The Zumwalts were comfortable, but not wealthy in those days. "Dad never dunned a patient for a payment. During the Depression many people he attended could not pay," Elmo Junior remembers. "Sometimes instead of money they would give us a dozen eggs, or a chicken or maybe a basket of tomatoes from their garden. Dad was a gentle, joyful man who loved his work and his family. I can remember when I was only five or six he gave up golf because he was spending six days a week in his practice, and the seventh on the golf course, which didn't give him much time with the children. He loved golf, but he loved us more, and quit the game with no regrets—which I think shows you the kind of man he was."

The Zumwalts enjoyed an almost idyllic life together. Elmo Junior picked up the nickname Bud when little Saralee fumbled the pronunciation of "brother," instead coming up with "budda." Each child survived its own share of scrapes. Bud told me how close his family was.

"Sundays were always family days. My dad had been born in Tulare, where his father had grown up. After completing his education, my grandfather had moved to nearby Richmond, where he was a high school principal. He was one of eleven children, so there was family all around the Tulare area. One of my dad's aunts had six children and was the local matriarch. Her home became our gathering place. On almost every Sunday, the whole clan would meet there for dinner and games of baseball, touch football, and horseshoes. I always had the sense of being deeply loved and trusted by my parents."

However, in 1932, when Bud was twelve, the first of several tragedies befell the Zumwalts. One day his brother Bruce Craig just gave up on a football game and went home in tears. The next day he was in the hospital with what the doctors thought was polio, but when his condition worsened over the next few days, he was transferred to a hospital in Los Angeles. While Bruce Craig's parents were with him in Los Angeles, Bud and Jim stayed with a neighbor named Fred Hopkins. A few nights later the telephone rang.

"The next morning Fred took Jim and me hunting," Bud recalls, "and when we were out in the fields, he called me aside and said, 'Bud, I want you to know that your brother Bruce Craig died last night.' I began to cry and I can still remember being angry at my little brother Jim because he didn't cry. I shouted at him. 'Don't you understand? Bruce is dead. He's dead!' I was twelve years old at the time, but Jim was only seven and did not understand what that meant. It turned out that Bruce Craig had tubercular meningitis, which was incurable in those days. My parents always felt especially bad about losing him because even though they were doctors they could not do anything to prevent his death."

Bud's mother had wanted him to follow in the footsteps of his parents and become a doctor. But both his parents believed Bud needed discipline. Although he was on his high school debating team, played tackle on the football team, and was an Eagle Scout and his class valedictorian, he was kind of wild. He ran with the kids who broke windows on Halloween and played "touch" with their cars at eighty miles an hour. One time he even ended up in court for throwing eggs at a hitchhiker from a passing car and was sentenced to do his family's housework for two months.

Bud's father hoped Bud would attend West Point. He had been in the Army medical corps in World War I and valued his military service, and thought his son would also benefit from it.

A wealthy oilman named P. M. Longan came to Tulare and changed those plans a bit. He captivated Bud's imagination with his adventures of going to sea. Another young man was hooked by the lure of the Navy. In 1939, eighteen-year-old Bud Zumwalt was awarded Senator Hiram Johnson's appointment to Annapolis and the small-town boy was about to fulfill his father's dreams. The second tragedy to affect the Zumwalts almost put an end to that dream.

ADMIRAL:

Just a short time before Bruce Craig became ill in 1932, my mother had been scheduled to go to San Francisco to have a breast lump examined. But because of my brother's illness and death, six months passed before she returned to San Francisco and actually underwent the biopsy, which revealed cancer. She had a mastectomy, but she was never the same happy woman she had been before her cancer, and Bruce Craig's death.

In the spring of 1939, I was preparing to enter the Naval Academy, but it was a troubling time. After more than five years of quiescence, Mom's cancer had recurred a few months earlier. The X-ray treatments failed to stop the disease. I realized she would not live much longer. I have often thought since then that if she had had the surgery when she was originally scheduled, she might have been completely cured.

That June the day finally came for me to leave home and go East. I had my bags packed in the living room. Dad was getting ready to drive me over to Corcoran, where you had to catch the train for Annapolis. By then, Mom had to have full-time nursing care and when I went into her bedroom to say goodbye, the nurse left us. Dad and Jim were there. Mom kidded me about going off on my big adventure. She made me promise that I would not come back when she died, but she said it in a lighthearted way to avoid being emotional. I promised, and we bade each other a rather casual goodbye.

As I left the bedroom and walked out the front door, I knew that was not the way to leave. I knew I would never see her again, so I returned to her room. She was weeping openly. I told her that I didn't want to go, but she insisted that I must, that I would be letting her down if I stayed. I moved beside her bed and leaned down and put my arms around her, and we both cried. Three months later Dad called me in Annapolis to tell me Mom had died.

We were both shattered. I said I would be right home, but he told me I should not come back because there was nothing I could do. Besides, he said, I had promised Mom that I would stay at school. Reluctantly, I agreed to honor my promise to her and did not return to California. I have always felt thankful that I followed my instincts and went back to see my mother that second time as I left home. It taught me a lesson and has always made me aware that you never know when you will see someone you love for the last time.

Right after the Japanese had surrendered, I was just three years out of the Naval Academy and a twenty-four-year-old lieutenant acting as prize crew captain of a captured Japanese gunboat. We had found their minefield charts and were sailing up the Yangtze River to Shanghai to help clear the river of Japanese mines. I spent several weeks in Shanghai and one evening a former guerrilla fighter invited me and a number of other naval officers to a dinner party.

It was at that dinner party that I met Mouza Coutelais-du-Rouche, the niece of the hostess. Mouza's father was a French national, as was Mouza, and her mother was a White Russian. Shanghai had a sizable Russian population at the time because many Russians who had originally fled to Manchuria after the 1917 revolution later emigrated there when the Japanese invaded Manchuria.

Mouza's parents were among those who had fled to Manchuria, and she was born there in 1922. Her father, who had lost a fortune in Siberia, ran an ice cream parlor in the city of Harbin. Mouza's mother was diagnosed as having cancer in 1940 and she and her husband went to Rockefeller Hospital in Peking for surgery while Mouza remained in Harbin with her grandmother. Her mother's treatment was not successful, so Mouza took her mother to Shanghai to be cared for by her mother's sister, while Mouza's father returned to Harbin. After her mother died the following year, the Japanese would not permit Mouza to return to Harbin. Nor would they allow her father to visit Shanghai.

Mouza remained in Shanghai with her aunt and uncle, and never saw her father again. Much later we learned that when the Russians took control of Manchuria at war's end they had cut off her father's means of support and he had become malnourished and succumbed to pneumonia in 1946.

When I first saw Mouza at that dinner party in Shanghai, my heart literally stopped. She was a tall, beautiful, poised young woman with a radiant smile that filled the room. I was transfixed by her. She understood English and spoke it with what I thought was a delightful Russian accent, and I talked her into teaching me Russian. Over the next several days we spent a lot of time together, and I knew I had fallen in love.

On October 22, 1945, five weeks after we had first met, Mouza and I were married in a Russian Orthodox ceremony. Members of the *Robinson* crew provided an honor guard, and as part of the ceremony, we each lit one candle. Mouza's burned out first, which in Russian Orthodox tradition meant that she would die before me. She told me she had hoped that would happen, because she did not want to outlive me.

I was scheduled to leave with my ship the morning after our wedding, so I bade Mouza goodbye at 4 AM. When I arrived on board the *Robinson,* my bags were packed and the executive officer, Lt. Commander "Tex" Winslow, told me that I had been transferred to the *Saufley,* the *Robinson*'s sister ship, which was due in port in one week. I was to be the *Saufley*'s new executive officer. I thought it was miraculous that the Navy had done something right. Usually, transfer orders don't arrive until after you have already set sail. As it turned out, the *Saufley* did not leave Shanghai for the United States until early December, so Mouza and I had several weeks together before we were forced to part. She was pregnant with Elmo when the *Saufley* finally left port.

Elmo was born in Tulare on July 30, 1946. I was with the *Zellars* in Newport, Rhode Island, that day. Mouza had been able to leave Shanghai a few months earlier after I had walked into the State Department and convinced them that the newly passed "GI Bride" law—which permitted servicemen's wives immediate entry into the United States—applied to my wife. She arrived in the States and joined me in Charleston, South Carolina, after travelling to Seattle by troop transport with a number of other service wives and being seasick the entire voyage. After four months she flew to Tulare so that my father could deliver Elmo.

When I arrived in Tulare nine days after Elmo was born, Dad showed me the birth certificate. It read:

> Born: Elmo Russell Zumwalt III
> Father: Elmo Russell Zumwalt, Jr.
> Attending Physician: Elmo Russell Zumwalt

Dad told me that Elmo had a heart murmur. He said in most cases these heart problems spontaneously go away, but Mouza and I were worried nonetheless. In every other respect, Elmo appeared to be a normal, healthy baby boy.

During the next two years, we moved twelve times up and down the East Coast, from Maine to Virginia, as I sailed with the *Zellars* as executive officer. We all grew weary of these moves, and I entertained thoughts of leaving the Navy.

I had not planned to make the Navy my career when I entered the Naval Academy in 1939. I was mostly looking for adventure and the free education that would help my parents out financially. I also believed that war loomed on the horizon, and I felt an obligation toward my country. Once in the Navy, though, my career went well, but Navy life was hard on my family. There was the constant moving as well as the terribly low military pay.

When Elmo was about six months old, I sailed down to Guantánamo Naval Base in Cuba for a shakedown cruise. When I returned home six weeks later, Elmo began screaming and crying the second he laid eyes on me. I was heartbroken that he'd forgotten me in so short a time, but I knew these long absences from home would be another fact of life for us.

I reached the point where I actively planned to leave the Navy, and had even been accepted to medical school. But my doubts about remaining with the Navy ended when I had the privilege of meeting General George C. Marshall and his wife at their summer home in Pinehurst, North Carolina. The general and I talked for several hours that day and I must say I was very pessimistic. Besides my personal difficulties with Navy life, I thought the military budget was being slashed far too much in light of the growing Russian threat and, to make matters worse, I told him I thought the public approved these military reductions.

General Marshall, whom I regard as one of the greatest Americans who ever served this country, had just retired from his post as Secretary of State. He listened patiently to the complaints of a young naval officer, and then spoke about the great qualities he found in the American people. He said this country had sprung to life when war had broken out, and had become incredibly productive in a very short time.

"Young man," he said, "don't ever sell the American people short. They have vast reserves of hidden strength ready to use when the crisis is clear." Then he peered at me over his glasses and said, "And when the time comes, your country will need dedicated career men like you." I never second-guessed myself about my choice of career again.

In February 1948, the Navy assigned me to teach NROTC at the University of North Carolina. It was one of the few times in my Navy life that I would be in one place on land for a long period of time.

We moved into Victory Village, a university-provided housing

area for married veterans. The small houses rented for $35 a
month.

What made Victory Village so special was the great feeling we
all had there. People were out of the service, happy to be alive, and
happy the war was over. There were a number of foreign brides
from Germany, Czechoslovakia, Spain, and France. This gave Victory Village a very cosmopolitan atmosphere. I have never been in
a place like it. It was Mouza's first opportunity to sink roots in this
country and to make friends. Living there helped stabilize our
family life. Also, the area in and around Chapel Hill is remarkably
beautiful and filled with rolling hills and lovely wooded areas.

Elmo was eighteen months old when we first moved there, so
he had already begun to walk and talk. We knew even at that age
that he was a very talkative little chap. He was also exceedingly
good-natured. We lived next door to a wonderful couple named
Jim and Caroline Caldwell. Caroline had had a daughter, Meredith, by her first marriage. Meredith was eleven years older than
Elmo and often babysat for him. Jim had served in the Burma
theater as an intelligence officer during the war, having interrupted his work on his Ph.D. in history. He was back at the
University of North Carolina to complete his doctorate, and he
also was a history instructor there.

Elmo was quite taken with both Jim and Caroline, but especially Caroline. He used to toddle over to their house where Caroline would read to him or just let him play. Elmo was also a very
big eater, and we didn't learn until much later that every Sunday
morning after breakfast at our house, he would walk over to the
Caldwells' to have another one. They always served waffles and
baked apples on Sunday and Elmo loved to eat them. It was the
beginning of a lasting friendship between our families, despite the
untimely death of Caroline from cancer in 1958. Jim, who became
a full professor of history at Carolina, later remarried and we were
all befriended by Betty, his new wife, a warm and gracious
woman.

On Thanksgiving Day 1948, our second son, Jimmy, was born.
We made it to the hospital just ten minutes before his birth. Elmo

was two and a half and seemed to accept Jimmy almost immediately, although as they grew older normal sibling rivalries developed. Our two daughters, Ann and Mouzetta, were born several years later.

After our stay in Chapel Hill, we moved to Charleston, South Carolina, in June of 1950. I had been promoted to lieutenant commander and was given my first command, a destroyer escort, the USS *Tillis*. Mouza and the boys moved back to Chapel Hill to be among friends during my absence.

One year later, the Korean war mobilization caused my transfer to the battleship *Wisconsin*, where I served as navigator. Leaving my family to go to sea was always painful. The worst time was the week before I left. I always had a sense of foreboding that something would happen and I would not be there when they needed me. I felt I could cope with anything as long as I was there with them. My foreboding became a reality for me this time. I received a telegram from the NROTC office in Chapel Hill saying that Elmo, who was then five, had been stricken with polio. Not unless you lived through the 1940s and '50s with children can you quite appreciate how terrifying polio was for every parent. I was horrified and deeply worried, and had no idea of the extent of the disease. I thought only in terms of permanent paralysis.

Communications in those days were not as advanced as they are now, and it was impossible for me to contact Mouza directly. I was desperately anxious to get back to Chapel Hill, but I thought there was very little prospect that I could.

But the captain of the *Wisconsin*, Captain Thomas Burrowes, was a devoted family man. He did not hesitate to give me emergency leave to be home with my family, even though he assumed great risk without his official navigator. I have never forgotten his act of humanity and kindness.

MOUZA ZUMWALT:

At about six in the morning Elmo came into my bedroom, and the only thing he said was, "Mommy, it hurts." Then he collapsed to the floor. He wasn't able to stand, and the first thing that went through my mind was polio. It was always in the news in those days. I knew they were treating polio victims at Duke University Hospital, which was about twelve miles away, so I just put Elmo into the car and rushed him there. I didn't even take Jimmy with us, since I was afraid he would be exposed to polio and get it too. I did not stop to think that he already had been with Elmo almost continuously. I drove to Duke as fast as I could and took Elmo directly to the hospital, but the doctors and nurses would not let me stay with him because it was a quarantined area.

I sat on a bench in the corridor, just outside the quarantined area. A couple sat across from me and did not say a word. They got up and moved next to me, one on either side. Then all of a sudden they put their arms around me. I didn't know what they were doing.

Just at that moment I heard Elmo scream. They were inserting a needle to remove spinal fluid for a test. This couple had brought in two of their children for the same test, one the day before and his brother that morning. They knew I was alone, and that I was going to hear Elmo scream when they inserted the needle. They wanted to comfort me when it happened.

I had to get word to Bud. Some people told me that the Navy would never let him off the ship, but I wanted him to know, so I had the NROTC send the telegram. I was surprised and relieved when Bud arrived the next day. By then the news about Elmo was a little more encouraging. The doctors told us that although there was paralysis in Elmo's neck muscles, they were not sure if it would be permanent. Within ten days, Elmo had improved greatly and was released from the hospital. He needed physical therapy for quite a while, but gradually all the strength came back to his neck muscles, and there have been no lingering effects from the polio.

Bud left to return to the *Wisconsin* when we were sure Elmo was going to be all right. It was always difficult for me and the boys when Bud was away. I think, even at an early age, his father's absences began to have an effect on Elmo. He had become very serious when he was still young. I think he felt he had a responsibility as a man of the house.

ADMIRAL:

In 1952 we moved to Newport, Rhode Island, again. I was in a one-year junior command and staff course at the Naval War College there.

With one exception, no matter where I was stationed, I always chose to live in the civilian community. Throughout my career, I had observed that the children of military people became inbred, and were often more sexually promiscuous than kids in civilian life. I also did not think they were motivated academically. Because these kids moved so often, they tended to cling to each other instead of befriending people from other backgrounds. I did not want my children to grow up in that kind of incestuous environment. I think, as a result, my children have never felt like military youngsters, even though I was a career military officer, and that's the way we wanted it.

Except for his bout with polio and having his tonsils removed when he was about two, Elmo had been in good health. When we moved to Newport, he was six and went into the first grade. This was his first extensive exposure to other children, and to the colder weather of the Northeast. He began having one bronchial attack after another. He was continually sick, and it was very upsetting to us. My father insisted, by telephone, that there must be some basic cause, so Mouza and I took him to the Navy doctors at the base and after a complete examination, including X rays, they told us that Elmo's lungs were clouded, and diagnosed him as having tuberculosis. We were heartbroken, and I called my dad to break the news. But he said, "Bud, I'll guarantee you he doesn't have tuberculosis. That child has been too well cared for and his diet is too well balanced. Get yourself a specialist and find out what's really the matter with him."

We made an appointment with a doctor at Children's Hospital in Boston, which then had and still has a reputation as being one of the best pediatric hospitals in the country. They diagnosed Elmo as having an atrial-septal defect in his heart. That meant that the septum, the wall that separates the left and right sides of the heart, had a hole in it so the oxygenated blood from his lungs mixed with the unoxygenated blood. This may have been the murmur Dad first heard at Elmo's birth. The other doctors had missed it. Remember, this was 1952 and heart surgery was still highly experimental and dangerous. The doctors told us Elmo was too young to be operated on at this time.

After we left Newport in 1953, I was assigned to the Navy Bureau of Personnel in Washington. We bought a house on a cul-de-sac in Annandale, Virginia, that on and off became our home for the next fifteen years. As much as any place, all of us think of it as home. In fact, our daughters were born while we were living in Annandale, Ann on December 26, 1953, and Mouzetta on March 30, 1958.

We started taking Elmo to the Johns Hopkins Hospital in Baltimore where the late Dr. Helen Taussig took him as a patient. Dr. Taussig was a nationally recognized pediatric heart specialist, and I was amazed at the way she diagnosed him. She was beginning to grow deaf, so instead of using her stethoscope, she placed her hands on Elmo's chest and by feeling his heartbeat was able to make the diagnosis. She later had it confirmed when a team of specialists inserted a long plastic tube into an artery in Elmo's arm. Using a fluoroscope to guide them, they pushed the tube up Elmo's arm and directly into his heart, a procedure called cardiac catheterization. This enabled the doctors to measure the blood-flow pressures inside Elmo's heart, and determine the severity and precise location of his defect.

Dr. Taussig and the other physicians told us that, without surgery, Elmo had a life expectancy of maybe twenty-three or twenty-four years. His heart was already about twice the normal size because of the tremendous overload this defect had put on it. While we jumped around for the next few years, moving to San Diego, then back to Washington, we knew eventually surgery would be needed, so we kept in contact with Dr. Taussig.

Elmo did well during his first years at school. In Annandale, Virginia, he adored his third grade teacher, Mrs. Dona Weakley, who was his first love. She is a beautiful, cheerful woman, and Elmo, and our entire family, have maintained close contact with her through the years. Jimmy and Ann also had her as a teacher, but she had left the school by the time Mouzetta began attending.

When Elmo went into the fifth grade, in Annandale, he ran into a terribly destructive teacher. Because of his health problems, Elmo was the smallest in his class, and for some reason this teacher put him next to the two biggest boys in the class, which made him look absolutely puny. One day we were called in for a meeting at which she told us that parents sometimes may not want to admit to a problem. Mouza and I asked her to be more specific and she told us that there was something wrong mentally with Elmo. She even used the word *moron,* and went on and on about how incapable he was of doing even the simplest schoolwork.

I knew Elmo well enough to realize that this simply was not true; in fact I had always thought of him as very bright. But this was very disturbing for us to hear. Since we had noticed Elmo appearing more subdued, I made an appointment with a psychologist at George Washington University, who tested Elmo. The results showed he possessed superior intelligence, and I brought those results back to this teacher, but she disregarded them. She continued to put Elmo down. To this day he has not gotten over it. Despite all his confidence and successes since then, he has always been terribly insecure about academics.

When Elmo was twelve, Dr. Taussig suggested that he begin to think about having heart surgery. She wanted it to be his decision as much as ours.

I remember vividly the ride home from Johns Hopkins back to Washington. Mouza, who normally went with us, had not come with us this time. Elmo rode in the front seat with me. He was in a very reflective mood. Going back as long as I can remember,

Elmo seemed to have an uncanny ability to look at himself objectively. I suspect it may have come from the fact that at an early age he knew he had a heart problem.

He asked about the pluses and minuses, and how long he would live if he had the operation, and how long he would live if the doctors did not operate, and then he asked me, "Will I be able to go to the Naval Academy if I have it done?"

I said, "Yes, I think the chances are that you will."

And he replied, "Okay, I'll have it done."

That was it; there was never any more discussion. Dr. Frank Spencer, who was a protégé of Dr. Alfred Blalock—one of the pioneers in cardiac surgery—would perform the operation.

A week before his scheduled surgery, Elmo suffered a ruptured appendix, causing a delay of several months for the operation. During that time, we asked a minister, the Reverend Hubert Beckwith, whether we should talk to Elmo about the possibility of death. The minister advised us to answer all Elmo's questions truthfully, but not to volunteer information. Elmo never brought up the question of death, and Mouza and I assumed that he was not thinking of it.

But the day of surgery, we were in his hospital room and he was already groggy from a sedative. Suddenly, he reared up and said, "Mommy and Daddy, I want you to be sure to put daisies on my grave." And then he lay back down and went to sleep again.

Elmo *had* known all along what his risks were, but he had not wanted to worry us, and that was just his last-minute way of letting us know that he was aware of the danger he faced. We were both in tears as he was wheeled out.

The operation took more than two hours and the wait was agonizing. This was 1958, and the doctors were not using a heart-lung machine, so they cooled Elmo with ice, and then had only nine minutes in which to get inside his heart and make the repair. The risks, we knew, were fairly high.

There were four couples in the waiting area, all with children having heart surgery. A doctor walked in and spoke to one couple. They began to cry, picked up their belongings, and left without saying a word. Another couple spoke to the doctor, and they were very tense because the results were uncertain. The third couple received good news. We had watched the doctor—he was the same physician in every case—and noticed that when he had good news, he entered the waiting room with a broad smile on his face. So we sat there knotted with tension until the doctor walked in smiling, and told us Elmo's surgery had been successful.

We learned that besides the hole in his heart, Elmo had two previously undetected anomalous veins, and Dr. Spencer had to change his strategy during surgery so those veins would not cause Elmo a continuing problem. Elmo was in pretty good health going in, and I think that speeded his recovery. Within a few days, he was doing very well and wanted to leave the hospital.

We had never let him ride a bicycle because of his health, so his reward after surgery was a bike. After he returned home, Elmo began riding his bike. He became more and more adventurous until one day he shot down a hill and rode through a stop sign. A speeding car hit his rear wheel, knocking his bike around and flipping him ten feet in the air. His head landed on the grass, just missing the curb by inches. The young girl driving the car rushed Elmo home. She was scared to death, and Elmo looked white as a sheet, but he was not hurt. We came *that* close to losing him after all he had been through.

The heart surgery proved completely successful, and within a few months Elmo's heart size returned to normal. The bronchial attacks ended, and the doctors assured us that in every way Elmo could be said to have a normal heart. He acted as if he did. He rode his bike, played sports, and, except for some occasional bouts of pericarditis—an inflammation of the sac surrounding his heart caused by surgical scars—showed us that he was a healthy young boy.

As a surface-ship sailor, I continued to go off to sea, usually for six months at a time. In my absences, Elmo became a kind of surrogate father to the other children. He turned into a real Mr. Fixit around the house, repairing leaky faucets or doing small carpentry work. He also became very intense. I think his intensity might have been caused by his new sense of responsibility, his illness, and, in good measure, by his born-and-bred character. He had a fine sense of humor and played jokes on everyone, but he had this deeply serious side even at that young age.

Jimmy, on the other hand, is much more relaxed. He is quick-witted and was forever teasing and kidding his siblings. Ann, the oldest of our daughters, is more like Elmo. She is more serious and more talkative, but not to the same extent as Elmo. Mouzetta is a free spirit, especially so when she was young, and like the other three, she has a wonderful sense of humor.

Elmo has always been protective of his brother and sisters. He and Jimmy had a healthy rivalry and fought a good deal as young-sters, but once when they were playing on opposite sides in a touch football game an argument erupted between Jimmy and one of the players on Elmo's team. The argument became heated and this fellow pushed Jimmy. Elmo stepped in and pushed the fellow back and said, "Keep your hands off my brother." I guess the moral was, Nobody can whack my brother except me. He was just as protective of his sisters, and has kept those qualities to this day.

Dr. James Caldwell:

The first time I met Bud and Mouza was in the spring of 1948 and I liked them immediately. They are both outgoing, friendly people.

Although it was obvious Bud was very competitive and driven, he has never fit the military stereotype of a career officer. He has a wonderful sense of humor about everything, including himself, and is very open to things. I grew to admire his integrity and his honesty, traits Elmo and, I think, all his children share.

Elmo was especially fond of my first wife, Caroline, and she of him. It was impossible not to love Elmo. He would talk to anyone and trusted everyone. I remember once Mouza was looking for him. He was just a little tyke, couldn't have been more than two. She heard horns honking on the highway that ran near Victory

Village. She ran toward the road, and there, right in the middle of the highway, was Elmo, with another little guy about his size, holding up their hands like policemen and stopping the cars. The people in the cars were all in stitches, but Mouza was scared to death. She gave Elmo a pretty good spanking.

The Zumwalts moved to Charleston, but after Bud went to sea, Mouza returned to Chapel Hill and we continued to keep in close touch with them over the years. When Bud came home, he would spend every minute with Mouza and the kids. He was fiercely protective of them. He always tried to understand each child's feelings and special qualities, even when they were very young. I know he thought his own father was a man of great patience and understanding, and as a parent he brought those qualities to his family.

TWO

★

ELMO:

One of my high school friends once said, "Elmo, you were born an adult." I have never forgotten that, and in many ways there is a lot of truth to it.

I am not sure why I became so responsible so young, but I think it was probably a combination of things. Although I really never thought of myself as physically disabled, even before my heart surgery I remember getting terrible headaches when I exerted myself too much. I know I became tired faster than other kids. I became anxious just before my heart surgery, and when you are twelve years old and faced with your own mortality, it has a sobering effect on you. But that period of my life was harder on my parents than on me. Mom has told me how bad she used to feel seeing me look out the window at other kids playing, because I was not well enough to play with them.

I also think Dad's long absences from home had a way of making me grow up fast. As the oldest child, I felt protective of my family. I became a sort of third parent. I can remember missing Dad, and thinking we really did not have a complete family without him. It was exciting every time he came home from sea. We would all go down to dockside and watch his ship come in. I was always proud of him, even though being a naval officer took its toll on the family.

Although Dad has always been a workaholic, he found time for all of us, and the quality of that time is memorable. I can remember touch football games he would play with us after he came home, and picnics and camping trips in the mountains. He took us to Cub Scouts and when he was home he went to all our school functions. He was very patient with us.

Both Dad and Mom opened us up to how other people felt, and instilled in us a strong sense of caring for people who were in difficulty. Dad has always been direct with all of us. He was not embarrassed if we saw him cry, and he did when he spoke of his mother and his brother, Bruce Craig. I don't think he has ever gotten over their deaths, and I don't think he ever will. He was openly loving with us, and still is. He has always hugged and kissed us, and shown us affection in all kinds of ways.

Dad developed remarkably close relationships with all of his children, despite his long absences. It may sound unbelievable, but in all my years of growing up, I can never remember him losing his temper at me, or at my brother or sisters, even when he had good reason to get mad. I have asked them and they can't ever remember him losing his temper, either. He is a great believer in teaching and leading by example, both with us and in his naval career. When we did something wrong, he would tell us he knew we could do better, or that we had disappointed him, but he would never strike out at us. Mom was the stronger disciplinarian.

He never put pressure on us to perform, but we all realized he was successful, and I think all four of us grew up feeling that we had to make something of ourselves. When I was young, I had wanted to be a career naval officer and attend the Naval Academy because I sensed Dad was deeply satisfied by his work, not because he ever said he wanted me to follow in his footsteps.

I remember even at a very early age thinking there was a star quality to Dad. When I was about ten years old, Dad had taken command of the *Arnold J. Isbell,* an old World War II destroyer. It was his first full ship command, because his earlier command of the *Tillis* had been cut short by the Korean war. Before he took command, the *Isbell* had stood last in battle efficiency out of a squadron of eight. By the end of his first year's command, it stood second, and at the end of his second year, it stood first, having earned an "E" for excellence in every category. I can remember the *Isbell* officers in our home in San Diego, talking about Dad with great affection and a sense of awe. They talked as if he had created a miracle.

Despite Dad's devotion to his military career, I never had the feeling that we were a military family. In fact, Dad is an *un*military type of person. Almost all my good friends came from non-military families, and we never lived on a military base. The only time we lived a military existence occurred during Dad's second tour in San Diego, when I was in high school. The area we lived in was saturated with military families, and I did not like the atmosphere. Because the military is so structured, kids can easily compare their father's career with the careers of their friends' fathers. It's a way to gain status, and the comparisons can cause jealousies, from which I was thankfully spared.

As I think back, we were typically middle-class, especially during my earlier years. A young naval officer with four kids is about as middle-class as you can get. I remember Dad was terribly concerned about what would happen to us if he were killed. The Navy widow's pension at that time came to $55 a month, and even by the economic standards of those days, that was not enough money for a family with four kids to live on for a week. Because Mom had no training to work in this country, Dad was afraid if he were gone we would be destitute.

To protect us, he bought loads of life insurance during those early years, and we were insurance-poor. From the bedroom late at night, I often heard Dad ask Mom, "How can we possibly pay all these bills?"

I must also say that for all of Dad's brilliance, he was no business genius. Once he borrowed about $100 I had made from my newspaper route to invest in an oil well. It went bust. He never gave up investing in oil wells, and they always failed.

Mom was not a spendthrift by any means, but with so much of Dad's salary going into life insurance, there wasn't much left to live on. I know those memories have left their mark on me as an adult because I am very careful with money and live in fear of debt.

As Dad rose in the Navy, our financial situation did not change dramatically, but his importance did. For instance, at the time of the Cuban missile crisis he was the Director of Arms Control for Assistant Secretary of Defense Paul Nitze. He was totally absorbed by the crisis. He even slept at the Pentagon. I realized then that Dad was among the policy makers of the country.

Paul Nitze was one of the major architects of the Marshall Plan and had served every president since Truman. He came to our house for dinner on occasion, and I absorbed a lot about foreign policy just listening to him and Dad. It was a process of learning current events and history from people who shaped them.

Paul Nitze was a multimillionaire, as was his wife, and they invited our family to spend the summers at their guest house on their farm on Maryland's Eastern Shore. I had never known how the aristocracy lived until I saw the Nitzes' summer place. There were 2,500 acres, a waterfront that seemed to go on forever, and the guest house in which we stayed was far more palatial than any house we had ever lived in before.

I did not spend my summers on the Nitze farm lolling around. When Dad was young, he worked on a tractor in the intense summer sun of the San Joaquin Valley, and he said it taught him some of the best lessons of his life. He said he learned just how hard physical work was, and just how little you earned doing it. He thought my brother Jimmy and I could benefit from the same experience, so he had us pick tobacco on the Nitze farm.

It was backbreaking work. We spent the entire day in the hot sun with our heads down by our knees cutting those damn tobacco stalks with a knife. I got one of the great breaks in my life when I broke out in a rash that looked like poison ivy. It turned out that I was allergic to the tobacco, and could not cut it anymore. Jimmy took off his shirt and rolled around in the tobacco hoping to get the same allergy, but he wasn't as lucky as I, so he had to keep on cutting it. I tried to convince him that it was good for his character. My fun didn't last long, because there were other chores to do, but, thankfully, none as tough as picking tobacco.

As I think back on my upbringing, I can see Dad did a number of things to help shape my character and the character of all his children. In many ways, he was a firm believer in the Spartan ethic, of being strong and standing on your own two feet. I say all this to provide some understanding of a story that is still painful for Dad to talk about, but I think it illuminates what he tried to do as a father.

I was six years old when we moved to Newport, Rhode Island, while Dad spent a year at the Naval War College there. One or two houses away lived a boy nicknamed Tiger. He was one of the meanest kids I ever knew. He seemed to relish beating the hell out of anybody smaller than himself. At six years old, and small for my age anyway, I was a good target for Tiger, who was two years older than me, and big. I ran away from him every time he got into his real mean moods. He really scared me.

Once Tiger came after me and I ran home. When I reached our front door, Dad was standing inside and locked the door on me. I pounded on the door but he would not let me in. I had to face Tiger head-on. I knew I didn't have much endurance, so I started screaming at Tiger and acting crazy to try to scare him. He didn't scare, and then when he came after me, I fought as hard as I could.

This happened more than once, and Dad would never let me in the house when Tiger was after me. I could not whip him, but I fought him hard enough to take some of the fun out of it for him. He gradually stopped bothering me as much, and as I became a little braver, I enlisted the help of a friend and tried to scare him back.

When people hear this story they ask, "How could your father do that to you?" Dad has told me several times that it was the most difficult thing he ever had to do as a parent, but he knew he would not always be there for me, and I had to face Tiger alone. I should also say that Dad forced me to take on Tiger before he realized I had a heart problem.

I think this incident has had a lot to do with my philosophy of facing problems head-on. It has been a lasting lesson, and I have often told Dad that he did the right thing when he locked the door. I think I have been a happier and more successful person because of it.

Another incident a few years later also had a lasting impact on me. After my heart surgery, I suffered chest pains caused by pericarditis. Pericarditis was a common aftereffect of my type of surgery in those days, and the first time it hit, about a year after the surgery, we were living in Norfolk, Virginia. Dad had been assigned to command the *Dewey,* the Navy's first guided missile frigate, which was another early sign that his career was moving rapidly upward.

I was taken to the Portsmouth Naval Hospital, which isn't too far from Norfolk. I was thirteen at the time. While I was there, I got to know a boy named Leroy, who was a little younger than me. He had had heart surgery twice, but the surgery proved unsuccessful and he was failing. I realized Leroy would not live very long.

Day after day Leroy cried for his mother and father to visit him, but they never came. All the other parents, including Mom and Dad, visited with Leroy and held his hand, trying in their own way to substitute for his own parents. I remember one of the Navy corpsmen on the phone many times, begging Leroy's parents to see their son. At times Leroy fooled himself into believing they were coming. Once I was in radiology when Leroy's mother came in for an X ray, but she did not go to see him. A while after I left Portsmouth Naval Hospital, one of the corpsmen called my parents to tell us that Leroy had died.

Even now, twenty-five years later, it is difficult for me to talk about Leroy without being overcome. I don't know why his parents didn't come. I think they were just emotionally callous in a way I will never comprehend.

That incident made me question faith in God. I was a philosophy major in college, and I have thought a lot about religion and the Judeo-Christian definition of God. Although I think there is a force that started the life process, I do not believe in an almighty or all-loving God. I know my agnosticism started with Leroy, because I cannot reconcile a loving God with Leroy's suffering.

Dad has also questioned whether there's a God, but for other reasons. He witnessed war up close and is an avid reader of history. He could never reconcile the extermination of six million Jews, or the killing of twenty million Russians during World War II, with the existence of a God, at least as we understand that God.

One other childhood experience has had a lasting impact on me. It happened during the fifth grade, at the Masonville School in Annandale, Virginia. In the third grade, my teacher was Mrs. Dona Weakley, who to this day remains my all-time favorite teacher. Mom and Dad were worried that I had fallen behind in school because of my illness, so Dad dropped me off at school early on his way to work every day and Mrs. Weakley would be waiting to help me with reading. She hugged me a lot. I found out much later that she knew of my heart condition, and was afraid I would overexert myself playing during recess. So she hugged me to feel how fast my heart was beating without bringing attention to what she was doing. After she held me, she would often ask me to help her with something, which was her way of slowing me down.

In the fifth grade, for whatever reason, my teacher had it in for me. She would call on me in class and before I could answer, she would cut me off with a condescending smile and say, "That's okay, Elmo, someone else can answer the question." She told my parents that they should love me for what I was, because I would never be able to accomplish anything academically. I was never confident of myself in school after that experience.

Although my brother Jimmy and I got along fairly well, we had our share of fights when we were growing up. I think in some ways Jimmy resented the fact that Mom and Dad paid so much attention to me because of my illness. I cannot blame him for that. I would have felt the same way if the situation were turned around.

Our most memorable fight occurred when I was fourteen and Jimmy was twelve. By that time, Jimmy was as tall as I was, and a lot stronger. I can't remember what we were fighting about, but it went on for hours. At one point Dad came home and dragged us into the backyard and said, "If you two want to fight, do it outside." We kept on fighting and this time Jimmy got on top of me and no matter how hard I tried, I could not move him. It came as a big blow to me because this was the first time he had ever beaten me in a fight. I went into the house yelling, "He beat me, he beat me." Jimmy was so shocked he did not know what to do. That was our last physical fight. I think Jimmy knew he could take me, but he never tried. And I sure did not want to take him on anymore.

I studied hard in high school, but good grades did not come easily. At least one guidance counselor suggested I not consider college. She said I would do myself a favor by learning a trade. After I graduated from college, I went back to see these counsellors and told them they had better be more careful about judging people in the future.

I had three close friends in high school, Steve Spiller, John Enos, and Dick Anderson. I usually played by the rules in high school, but at the end of our senior year, Dick Anderson and I played hookey for the first time. We drove Dick's car to Great Falls, Virginia, a beautiful place along the Potomac River. This day of all days, Mom had a flat tire on our car. She called the school to ask me to come home at lunchtime to fix it. When I arrived home later that day, Mom and Dad knew what I had done. They didn't punish me when I convinced them it was the first time I had skipped school, but I still had to face the vice-principal and suffer some grief from him.

After my high school graduation in 1964, I had a pick-and-shovel summer job, working on the foundations of houses after the backhoes had dug them out. I was seventeen at the time. Many of the other construction workers had been laid off from West Vir-

ginia coal mines and had only finished the fifth or sixth grade. I
realized I made a mistake when I mentioned that I had graduated
from high school, since relative to their education, I guess it
seemed as if I had been bragging.

The second mistake I made was to tell them that I had wrestled
a little bit in high school. They began jumping me so that I could
show them how I wrestled. They were so strong and mean that it
reached a point where I had to fend them off by swinging my
shovel at them. Usually they would lose interest after a few minutes and go back to their jobs. When I told Dad about it, he said,
"Look, I know you're not a quitter, but this is absolutely ridicu-
lous. Getting beat up is not part of the job. Why don't you just
quit?"

I told Dad it was my job and I was going to stick with it. I was
so naive that I thought everyone had to put up with this sort of
thing on construction jobs.

Things came to a head one Saturday when Mom, Dad, and
Jimmy picked me up after work. Jimmy walked over to the construction site to get me, and by then Jimmy was built like the
bottom of an oak tree. One of these construction workers asked me
if he was my brother and I said he was.

He started yelling at the top of his lungs, "He sure is an ugly-
looking son of a bitch." This guy had never laid eyes on Jimmy
before, but he wanted to fight with him. Jimmy kept walking
toward me and the worker kept yelling, now joined by a friend of
his. Jimmy knew what I had been through and he yelled back at
them. Then the biggest man on the construction gang, a fellow
about six-four and built like a professional football player, said to
Jimmy, "I'm gonna beat your ass."

I was trying to stop the fight because I thought this guy would
break Jimmy in half, so I said, "If you fight here, we'll all be fired
for fighting on the job."

This big guy told Jimmy to go to a nearby hill, away from the
construction site. As they were walking, I kept trying to talk the
fellow out of fighting my brother, but another worker kept egging
him on. When they reached the hill, the big guy jumped Jimmy,

but Jimmy, who had wrestled in high school, knocked him off his feet.

They rolled toward a ditch and the big guy kept Jimmy down. He was just about to smash Jimmy in the face when, all of a sudden, I saw a white streak fly by, pounce on this fellow, and rip him off my brother. It was Dad, dressed in his Navy whites. The big guy pulled his fist back and was about to take a swing at Dad. But Dad's uniform must have startled him, because he stopped. Dad told him he ought to be ashamed of himself for picking a fight with a fifteen-year-old boy, and the three of us went back to the car and left before another battle developed. If he had hit Dad, I know Jimmy and I would have jumped in, and the police would have come and all of us would have been arrested. When I reported to work on Monday, the foreman had heard about the fight and transferred me to another crew. I never had another problem on the job.

My high school grades were not good enough to get me into the Naval Academy. It was a disappointment to me, but not a bitter one. I had pretty much resigned myself to the fact that I was not academically strong enough for Annapolis. To tell the truth, I also think I had some fear of the Naval Academy because of my insecurities about school. I was accepted at Elon College in North Carolina. I did well enough there in my freshman year to transfer to the University of North Carolina at Chapel Hill. I thought the Carolina campus was beautiful and the academics were a challenge.

I also was reunited with Dr. James Caldwell, our old friend from Victory Village. He had become a history professor and remained close to our family. At Carolina, I enrolled in the NROTC program. At that time, 1965, Vietnam still seemed a very distant war.

Originally, I had wanted to major in English or history, but I took a few philosophy courses and found they stretched my mind. I became convinced that I would gain more from majoring in philosophy than English or history, even though people give you a funny look when you say you're a philosophy major.

During my senior year in college, I met Kathy Counselman, a sophomore at Marymount College in Virginia. My mother had taught Russian for a number of years, and Kathy's mother had been one of her students. They became friendly and Mrs. Counselman invited my mother to lunch one day. When Mom saw Kathy's picture on the piano, she said she had two sons, and maybe they ought to all get together. During the Christmas break, Mrs. Counselman invited my whole family for dinner.

Jimmy, who is usually the quietest member of our family, especially around people we do not know well, was the life of the party. He told jokes and had everybody laughing the whole night, while I stayed in the background.

I was very attracted to Kathy. She had long blond hair and a beautiful face, but she also was intelligent and thoughtful. I have always been a leg man and I thought she had beautiful legs. As we were leaving the Counselmans' later that evening, Mom invited Kathy to join us the next night. We had tickets to a play. Kathy accepted, and I found I was even more attracted to her at our second meeting.

After I returned to Chapel Hill, I wrote Kathy twice without receiving an answer, and thought that was the end of it. Then I received a warm, friendly letter from her and I thought maybe there was hope for me. We saw each other a couple of times before my graduation in June 1968.

I remember graduation well, because Dad was the speaker for the NROTC graduates. In his speech, he mentioned me and my early heart problems and how I had persevered, and I remember squirming in my chair when he did it. Fortunately, he didn't dwell on me and my problems. My old friend from high school, Dick Anderson, had just graduated from the University of Virginia and came down for my graduation and shared my happiness.

I also had a three-year Navy obligation to fulfill.

DICK ANDERSON:

Elmo and I grew up in the same neighborhood in Annandale, right around the corner from one another. My earliest memories of him are as a twelve-year-old who had just had heart surgery. After I got to know him a little, I learned how much he loved his family, and I remember how much he talked about them, especially his father. It was unusual.

Elmo's home was always open to his friends. Mrs. Zumwalt often cooked breakfast for all of us, and that was not a common thing in that neighborhood. The admiral always acted in a friendly way and took an interest in Elmo's friends. He wasn't what you would think of as a military man, certainly not a disciplinarian. He would invite us to the Pentagon to play handball, and he would play touch football with us in the yard. One time I was invited to dinner at their house with Paul Nitze, and he talked all through dinner about the Marshall Plan. I was sixteen at the time. That's just the way the Zumwalts were; if you were a friend, you were always welcome in their home.

Elmo has a serious side to him, and he studied hard, but always provided lots of laughs. He liked to tease people, but he kept his teasing in bounds and no one got hurt. His brother Jimmy went around with us, and he was a master at teasing.

Elmo was a maverick in his car. His dad drove fast and so did he. Sometimes with a carload of people, especially people who didn't know him well, Elmo would drive down a hill and start yelling that the brakes had gone. Then he would pound his foot against the floorboard. Everyone would dive down in the car, and he would start laughing.

Elmo also had a feisty side to him. He got into a lot of scuffles in high school. He would never hesitate to go up to a bully and tell him to leave someone alone. I remember one morning he got into a fight at our bus stop with some guy who was pushing people around. He would always speak his mind to protect the weaker boy. I'm not saying Elmo usually won in these encounters, just the opposite. He usually got the worst of it, but he wasn't afraid of anyone.

Kathy Counselman Zumwalt:

I was a freshman in college when my mother told me she had invited the Zumwalts over for dinner. She said she wanted me to meet Elmo Zumwalt. I did not like the idea of this "arranged" meeting in the first place, and when she told me his name I thought, Elmo? With a name like that, how good could this guy be? I was not looking forward to the evening.

I invited a girlfriend over because I knew Elmo had a younger brother. I refused to dress up to impress the Zumwalts, which was why I wore knee socks and shorts. I did not know at the time that Elmo loved legs. During the entire dinner, Elmo was somber and serious while Jimmy was cracking one joke after another.

After dinner, I asked if anyone wanted to play cards. Elmo looked at me and said, "I don't play cards." I thought, "Oh, boy, this guy is loads of fun." Needless to say, Elmo did not make a great first impression on me.

As the Zumwalts were leaving our house that evening, Elmo's mother asked me if I would like to join them the next night. She said they had tickets to a play at the National Theater in Washington. What could I say? "No thanks, one evening is plenty"?

I accepted, but later that night Elmo called me on the telephone and said he realized I was put in an awkward position. He said he would personally love for me to come to the play with them, but he would understand completely if I did not want to. I did not think many guys would be thoughtful enough to do something like that, and I was impressed by it. I began to think there was probably more to him than I had realized. I told him I would love to come.

The next night Elmo seemed far more relaxed. He kidded his father a little bit and I began to see he had a sense of humor. I also found him physically attractive.

After we both returned to school, we exchanged letters and I visited him at North Carolina. After he graduated from college, we dated for a brief time in the Washington area before he went on active duty in the Navy.

I was only nineteen at the time, and I was not thinking of marriage, but my attraction to Elmo was deepening.

★

VIETNAM

THREE

★

At the time of Elmo's college graduation the Zumwalt family underwent great changes that would shape us and our destinies forever after. Elmo was beginning his military career and mine was moving into an entirely new arena—Vietnam.

When we arrived back in Annandale after his graduation, we all drove over to see Elmo's third-grade teacher, Dona Weakley, because he wanted her to see him in uniform. Elmo's sense of loyalty runs very deep, and he had never forgotten her.

I was proud, as any parent would be, that my son had graduated from college, but I was especially proud of Elmo because I knew how difficult academics were for him. He still lived with the scar of that fifth-grade teacher. I think he spent so much time worrying about school that he never really learned how to study. The fact that he had graduated from a first-rate university was a testament to his tenacity, a quality I had always known he had in abundance.

No matter how often we told him that he was bright, he never really felt it in his gut. In high school I had persuaded Elmo to take a public speaking course. I had hoped it would instill some confidence in him, as it had in me when I was in high school. I had had a speech problem that stemmed from the fact that I was born a natural left-hander and was converted, as were most left-handers in those days, to the use of my right hand. The theory then was that you were better off learning to write with your right hand. Now, of course, we know that isn't true.

Before I went to the Naval Academy, I was examined by a wonderful specialist who told me that I had a slight tendency to stammer when I began a statement. I have it to this day, but it is not noticeable to most people. The specialist encouraged me to continue my public speaking because my tendency to stammer would get worse as I grew older, and public speaking would help keep it in check. Being converted from a left-hander to a right-hander, I was told, causes a signal in the brain to lag, which contributes to the stammer, as well as to the deterioration of one's handwriting. Mine has always been notoriously atrocious.

So a public speaking course helped me in many ways, and I had thought it could do the same for Elmo. Elmo did so well in his public speaking course that his teacher recommended he give the graduation speech that summed up his class's years at Annandale High. Elmo had a lot of misgivings but gave the speech at the graduation ceremony at Constitution Hall in Washington. Unfortunately, his success as a speaker did not give him added confidence in academics when he entered college.

Every father takes pride in the fact that his son wants to follow him in his profession, but I also know the father's achievements can place an unfair burden on the boy. The father of one of my classmates, Jim Holloway, had been an admiral, and I think Jim, although an outstanding naval officer who succeeded me as Chief of Naval Operations, always thought he was being compared to his dad. Following in a father's footsteps puts a lot of pressure on any young man. But I also knew Elmo had his own mind, and would not do something just because I had. He would make his own choices.

My official orders to report to Vietnam came through in July 1968, and I was due to report there in September. For years I had seen our deepening involvement in that war. In the early 1960s, large-scale American involvement was actively discussed within the military and the government. The tone and substance of many of those meetings convinced me we were going to take a stand there. During much of that period, I was an assistant to Paul Nitze, first when he was Assistant Secretary of Defense, and later when he was Secretary of the Navy.

My relationship with Paul Nitze had a profound effect on me and my career. Paul examined everything with great intellectual vigor. By serving under him, I was able to expand my intellectual scope and sharpen my administrative skills. The final benefit my service with Paul conferred on me was the two stars of rear admiral in July 1965. My classmate Jim Calvert, who had commanded the second submarine to travel under the North Pole, and I were selected two years before other members of our Naval Academy class technically came "into the zone" for promotion to flag rank. Normally, before a captain is selected to flag rank, he must have a capital command, generally a destroyer, or a cruiser squadron in the case of a surface sailor like me. But Paul's fitness report about me strongly recommended that tradition be waived, and the selection board took his recommendation.

Throughout the early 1960s, Paul argued long and hard against massive American ground intervention in Vietnam. If we did intervene militarily, he said, it should be with air and sea power. I agreed completely, having prepared some of the "talking papers" with which he debated Defense Secretary Robert McNamara and other National Security Council members.

Although I thought a communist takeover of South Vietnam was clearly undesirable, I did not think it posed a direct threat to the United States. We also did not have a treaty, or any other commitment, with South Vietnam that would make a failure to send troops a failure to keep our word. Most important, I did not consider South Vietnam to be a viable national entity capable of repelling Hanoi's aggression. Moreover, the war would impose a substantial drain on our military strength at a time when the Soviet Union was furiously building up its own military arsenal. I think these fears were justified. Many of the Navy's resources were simply gobbled up by the war effort, and we lost many of our forces that we needed to control the seas, particularly antisubmarine ships, planes, and weaponry.

So, in addition to wanting to avoid all the sorrow that war brings, I felt deeply that it was not in our country's interests. Both Paul and I thought it was the wrong war, in the wrong place, at the wrong time. It was for all these many reasons that I wanted to see America's commitments to Vietnam reduced when I was named commander of the in-country naval forces in Vietnam. With my new command came my third star.

Before I left for Vietnam, Mouza, our daughters Ann and Mouzetta, and Kathy, the beautiful young girl Elmo was dating, drove up to Newport, Rhode Island, where Elmo had gone to attend Navy communications school. I hoped he would not come to Vietnam, because if something happened to me, he would have to look out for the family. I told him how I felt, and he seemed to agree, but I also sensed that he did not think it was fair for others to be over there fighting, and for him to remain on the sidelines. But I still got the impression that he agreed it was risky for the family for the two of us to be there at the same time. We said our goodbyes and I began my final preparations to go to Southeast Asia.

My orders regarding my third star had read that I was not to be "frocked" until I left the continental United States. I left San Francisco with Mouza, Jimmy, Ann, and Mouzetta on board the flight, along with Howard Kerr, a brilliant young lieutenant I had selected to be my aide in Vietnam. Howard went on to become an aide to President Ford. In his thoughtful way, Howard had brought some champagne and my three-star boards, and as we flew out of San Francisco, he opened the champagne. Then Mouza and Howard's wife, Patricia, each put on one of my boards. I was forty-seven years old, and a vice admiral.

Mouza and the girls and I arrived at Clark Air Base in the Philippines. I knew living at Clark was going to be very difficult for my family. It was the first time they had ever lived on a military base, and the fact that they were the only Navy family on the base did not make it easier for them. There are service rivalries even among the families.

But for them the hardest part would be seeing all the wounded young men coming in from Vietnam to the hospital at Clark. I know from talking to Mouza and my daughters since then that they were deeply affected by it. Mouza worked tirelessly as a Gray Lady, visiting the wounded. She invited many young servicemen to our home for dinner.

Besides a number of briefings at the Naval Base at Subic Bay, Howard and I went through a survival course there. They put us down in the jungle with only a machete. We learned to make passable coffee from nuts that fell from trees and we were taught how to find and collect fresh water from certain vines. I also learned how to fish without poles or string. It was not particularly difficult training, but, I thought, a valuable one.

I bid my final goodbye to Mouza and our girls, and flew to Vietnam to undertake what I clearly realized was the biggest challenge of my naval career to that point. I sensed strongly that our military involvement in Vietnam would have to be rapidly curtailed. I thought if Richard Nixon were elected president in the upcoming 1968 elections, we had three years before our military forces would be removed. If Hubert Humphrey won, that would be cut down to one year.

I had an additional obstacle. I felt my assignment to Vietnam was Admiral Tom Moorer's way of getting a thorn out of his side, namely me. The Navy has three major components—submarines, surface vessels, and aviation—and within the Navy each of these is a jealously guarded turf. Moorer, the Chief of Naval Operations, was an aviator and he wanted the aviation community in control of the Navy. I think he saw me, a surface sailor, as a possible threat.

But there were also personal differences. Being as close as I was to Paul Nitze, Paul often told me things about the Navy while he served as Deputy Secretary of Defense. Whenever I received this information, with Paul's knowledge and consent, I would stop by Moorer's office and pass it on to his executive assistant. It became clear to me after a while that my passing on this information irritated the hell out of Moorer. He resented the fact that I was getting information that he did not have.

I believe the reason Moorer wanted me in Vietnam was that no rear admiral had ever left Vietnam and obtained another job that led anywhere. This was Moorer's way of getting rid of me: *Promote the son of a bitch and nobody will ever hear from him again*.

I took command of what was called the brown-water navy, the ships that patrolled the inland rivers and coast of Vietnam. I did not command the Seventh Fleet that patrolled the South China Sea from which the carrier-launched planes were flown.

When I arrived I made a ten-day tour of Vietnam to assess the situation as quickly as possible. I found things far worse than I had imagined. Morale was terribly low for many Navy people eager to do their job. At command headquarters in Saigon I perceived what I can only describe as a country club atmosphere. Saigon seemed a world away from the war.

Many officers were more concerned about their tennis dates and dinner plans than putting out a maximum effort to fight. In addition, there was a terrible split between the Navy and the senior Army command. The Army was running the show and the supreme commander, General Creighton Abrams, wasn't even talking to my predecessor, Rear Admiral Veth. One of the first things General Abrams told me was that he was getting no help from the Navy in fighting the war. He said he had never offered the Navy the chance to contribute briefings at the Saturday commander's conference, but would offer me that opportunity. "But it'll last only as long as you produce," he said.

It was clear to me that there was a lack of good strategic and tactical planning at all levels, and I detected no sense of mission. The Navy's attitude basically was that the war was the Army's job. I needed to turn that attitude around, and I needed to do it quickly.

General Abrams had a reputation for being a tough man who ate people alive. He certainly proved a tough disciplinarian. I might add that he was also the finest commander under whom I had ever served, and a man who cared deeply for his troops. He was meticulously honest in his war reports back to Washington. In one of the first briefings I attended at General Abrams's headquarters, all of the most senior commanders were there to make presentations. Abrams had just returned from Washington, where he had met with President Johnson. He was obviously tired and grouchy from his long trip back. In his earthy way, Johnson had told Abrams, "General, I want every Vietnamese who carries a peter to be in uniform and to be in this war effort, and I want us to get out as fast as we can." Abrams had heard the message loud and clear.

Abrams opened the briefing. The Air Force was first up, and a colonel rose out of his chair. He really looked slick, and he had a lot of slides with different colors and numbers. He even put the Air Force Command's thunderbolt log on these slides. It was an impressive visual display and he moved through it flawlessly. He reached the part where he said the Air Force would transfer most of their resources over to the South Vietnamese by 1976. That was at least five years too late. General Abrams put his hand to his head. The next thing I heard was a fist smashing the table, and Abrams yelling, "Bullshit! Bullshit! Bullshit! That's all I ever get out of the Air Force."

He was enraged that the Air Force did not understand the urgent timetable for the United States to depart Vietnam. He said they were in a pressure cooker and did not have anything near an eight-year timetable to Vietnamize the war. And he said the next administration that emerged after the November 1968 elections, whichever it was, also would not give anyone that much time. I knew he was absolutely right. Americans were fast running out of patience with the war.

The general's chief of staff, Major General Corcoran, approached me and suggested that Abrams was very tired, and asked if I would like to rework my presentation and schedule it for another time. I said no, I was ready to go.

General Corcoran said, "All right, Bud, if that's what you want to do. I'll go tell Abe. Let's give him forty-five minutes to clear his head and come down from the emotional level he's on now."

When I was called upon, I laid out an entire plan for a rapid Vietnamization of the war, which I thought was possible and necessary. In effect, I planned for the South Vietnamese Navy to wage the in-country naval war essentially on their own within three years.

Unfortunately, my Navy superiors in Hawaii and Washington were lukewarm to my idea of turning over so much U.S. Navy equipment to the South Vietnamese so quickly. They doubted the ability of the South Vietnamese Navy to put this equipment to full use in so short a time.

I said step one was to select young Vietnamese men to learn a few basic English words—I had even picked out the building in Saigon where that language training would take place—and then these Vietnamese should join the American crews aboard the riverboats. They would learn how to operate the boats, and in turn train their fellow South Vietnamese, and gradually they could begin replacing American crews. When I finished giving all the details, an Air Force officer began to criticize it. Abrams cut him off. "The Air Force has already dug themselves into a cesspool here today. Bud Zumwalt may be doing the same thing, but so far he's making some sense."

Abrams told me to move ahead, and at the end of the meeting, he asked me to accompany him back to his office for a private talk. As we walked, he put his arm on my shoulder. Much later, I found out how important my briefing that day would be for me. When Defense Secretary Melvin Laird visited Vietnam a few months later, in part as a result of that briefing, Abrams recommended to Laird that I should be considered when it came time to name a new Chief of Naval Operations. I also met with Laird on that visit, and I later learned that when he returned to Washington he spoke to Navy Secretary John Chafee and said, "When you're making nominations for the next CNO, give me three names, but make sure Zumwalt is one of them."

I had to make radical changes within the naval operations staff I had inherited to do the job in Vietnam. I felt the level of competence hovered around zero. Vietnam was a dumping ground for weak naval officers at the commander and captain levels. Fortunately, I was blessed with a magnificent intelligence officer named Rex Retanus, who later became a vice admiral, but he was one of the few bright lights. I had to remove the assistant chief of staff, and later the chief of staff, by generating "opportunities" for them to serve back in the States. I think the second-rate Navy effort at that point grew out of decisions deliberately made by Admiral Moorer. Air strikes meant glory for the Navy. He did not want to waste the Navy's resources fighting the war inside Vietnam.

Every night from ten to eleven o'clock I phoned the Navy personnel detailers in Washington and leaned on them one at a time to get me the officers I needed. I knew the names of some officers I wanted, and members of my staff knew others. I got my choices, not because the Navy's policy changed, but because I pulled them in one by one on my own. I had to work on that problem for countless hours while in the midst of fighting the war.

Obtaining good officers was difficult since many good naval officers perceived that Vietnam service would be of no help to their careers, and more likely a step backward. I had always thought that when your country was at war, you sent your best men to fight it. I knew there were personnel detailers in Washington telling good naval officers not to go to Vietnam, and offering them a year at the Naval War College instead. In effect, these military officers were dodging the war just like the young men who ran off to Canada.

Turning the war around from the naval point of view was clearly a challenge. I went into the field every day to size up the situation, to see what was needed, and also to show the men who served under me that I was not going to run the war from a desk in Saigon. I wanted them to know who I was, and that I had to understand what they were up against. There was no precedent for the Navy fighting this kind of war. No course on it had been taught at the Naval Academy. We had to experiment, and make up tactics and strategies as we went along.

The continued infiltration of enemy arms and men into South
Vietnam was the major problem we faced. Earlier, our patrols off
the Vietnam coast and on the major rivers had dramatically slowed
the supply of arms shipped along these routes. But the Viet Cong
had changed their strategy. They divided into smaller units and
used sampans and other small boats to bring in arms at the rate of
several hundred tons a week. Their highways were the smaller
rivers and canals that cover the southern delta of South Vietnam.
It became clear that we had to shift our attention away from the
coastal waters and the major rivers, and concentrate on these hundreds upon hundreds of smaller waterways.

While I worked with Paul Nitze four years earlier, we began
the procurement and military conversion of a hundred boats that
had been built to resupply the oil rigs in the Gulf of Mexico and
other areas. These boats were fast and light, and were named
Patrol Craft Fast, or PCFs, but we called them swift boats. They
had proved effective for the coastal and major river patrols, so we
deployed them into the narrow canals and rivers. We moved slowly
at first, then deployed the swift boats more rapidly when they
proved effective. I called them my brown-water cruisers.

The swift boats were just part of our plan. We also deployed the
faster, but less heavily armed, PBRs—Patrol Boat River—which I
called my "destroyers." Then I persuaded General Julian Ewell,
commander of the Ninth Army in the delta, to release most of his
old World War II LCMs, which had been converted into heavily
armored troop carriers, as well as howitzer mortars, and command
communication boats that had been used to support the Army
troops. The LCMs were my "battleships." We needed this river
armada to prevent the infiltration of weapons that were killing our
soldiers.

The major areas of infiltration occurred along the Cambodian
border, and into South Vietnam, and that was where I thought we
should strike hard and fast with our river patrols. But in doing so,
we paid a price: Navy casualties began to rise significantly as we
became more directly engaged in the war. General Abrams saw it
as tragic good news, a sign that the Navy was doing its share in

taking casualties and increasing the overall efficiency of the war effort. Heavier Navy casualties meant the Army took fewer casualties, which showed our efforts were succeeding. General Abrams also knew I shared his sense of urgency about turning the war over to the Vietnamese as quickly as possible. As a result, the general and I began a close, warm working relationship. But that didn't mean he became mellow.

I remember one Saturday morning he sat at the end of the conference table, smoking his big cigar.

"Gentlemen," he said softly, "we had a very sad thing happen this week. The finest division commander we've ever had in Vietnam—happened to be a Marine, but nevertheless the finest division commander we've ever had—made a mistake. That fine division commander had a friend, and that friend was a member of the press, and that commander took that newsman in his helicopter on his final rounds, and he trusted that friend, and he confided in that friend, and the next day he found himself in the headlines. That commander has been embarrassed, and this command has been embarrassed, and, gentlemen, with regard to the press, that magnificent commander forgot just one thing: THEY'RE ALL A BUNCH OF SHITS!"

He punctuated his blast by pounding his fist on the table. I started laughing. Then I looked around the table. Nobody else was laughing. Then I looked at General Abrams, and he was drilling two holes right through my head, and I realized he had not meant this to be funny. This outburst was the lesson for the week.

General Abrams had many attributes I admired. He never chewed out an enlisted man, and he had a deep sympathy and feeling for those who fought. And he did not abide those who, for apparent political gain, periodically came to Vietnam for a "tour." Once we were visited by John Warner, now a U.S. Senator from Virginia, but then Under Secretary of the Navy. He walked into General Abrams's headquarters, acting every bit the VIP. He sat down in front of General Abrams's desk without being invited. Obviously unaware that Abrams was getting guidance directly from the President, Warner began to impart some of his instant wisdom on the war. Abrams gave him a hard look. Then the general reached over and took one of his cigars from the cigar box on top of his desk. Without being asked, Warner started to take a cigar for himself. Before his hand reached the box, Abrams slammed it shut, nearly taking off Warner's fingernails. He then pulled the box back and put it in his desk drawer. Then he bit off the tip of his own cigar, and lit it. John Warner had learned his place when he was in the presence of General Abrams. It's also my opinion that if General Abrams had been commander throughout the war, it would have turned out far better for us.

When we first began the patrols along the canals and smaller rivers, I think we caught the Viet Cong off guard. But it did not take them long to respond and set up ambushes, because the canals and rivers were often so narrow the men in the river patrol boats could easily be hit from either side by enemy fire. The swift boats and PBRs were especially vulnerable because they had so little protection. Swift boat hulls were made of aluminum only one-eighth of an inch thick. The PBR hulls were fiberglass. The enemy could hit them with B-40 rockets, which are like the old bazookas, automatic weapons, and hand-held rockets. And under cover of the dense foliage that grew along the riverbanks, the enemy attacked the boats without being seen. Our river patrol casualties reached an unacceptably high rate of 6 percent a month. That meant anyone serving a year's combat tour on the riverboats had a 70–75 percent chance of being killed or wounded. We had to reduce those risks considerably.

I thought one way to save American lives was to remove as much of the jungle cover as possible. By destroying the foliage along the riverbanks, we could push the enemy farther in, and make it much more difficult to ambush our patrol boats. Agent Orange had been used in other defoliation efforts, and I wanted to increase its use. My logistics officer checked with the Army and Air Force logistics people about possible injurious effects of Agent Orange on humans, and we were told people would not be harmed. You trust those things. But I must say, had I known that Agent Orange would cause some human harm, I probably would have used it anyway. I knew that not using it would cost many more American lives.

Like General Abrams, I felt deeply for the men who were fighting in that war. I knew the people around me said I suffered when I visited the scenes of the firefights that involved our boats. I still remember every time I gave an order to send some young men into danger. Personally, it is much more difficult to send other young men than to give orders for your own ship to go into battle and for you to go with them. To this day, I am unable to visit the Vietnam Memorial because of all the names of the young and valiant men that I ordered into battle, men who did not come back. I just cannot face doing that, and I'm not sure I ever will.

I ordered the increased use of Agent Orange along many of the riverbanks our boats began to patrol. The Air Force was in charge of spraying Agent Orange, and called their defoliation efforts "Operation Ranch Hand." Twenty-four C-123s were assigned to Ranch Hand. Every week they dropped thousands of gallons of the defoliant on the jungles of Vietnam. As more and more Agent Orange was sprayed, our patrol boat casualties began to drop significantly, so our strategy was obviously succeeding.

Four or five months after my arrival in Vietnam I received unsettling news. A detailer from the Navy Bureau of Personnel wrote to me that Elmo had volunteered to come to Vietnam to serve as a swift boat commander. I had had a strong premonition about it. I thought Elmo had courageously overcome so many obstacles in his life—polio, his heart condition—it would be one of those tragic ironies if he were killed in the war. I knew what our men were up against out there in the rivers, how dangerous and tough the job was.

I was also filled with considerable guilt, because I had in my hands the power to deny his request. The detailer from Navy personnel asked me what I wanted to do. I did not want Elmo to come, but as it turned out, I really did not have much of a say in

the decision because, at about the same time, I received a letter
from Elmo. He told me of his intention to serve in Vietnam, and
politely, but firmly, asked me to keep hands off. He told me I
would not have been the father he thought I was, or wanted me to
be, if I interfered. So I told personnel bureau to handle Elmo's
request as they would any other, and I sent them a copy of his
letter.

HOWARD KERR, CAPTAIN, USN (RETIRED):

I was a lieutenant and had just finished my master's degree at
the Fletcher School of Law and Diplomacy at Tufts University. I
had been offered my first ship command when a friend of mine
from Washington called me and said that Admiral Zumwalt had
been named commander of our in-country forces in Vietnam. He
asked me if it would be all right if he mentioned my name to the
admiral as a possible candidate for his staff. I thanked him, but
told him I had really decided to take my ship command. He
recommended me to the admiral anyway.

Soon after that, I received a call from the admiral, asking me to
be his aide. I told him it would be impossible for me to turn down
a ship command for a staff job. He was very gracious and wished
me luck. After I hung up, I picked up *The New York Times* and
my eye caught this article that said the Navy had just named Elmo
Zumwalt the youngest three-star admiral in history. I reconsid-
ered, called the admiral the next day, told him why I changed my
mind, and said I wanted to join him. I realized the chance to
watch and learn from him was too great an opportunity to pass up.
It was one of the best decisions I've ever made.

What I remember was how quickly he sized up and acted on
the situation that faced him in Vietnam. When we were leaving
the plane at Ton Son Nhut Airport, after arriving in Vietnam, he
turned to me and said, "Well, Howard, this is day one. Let's get on
with it."

And he did. His dual objectives were to stop the arms infiltration, and Vietnamize the Navy war effort. To do it, he moved

extremely quickly to remedy what we regarded as a bad situation for the Navy. He literally shook the Saigon naval staff to its marrow. The tennis matches ended. The happy hour ended. People began arriving very early in the morning and working all day and well into the night, including weekends.

The admiral himself was tireless. Eighteen-hour days, seven days a week. That was his routine. Those who refused to change lost. Some left, others were miserable in their jobs. The admiral demanded creative, innovative thinking and commitment.

In all my time with him, I do not recall the admiral ever bawling anyone out. He wasn't a table-pounder or an ass-chewer. When he was sure someone could not do the job, he simply removed him. He thought the best way to get across what he wanted to do was to meet and talk with people and lead them by example.

People in the field didn't have to wonder who he was, he was out there with them every day. When he talked to a junior officer, or an enlisted man, and they said something that made sense to him, he made certain something happened as a result. And the men knew that. That's the way he ran his command. He was always open to ideas.

Going out into the field involved a lot of risk. But I think he felt it had to be done that way, and I can't recall the admiral ever showing concern about his own personal safety. But I know he was concerned when he learned Elmo had volunteered to come to Vietnam to fight in the swift boats. The admiral took out a sheet of stationery and sent a handwritten request to Elmo's Navy detailer back in Washington, asking that if he were killed, Elmo be removed from the combat zone.

FOUR

★

ELMO:

After I finished the Navy communications course in Newport, Rhode Island, I was ordered to report to the *Claude B. Ricketts,* a guided missile destroyer stationed in Norfolk, Virginia. The ship's captain, Commander Thomas Mullane, had been the weapons officer on the *Dewey* when Dad commanded that ship. Dad and Commander Mullane had maintained a close friendship, and Dad knew he was one of the up-and-coming young officers. Although I had been on NROTC summer cruises before, I had never been on a ship where I was an officer with duties and responsibilities, so this was an exciting time for me. It was also the fulfillment of a childhood dream to be a naval officer. I was the electronics officer on the *Ricketts,* and we took cruises to the Caribbean where we test-fired the missiles.

In pretty short order, I realized I did not want to spend my life in the Navy. I had seen the Navy through Dad's eyes, which helped explain why I wanted to be a naval officer, but when I dealt with the nitty-gritty of Navy life I soon learned I did not like it. For one thing, I knew how hard that life is on families and I had decided I wanted to get married and raise a family. I did not like going to sea for months at a time. It was godawful to get up before dawn to take a 4 AM to 8 AM watch, and then be in the midst of a storm so violent that destroyers would disappear in front of you because the seas were so high. I knew I didn't want to spend a lifetime doing that.

After four or five months with the *Ricketts,* a Navy detailer came on board while we were ported in Norfolk. Detailers are the guys who make assignments for Navy personnel. He asked me what I wanted to do in the Navy, and gave me a list of possibilities, one of which was to serve as an officer-in-charge of a swift boat in Vietnam. He said they were usually senior ensigns, or lieutenant j.g.'s. Even though I had made up my mind not to make the Navy a career, I wanted the opportunity. I had always thought that combat was the true test of an officer, and I wanted to take that test. Also, the commodore of our division of ships, a Navy captain, had been in charge of the swift boats in Vietnam. He said officers in charge of those boats had more responsibility than the men who operated the missiles on our ship. I told the detailer that I wanted swift boats. He said I had a good chance of getting them.

I had not forgotten the conversation Dad and I had had when he, Mom, and Kathy had visited me in Newport the previous summer. I realized that Dad's misgivings about my serving in Vietnam made sense, but I had made no commitment not to go there. I guess you could say that I was kind of purposely vague when I talked to Dad then. Despite his personal feelings about the war, I knew he had regarded his Vietnam assignment as the biggest challenge of his naval career. And in my own way, I saw the command of a swift boat as a challenge for myself.

Right after I had told the Navy detailer that I wanted to be considered for swift boats, Commander Mullane called me into his office. We were still aboard the *Ricketts.* He said he wanted me to think long and hard about my decision. He said for Dad to be the commander of the naval forces in Vietnam, and to have his son in the front lines of combat in jeopardy all the time, would be a terrible burden for him. I do not think I fully appreciated what he meant then, but I understood what he was saying. I told Commander Mullane as politely as I could that I hoped the system would not interfere with my decision. Knowing the kind of man he is, and knowing he and Dad were close, I figured he would get the word some way to Dad. So I wrote Dad and told him I understood my coming to Vietnam would place him in a difficult situation, but I did not want him to stop me from volunteering.

I know there are many people then and now who think I volunteered for Vietnam to prove something to my father. It's impossible for me, or anyone, to know what our subconscious motives might be, but as far as my conscious thoughts were concerned, I never felt that I had anything to prove to Dad. I saw becoming a swift boat officer simply as a test of myself. I did not know if I would pass this test, if I would prove a good naval officer or a coward, but I knew I wanted to find out.

In the spring of 1969, the *Ricketts* left for a Mediterranean cruise, and my orders to report to swift boat training came while we were in port in Spain. I flew back to the States on a military plane and had a few days in Washington to spend with Kathy before I had to report to San Diego.

The relationship between Kathy and me had deepened during the last few months. While the *Ricketts* was in Norfolk, I had had most weekends to myself. A friend of mine lived in Washington and drove back there on weekends. I would ride with him, and he would drop me off at Kathy's parents' home. Kathy had always loved horses, and had a horse of her own named Egypt that she kept at a nearby stable. We went riding frequently, although I never became much of a horseman. I think Egypt began to realize Kathy and I were getting close. He made his views known by wedging his head between us and pushing me away from Kathy.

We sometimes drove into Georgetown to go dancing. Kathy never let me forget the time the car I was driving suddenly jumped the curb and started up the sidewalk, scaring the daylights out of her. Kathy thought I was a lousy driver. Actually, she was wearing shorts and I became so enthralled with her legs that I forgot to watch the road.

I had always thought that the most important decision I would ever make in my life would be choosing the person I married. I thought it would be more important than the career I chose or anything else. I had seen some unhappy marriages and I did not want to make the same mistake myself. But the more I got to know Kathy, the more I appreciated her humor, sensitivity, intelligence, and other qualities. I also fell in love with her. Kathy felt the same way, which is why my decision to go to Vietnam upset her so much.

KATHY COUNSELMAN ZUMWALT:

When Elmo told me he had volunteered for Vietnam, I took it as a personal affront. At that point, I knew I loved Elmo and I could not understand why he wanted to go off to fight in that war for a year. I felt our relationship had reached the point where we both wanted to be with one another as much as possible. It seemed to me that going to Vietnam was more important to Elmo than our relationship. I could have understood if he were drafted and had no choice, but he asked to go.

I also opposed the war and Elmo knew this. I had transferred to Marymount College in Tarrytown, New York, and the students and teachers there were extremely antiwar. In fact, a group of people there were charged with conspiracy to kidnap Henry Kissinger as a war protest, and one of the nuns at Marymount was involved. I had marched against the war and signed petitions to end the fighting.

As much as Elmo's decision upset me, I respected him enough to realize going to Vietnam was something he felt he had to do. I never became angry at the men who fought in the war. I had nothing but sympathy for them. I objected to the war policy, so I did not hold Elmo's participation in the war against him. He is from a military family and we viewed the war differently. I respected his views.

But his decision to go made me realize just how deeply I loved him. Despite my misgivings and hurt feelings, I wanted to become engaged before Elmo went to Vietnam. But Elmo refused. He told me I was only twenty years old and a junior in college and that I had a long life ahead of me. He said he feared being badly injured or maimed in battle. If that happened, he did not want me to feel obligated to him when he came home. I told him it would make no difference, but he would not change his mind. He even said he thought I should date some other men while he was in Vietnam, to be sure I wanted to marry him. I was sure already.

He left for San Diego from National Airport in Washington. I kissed him goodbye and then I cried.

ELMO:

When I first arrived in San Diego in the early summer of 1969, I needed a place to stay and looked for leads on the bulletin board at the Navy base. I found another naval officer who advertised for a roommate to share expenses for a house a block from the beach in Coronado. Coronado is a peninsula near San Diego where the swift boat training would be held. I went over there to meet this fellow, Ken Norton. I liked Ken almost immediately.

Often, Naval Academy graduates make it known very quickly where they went to school and frankly consider themselves superior to non-Academy officers. Ken, who came from Lady Lake, Florida, was one Academy grad who was not like that at all. Although he outranked me—he was a lieutenant j.g. and I was still an ensign—he was very low-key and likable. In fact, when I first asked him where he'd gone to school, he just said, "in the South." It took a while before I found out he had gone to the Naval Academy, and still later I learned he had been on the Academy boxing team.

Ken was of medium height and prematurely bald. He had a muscular build, and wore a thick mustache. Ken was very proud of his dad, a retired Navy commander. He owned an old Jaguar sedan that he maintained himself. And it turned out that we were in the same swift boat training class.

What I remember most vividly from our first meeting is that after I had known Ken less than an hour, he said very matter-of-factly that he expected to die in Vietnam. I tried to talk him out of it, but I could tell by the way he discussed it that it was something he absolutely knew was going to happen. It was as if he knew his destiny. I told him I did not think that was my destiny, and I said talking about a premonition might somehow help it become true. Ken then dropped the subject.

Although quiet, Ken was a fun-loving guy. He enjoyed cooking, driving his car, and going to parties. But because he believed so strongly that he would die in Vietnam, he made out a will. I'm normally not superstitious, but I refused to make out my will. I was only twenty-two, one year out of college, and I did not have much to leave anyone anyway. But I really believed that if I made out a will I might be setting things in motion for my own death.

The Coronado amphibious base where we trained was about three or four miles from where we lived. Ken drove me there every day. During our training, he sold his Jaguar, and bought a 1949 MG TC, a classic car that he prized. It was beautiful, and I remember that he told me he had left it to his brother in his will.

Besides Ken and me, there was one other officer in our training class, Jeff Jones. The Navy had already assigned the crews we would take to Vietnam so we would all go through the training together. We were first introduced to the swift boat, a 55-foot-long aluminum craft powered by twin 550-horsepower diesel engines. Swift boats could reach a speed of 30 knots, and were armed with an automatic grenade launcher, an 81 millimeter mortar, and 50 caliber or 60 caliber machine guns forward and aft. That was not a lot of firepower compared to many other ships, but these boats had the advantage of speed.

Much of our training took place in classrooms. We were shown how the Viet Cong attacked swift boats, the types of mines and traps they set. We were also taught how best to protect ourselves.

I got to know my crew. Billy Nairmore was the engineman. He was a big, strong guy from Alabama but also one of the gentlest men I have ever known. He had just turned twenty and was the only married member of our crew. His wife, Alice, was expecting their first baby. Geoff Martin was the top gunner. He came from the Los Angeles area and had already served a year in Vietnam on the PBRs, another type of river patrol boat. Whiting Shuford, the after gunner, came from North Carolina. Whiting had dropped out of college to join the Navy. There was a fourth member of the crew whom, for reasons that will become obvious, I do not wish to name.

After the initial part of our training in San Diego, the Navy assigned us to the San Francisco area, where we learned to completely take apart and repair the swift boat and its weapons. We went on mock patrols on the rivers near San Francisco. But the hardest part of our training came in a course called SERE, which stands for Survival, Evasion, Resistance, and Escape. The Navy conducted SERE in the California mountains.

The week-long course began in the classroom, where we learned about dangerous insects, the different types of vegetation, anything we might encounter in the wilds of Vietnam. But the last forty-eight hours proved the toughest. We were driven deep into the woods and left with only a knife. We had to live off the land while an aggressor force came after us. We tried to avoid capture, but were caught and taken to a prisoner-of-war compound. We were on limited rations and became pretty hungry. My throat began to feel dry from lack of water. The aggressor force consisted of men trained to apply techniques learned from ex-POWs of the Korean war. They made this a very realistic exercise. We were kept awake through two nights, and very quickly got the feeling of what it was like to be tired, hungry, and thirsty.

Then they tested us psychologically. They put me in a black box for about thirty minutes. It was so small I could not move. I even feared my circulation would be cut off.

These "aggressors" would also play the tough-guy, nice-guy routine. One would slam you in the mouth, shove you against the wall, kick you. You really felt like taking him on, but you were in a situation where they had a lot more guys than you could possibly handle. The "nice guy" would try to persuade you to capitulate after the "tough guy" had pounded you. At one point, I was given a dose of torture. I was held upside down and someone put a handkerchief against my nose and mouth, and poured water over my face. I felt as if I were underwater. I kept trying to tell myself that these guys would not drown me, but I also kept thinking they might screw up and drown me accidentally. They tried everything they could to break us. They played officers against enlisted men, blacks against whites, anything to gain an advantage.

If someone had ever asked me before that experience if I would feel real fear in a training exercise, I would have said no. But I did feel fear. The treatment became so harsh that one of the men broke and capitulated to the aggressors. We did everything we could to talk him out of it, but he would not stick with us, and we all really turned against him. That's how realistic it was. I believe he was taken off the swift boats and given an assignment in a noncombat area.

Finally, they gave us a liquid and brought us back to normal living conditions. At that point, I think we all knew if we were captured it was going to be pretty miserable. That was the real lesson for me and my crew: to avoid capture at all costs. When the SERE training ended, I felt like I was getting out of prison.

After our training ended, and we were preparing to go to Vietnam, I had dinner at a restaurant with Billy Nairmore and his wife Alice. All the members of my crew, including me, were volunteers and bachelors, except for Billy. He had been a reserve petty officer who had been called to active duty. That was unusual, but it happened. I vividly remember the dinner because Alice and Billy had only been married a few months, and obviously were very much in love.

Alice is an outspoken woman in any case. She strongly opposed the war, and did not want Billy to go to Vietnam. She made her views known to me in no uncertain terms. Billy interrupted at one point and asked her if she knew that I was the son of the naval commander in Vietnam. She said she didn't, but it didn't make any difference. She told me that I had better make darn sure that Billy came back from the war alive. I'm normally the type of person who jumps in and defends my position, but in this case I just listened to what Alice had to say. I acknowledged the situation did seem unfair, and very precarious for Billy. I promised Alice I would do my damnedest to get us through Vietnam alive.

In August 1969, I arrived in Cam Ranh Bay in Vietnam along with my boat crew, and Ken Norton and Jeff Jones and their crews. On the last night before we left to assume our command duties, the three of us went to the officers' club. The beach at Cam Ranh Bay is one of the most beautiful in the world. The sand is almost pure white and the water is a crystal-clear blue. The officers' club sat right at the edge of the surf, offering a spectacular view. That night was very clear and warm. The moon glinted off the water. It was hard to believe, sitting there enjoying gin and tonics with friends, that a war was going on, and in very short order I would be in the middle of it. I wondered that night if the three of us would be there a year from now.

Ken Norton and I had both been ordered to Da Nang, to coastal division 12. Jeff Jones had been ordered to go down south. In Da Nang I was assigned my swift boat and began patrolling in the South China Sea, off the coast of Vietnam. Inexperienced crews, such as mine, were given a senior combat officer to ride along with them on their first patrols to show us the ropes.

That's where I first met Lieutenant j.g. Bob Crosby. Bob was a smart, experienced officer from South Hamilton, Massachusetts, and a Cornell graduate. He had a quick sense of humor and was patient with green crews. He spent a lot of time telling me what to watch out for on swift boat patrols. After I got to know Bob well, he and I talked together in the officers' barracks late one afternoon. Bob spoke in a quiet, reflective way, and said he had had an intense feeling—a premonition—that he was not going to make it through Vietnam alive when he had first come here a year earlier. But he said now that he was no longer on the dangerous river patrols, and was training crews in ocean patrols, he had been through the worst. He said he had only about thirty days left in Vietnam, and it looked like he was going to make it. I thought of Ken Norton's premonition of death, and I felt some reassurance for Ken that Bob had had similar feelings.

Like most people reaching the end of their tour, Bob took

precautions. He did not want to tempt fate. In our barracks at night, we sometimes received enemy rocket fire. One night the rocket fire was especially heavy, and I woke up to hear the rockets exploding just beyond the barracks. I was still in bed when I heard Bob running down the hall toward the bunkers, where there was more protection against the rocket fire. I came to appreciate his attitude more and more the closer I came to the end of my own combat tour. I was in constant fear that after all I had been through, as I neared the end, I would take a hit.

Sometimes we patrolled near the coast, and once we were joined by a South Vietnamese sailor who had lost members of his family to the Viet Cong. His hatred of the Communists consumed him. We made a tape in Vietnamese that insulted the VC and North Vietnamese. That tape said they ran like dogs, stank like rotten fish, and fought like chickens. We played it over the boat loudspeaker as we neared the coastline to draw the enemy out. It did not take long before someone opened fire from the shore. We were ready and fired back immediately. It's one hell of a strange feeling when you are shot at.

It was my first firefight. In the panic I accidentally loaded one mortar round on top of another that had already been put in the barrel. It could have exploded and killed all of us. But for some unknown reason, neither round went off. It was a stupid mistake on my part, one I would never repeat, but it gave me an appreciation of what combat can make you do.

Except for that one incident, the heavy seas proved to be the worst thing about the coastal patrols. Sometimes the waves rose so high they tossed our 55-foot boat around like a cork. When it was really bad, the only thing we could do was lie flat in the boat so we wouldn't get knocked silly. Other than that, we felt relatively safe on these patrols.

Long before I arrived in Vietnam, I had heard a lot of Navy people were wondering what kind of cushy job I was going to get. Some Navy people even harassed my crew for being on the boat commanded by Admiral Zumwalt's son. Hearing that kind of thing was not my reason for requesting river patrols, which everyone knew were dangerous, but I did not appreciate the fact that my crew and I were being unfairly judged before we were given a chance to perform.

I had made it a special point not to contact Dad when I arrived in Vietnam. I wanted to avoid even the appearance of receiving some special privilege. But that didn't end the talk, or stop Dad from wanting to see me. I knew that I would hear from him.

ADMIRAL:

I realized Elmo would be uneasy about meeting with me once he arrived in Vietnam, so I went up to Da Nang one time when I knew he would be there and caught him by surprise. It was wonderful to see him again after nearly a year. I felt a father's pride in seeing him in uniform, and in command of his own boat. I had already heard through the grapevine that Elmo was a good officer. I always knew he would be.

There is an age-old military tradition that senior military fathers can have their sons serve as flag lieutenants and aides, and many generals in Vietnam had done that. I thought it would be futile to ask Elmo if he would consider serving with me, but I asked him anyway. He said he appreciated my offer, but he did not desire Saigon duty. He wanted field experience.

He was the type of officer that I treasured as a commander, but as his father, I was scared as hell because I knew his boldness and courage could get him killed. I had seen these characteristics surface during his illnesses, and again in high school when he got into scuffles with those bigger guys. I had even asked him not to take on those fellows, but he did anyway. I often recalled the time I had locked him out of the house when he was six and left him to fight that bully, Tiger. This experience, coupled with his own stubborn character, seemed to have given Elmo a high level of physical courage, and now I was worried. I knew Elmo was smart enough not to do anything foolish, but I knew he would take intelligent risks. If you take enough intelligent risks, pretty soon the odds are going to get you.

I also knew Elmo faced additional danger because he was my son. I had already been the target of one assassination attempt. It had happened at the compound where I lived in Saigon. Every lunchtime, we played volleyball there, and I regularly participated. One time, a Viet Cong rode by on a bicycle and tossed a grenade over the wall. I was lucky because I happened not to be playing that day, and no one else was hurt because the would-be assassin threw the grenade into the wrong area. It exploded at a safe distance from everyone.

I knew the Viet Cong and North Vietnamese regarded it as a major victory to kill or capture a high-ranking officer, or his son. We had seen it happen with the capture of Admiral McCain's aviator son. We later learned the North Vietnamese were especially brutal to him. That was why I had strongly believed that someday I would have to tell Elmo's mother that something terrible had happened to him.

Elmo and I spent the night together at VIP headquarters in Da Nang, which really wasn't very VIP-ish. We talked about family matters over dinner. I told Elmo what I had heard from Mouza and the girls, and how Jim was doing at college.

We took a long walk along an isolated stretch of beach. Elmo told me what he had learned about the river patrol operations. He understood the tactics and overall strategy of their mission and expressed a strong desire to go to the southern regions around Sea Float, An Thoi, and Ha Tien, the areas of heaviest river fighting. I warned him that these places were very dangerous, which, of course, only brought a gleam to his eye.

I knew Elmo would never allow me to stop him, so I gave him two pieces of advice. I told my son that he had to be as meticulous as possible in obeying the rules of engagement, and I said he should be as tough as hell on his crew. I told him of postmortems I had conducted on the patrol boat firefights the day after. I said crews who took the casualties often turned out to be the ones who had let their guard down. I said riding herd on his crew wouldn't always make him popular, but that was one of the prices of command.

I knew Elmo well enough to realize that he would scrupulously avoid even the appearance of favoritism, which I think was one of the reasons he wanted to be in the areas of the heaviest fighting. It was his way of proving to everyone that he wasn't getting any favors because of my position. That meant he was going to be exposed to as much danger as any of the swift boats, and probably more.

Early the next morning, Elmo saluted me goodbye—with a smile on his face—and I returned to Saigon.

By the time Elmo had arrived in Vietnam the summer of 1969, the Navy had blockaded the river and canal system along the Cambodian border and enemy control of the delta had been reduced. I thought the Navy was uniquely suited to engage the enemy on the Ca Mau Peninsula, at the southernmost tip of Vietnam. This peninsula contains uncounted streams and dense mangrove swamps. It was hard to get to and even harder to get into.

For years, the Viet Cong had used the peninsula as a sanctuary. When our forces controlled neighboring areas of the delta, the Viet Cong would return to this area where they could not be reached. The U.S. Command had regarded the Viet Cong on the Ca Mau Peninsula as so firmly entrenched that it had evacuated as many of the inhabitants as possible and then bombed it with B-52s.

I learned firsthand how well the Viet Cong protected the area. Soon after I had arrived in South Vietnam, I had flown low over Ca Mau in an Army reconnaissance plane. The VC proved very alert, because on the first pass they fired at us; I could see the tracers. To get a better sighting, I asked Lieutenant Lew Glenn, who was with me, to tell the pilot to fly over the area one more time. This time the fire became more intense. Lew turned to me and said if I asked to fly over a third time, he would revolt. I didn't and he didn't.

Besides its tactical significance, Ca Mau was important for other reasons. It had been one of the most fertile and industrious regions of South Vietnam, but under the thumb of the VC it had become virtually inactive.

I learned another reason for its importance after I made a helicopter trip there in the presence of Admiral Tran van Chon, who was the overall commander of the South Vietnamese Navy. I came to hold Admiral Chon in the utmost respect. He was an extremely intelligent man, a devout Buddhist, and a true patriot. He had risen on merit, not through a coup.

I still recall the trip we made to the peninsula that day. He told me that in the early 1960s the Viet Cong had thrown the Vietnamese Navy out of this area, and he felt it would be a great triumph if we could take it back. I could tell by the way he talked about it that the idea of returning touched him deeply. It was not his own personal pride at stake. He felt it would also be good for the entire economy of South Vietnam.

It occurred to me that if the Navy could gain control of a section of the principal river that cut through the peninsula—flowing from the Gulf of Siam to the South China Sea—it might be possible for a resettlement effort to begin on the riverbanks and gradually spread up- and downstream and inland as the foothold expanded. The Army thought that it would prove even more foolish than a land base, but General Abrams, who had a quick and thorough grasp of tactics, overruled the IV Corps senior adviser. That was how Sea Float, as we came to call it, originated.

We actually assembled Sea Float in Saigon by tying eleven giant pontoons together. In all, Sea Float was about the size of a football field and was big enough for helicopters to land on. It also served as a base for our river patrol craft. Sea Float contained a galley, drinking water, medical and dental facilities, and a fuel supply for our boats and aircraft. After it was assembled, which took just over a month, we towed it in the open sea along the coast of Vietnam, and then into the Cua Lon River. We anchored this huge platform in the middle of the river at Nam Cam, where Sea Float became an instant island. Just getting Sea Float up that river and secured proved a feat in itself because the currents in the Cua Lon River are extremely swift, making this kind of maneuver very hazardous. After our man-made island was in place, one of the men called Sea Float an "apparition that just appeared out of nowhere." I suspect that is what it might have looked like to the Viet Cong and the North Vietnamese.

Sea Float was manned by two hundred personnel and we took great precautions against enemy attack. We placed nets upriver to stop any mines from being floated downstream. We also armed Sea Float with mortars and rockets, a Navy SEAL platoon, and we regularly threw hand grenades overboard in case the enemy tried to swim underwater to get at us. One time after we threw in a grenade, a dead Viet Cong floated to the top of the river.

Swift boats and the more heavily armored river assault boats tied up to Sea Float and we staged general quarters drills at night. We would send an alarm and the boats would move away from Sea Float and take their positions, the helicopters would lift off, and we would unleash a huge amount of automatic fire into the river-bank areas. Every fifth round from a machine gun consists of tracers to track where you are firing. All that firepower created an awesome sight. It was supposed to.

I figured the VC, the North Vietnamese, or both, were watching us. I knew if they witnessed one of our general quarters drills they would think long and hard before attacking Sea Float. That must have been the conclusion they reached, for despite the vulnerability of this small, man-made island in the middle of enemy territory, they never made an all-out attempt to destroy it.

Within a surprisingly short time, Sea Float's success became evident. The Vietnamese began resettling along the riverbanks. They planted pineapples once again, rebuilt pottery kilns, and renewed shrimping and fishing. More and more old inhabitants returned to the area. Our pacification team learned that the Viet-namese had given up a charcoal business at Nam Cam because the Viet Cong tax collectors would take all their money while they were en route to Saigon to sell their charcoal, which was used for cooking in Vietnam. The SEAL teams, working with the swift boats and the river assault boats, patrolled the rivers leading from Nam Cam to Saigon, and soon after Nam Cam's old charcoal business began to thrive again.

Perhaps Admiral Chon appreciated Sea Float's success most.

Despite the deep cultural differences between us, I came to regard him as a close friend. It pleased me personally, as well as militarily, to help him and his country establish a strong foothold in the Ca Mau Peninsula.

The fact that Elmo served in combat in Vietnam highlighted one of our cultural differences. In Vietnamese society, the sons of high-ranking people unashamedly used their influence to avoid battle. That did not bother me, as I simply accepted that fact as a part of Vietnamese life.

In all my dealings with Admiral Chon, I never tried to act as if I were running the show. I always began by asking his advice, and then made recommendations to him. Sea Float was established in this way. I found him a man of courage and honor. At one point, I had received an intelligence report of an impending Vietnamese coup. It was marked for U.S. eyes only, but I thought that was a stupid order and I told one of my aides to go to Admiral Chon in the middle of the night and warn him. Admiral Chon already knew that the coup would not happen, but my aide told me the admiral wept because I had thought enough of him to warn him against direct orders. An enduring bond of trust was forged between us.

I made it a practice to issue memorandums to my staff listing ideas I thought could expedite the U.S. departure from Vietnam. These memorandums were called "ZWI," for "Zumwalt's Wild Ideas." Sea Float remained one of my favorite wild ideas, and I visited it every month or so, often bringing along senior officers from the Army or Air Force who had thought Sea Float would never work.

We used Sea Float as a base for the river craft, but because of the heavy density of the jungle growth and the narrowness of many of the rivers and canals in that part of Vietnam, our boat crews were suffering very heavy casualties. The VC would rush in to set up an ambush, then dash out, all under cover of the jungle. Also, the Cua Lon River in the area where we placed Sea Float is only about 400 yards wide, so despite all our precautions, the jungle afforded the enemy too much protection when he decided to strike at us. That was why I wanted the area around Sea Float, and many riverbanks in the Ca Mau Peninsula, to be sprayed heavily with Agent Orange. I gave the order to do it.

I had strong feelings for the young men who were out in the field, fighting the war, risking, and sometimes losing, their lives. No commander who cares about his men can escape these feelings. I based my decision to use Agent Orange, like every other decision I made in Vietnam, on my desire to minimize casualties and end the U.S. involvement in the war as successfully, and quickly, as possible.

I especially remember two lieutenant commanders named Petersen and Elliot. I rode on each of their boats several times. They commanded in sequence the rivers on each side of the Parrot's Beak—that part of Cambodia that juts into Vietnam west of Saigon—during the operation we called Giant Slingshot, which was our successful effort to stop the infiltration of enemy arms and men into the area around Saigon. These rivers run along both sides of the Parrot's Beak and then converge to form a giant letter Y, which is where we derived the name Slingshot.

Within hours after I had ridden on the boats of these two young men, they were killed in separate firefights. I felt a sense of personal loss that remains with me to this day.

Every day Elmo remained in Vietnam, I feared he would share the same fate, and I will confess how I showed favoritism to him. Early every morning when I arrived at headquarters, I would look over the lists detailing the firefights our riverboats had been in the previous night. I always looked first to see if Elmo's boat had been hit. I have always felt a little guilty about doing that because I was the commander for all the brave young men in those boats. But I could not stop being a father.

FIVE

─────────── ★ ───────────

ELMO:

We broiled in the hot afternoon sun as our swift boat moved slowly along a river south of Da Nang. Our partner boat headed down one fork, while we took the other.

It was a manhunt. We were hunting the enemy, and they were hunting us. That's exactly how it felt on river patrols every day, every minute we were on them. We never knew when we came around a bend in the river, sometimes so narrow that we couldn't turn our 55-foot boat around, that someone wasn't lying in wait ready to shoot us. The only constants were fear and an obsession with survival.

The rivers were often beautiful and had picturesque names like Song Dam Doi and the Song Bo De. In the evenings, the sunsets were spectacular. But my appreciation of all this beauty faded quickly in the atmosphere of war.

We came to a wider part of the river. Along some of the banks were brown, stripped patches, evidence of defoliation. We approached an area where our patrol boats had been fired on before. Everyone on our boat was at the ready. On our left we spotted an enemy bunker sitting very low and almost invisible along the edge of the shoreline. No one was in it.

The enemy often fired at our boats from bunkers. They dug them deep in the ground so they could not be easily seen, then covered them over with layer upon layer of mud and straw, until they looked like a mound of earth. When the mud dried, they became as strong as cement. We could not penetrate these bunkers even with our 81 millimeter mortar. I wanted to blow the bunker up with plastic explosives to give the enemy one less protected ambush site.

We beached our swift boat and Geoff Martin, who was experienced with plastic explosives, and I hopped out. He stuffed a thick chunk of plastic inside the bunker and lit the fuse. I was only twenty or thirty feet away when it exploded.

My ears were ringing as I walked back to our boat. Suddenly I saw tracer rounds from automatic-weapon fire coming at us. A split second later I heard incoming rounds ricocheting off our boat.

"They're shooting at us," I yelled.

Whiting Shuford, our after gunner, was already returning fire.

Adrenaline pumped through my body. Every muscle tensed. Geoff and I dived back on the boat. Billy Nairmore gunned the engines. I ordered Billy to move out into the river where we could maneuver. I did not want to be pinned down on the shore.

They were firing at us from two positions along the riverbank about seventy-five yards away, protected by trees. I did not know if they were Viet Cong or North Vietnamese regulars, not that it made any difference at this point. Whiting and Geoff sprayed 50 caliber rounds into their position. I fired my M-16 at them, but that was a pop gun compared to the automatic weapons they were using.

After a few minutes, their firing eased, then it quit completely. I do not know if we hit them. We did not go to find out. Fortunately, none of my crew had been injured.

I did not think the ambush was planned. Planned ambushes often caught our boats in murderous crossfires. This time I think they saw us blow up their bunker and wanted to teach us a lesson.

My adrenaline rush began to subside. It was not our first river firefight, and I knew it would not be our last.

I had begun river patrols south of Da Nang, near the town of Hoi An, after a month on coastal patrols. It had not taken me long to realize why they were far riskier than coastal patrols.

Swift boats usually travelled in pairs and I had grown increasingly unhappy with my sister boat. I wanted to go up more uncharted rivers and canals, but the officer-in-charge of the other boat preferred to stick with routine patrols. A short time after the bunker incident, I asked the commanding officer of our swift boat group for another partner. He asked me who I wanted, so I requested Ken Norton, who had just come off coastal patrols and was now in the Da Nang area.

Ken and I began patrolling together. We saw eye to eye on tactics, and we had the same attitude on the war. We might not have agreed with all the reasons our country waged it, but we thought that as long as we were involved we should try to do the best job we could.

While in the Da Nang area, defoliation efforts were obviously under way. Dramatic changes took place before our eyes in many of the areas we patrolled. One week there would be thick green foliage, and the next we would see leaves and grass eaten away from the devastating effects of Agent Orange. We patrolled near the places where spraying occurred, and I suspect on occasion we ourselves might have been sprayed. At the time, I felt safer knowing that if anyone wanted to ambush us, at least they would no longer shoot us from point-blank range without exposing themselves to risks.

We conducted many of our patrols at night, because that was when the VC usually infiltrated. I do not think anyone who went on night patrol can forget his first one. It is an indescribable feeling. It was pitch black on the rivers, and often there was so much jungle growth that it looked like shadow upon shadow. We had to keep glancing at the boat radar to see where the riverbanks were, because radar was all we had to guide us. We hoped every little blip we saw on the radar did not turn out to be some VC sampan just waiting to fire at us. We had the feeling that we were in a dark closet, with the door closed, and someone was in there with a gun trying to kill us.

Sometimes we stopped along the riverbanks. We heard every sound, the rustling of the wind, the movement of a small animal. At first I thought every noise was a Viet Cong setting up an ambush, and I readied my M-16 more than once. But soon my hearing developed to the point where I could differentiate between normal jungle sounds and the sound of a human foot moving.

To train helicopter crews how to better react when we called for air support, a helicopter pilot once went on patrol with us. I'll never forget his remark: "Up in the helicopters we're the hunters, but down here you are the hunted." Much of the time that's exactly how we felt. We usually only found the enemy after he had found us first.

It had not taken me long to realize the truth in Dad's advice that I should be hard on my crew. I kept on them. I insisted that they wear flak jackets and helmets at all times. Everyone did, except for Geoff Martin. Geoff was our top gunner. He was a damn good shot and a valuable man to have in a firefight. But Geoff had been in Vietnam before, aboard PBRs, and he thought he knew a lot more about river combat than I did. I thought he probably did too, but I did not want any member of my crew killed because I had been negligent about getting them to wear flak jackets.

So one day Geoff and I had it out. I told him to put on his flak jacket. He said it was too hot and the enemy was not around anyway. I said I didn't give a damn about the weather, or where he thought the enemy might or might not be, I wanted him in his flak jacket. I thought that settled it, but a couple of minutes later I looked over at Geoff and he still had not put on his flak jacket. I told him I would put it on for him. He made a wisecrack and I challenged him to a fight.

"If I hit you, they'll court-martial me," he said.

I told him I'd take my bars off, and we would fight man to man.

He looked at me and said, "If it means that much to you, I'll put the damn flak jacket on."

I was relieved for a couple of reasons, not the least of which concerned the fact that he was bigger than me, and no doubt would have beat the hell out of me.

I kept us on maximum alert at all times. Sometimes when we waited quietly along a riverbank, I deliberately threw shells into the jungle just to keep everyone on their toes. It worked. They would all tense up and get ready to fire. Another time Geoff Martin fell asleep. I held an M-16 a couple of feet from his ear and fired. It woke him up real fast, and damn, was he mad. I did not care how angry my crew got at me or what kind of a son of a bitch they thought I was.

One of our gunners, Whiting Shuford, came from a wealthy North Carolina family and had lived a comfortable life. Whiting razzed the hell out of Billy Nairmore. Billy wasn't any more frightened than we were—and I'll be the first to admit I was scared the whole damn time I was on patrol—but he showed it more. That's what Whiting razzed him about. Knowing that Billy was married and had more to lose than the rest of us, I became annoyed at Whiting. I finally decided to turn the tables on him and I put him up in what we called the "peak tank." This was the forward 60 caliber machine-gun position, at the very bow of the boat, right in the area where we were taking our heaviest hits.

Whiting got mad as hell at me and requested a transfer. I told him the only reason he wanted to transfer was because I put him up in the peak tank. He then volunteered for any position on anybody's else's boat. The transfer didn't come through very quickly, and after a while Whiting was cured of picking on Billy. I rotated him off the peak tank and onto the after 50s, which was the second most important position on the boat. Whiting changed his mind, stayed with our boat, and always demonstrated great courage in battle. He and I began to get along a little better, and later became close friends.

Very early in my tour an incident occurred that made me realize it was risky to maintain a pattern that the enemy could observe.

We had turned up a narrow river earlier in the day, and our propellers became entangled in a fishing net near a sandbar at the mouth of the river. We tried to untangle the net, but the job proved hopeless, so we cut the net away and continued on patrol.

That evening we banked our boat on the same sandbar. This was the same place and the same time we always stopped to have dinner and relax for a while before going on night patrol. One of the guys was on watch, and others were sleeping. It was quiet and peaceful, when all of a sudden we were startled by a thunderous explosion. I had no idea where the explosion came from, but it was so close that at first I thought it might be our own or our sister boat. When I realized it wasn't, my immediate reaction was to get our boat under way and then try to figure out what had happened. I could feel the explosion ringing in my ears.

We prepared to move out into the river, and I then realized what had happened. The VC had floated a mine down the river and it had hit two wooden South Vietnamese Navy junks that had been lashed together and were patrolling just upriver from us. Nothing was left of the people on the boats, or the boats themselves. I am convinced that the fisherman's net we ripped earlier in the day belonged to a Viet Cong. He knew where we went ashore every night, and he set out to pay us back for ripping his net. It was by pure chance that those junks were hit instead of our boat. From that moment on, I never followed any pattern at all. My only pattern was to have none.

I realized that the Viet Cong or North Vietnamese would take a special satisfaction in killing or capturing me because of Dad. One time the swift boat base radio announced that Admiral Zumwalt's son rode on the 35 boat. I immediately had the numbers on my boat painted out, because I thought the enemy might monitor our radio. I also made it a point to tell the guy who announced my name that I did not appreciate being made a celebrity and a target.

After patrolling around Da Nang for several weeks, I volunteered to go to the southern part of Vietnam, where the river fighting was reportedly heavier. I headed toward An Thoi, a village on Phu Quoc Island in the Gulf of Siam. From there, we would patrol over to Sea Float in the Ca Mau Peninsula, and to the Ha Tien area near the Cambodian border.

Before we left, I felt I needed to talk to Billy Nairmore to see if he wanted to go with us, or to remain in the Da Nang area with another boat. Given the fact he was married with a baby on the way, I thought I at least owed him that. I told him I thought our risks would be greater in the south, but Billy said he thought we had a good crew. He felt close to us, and he wanted to take his chances with us.

We were short one crew member, because earlier one of the original members of my crew had been transferred to another boat. The transfer of crew members from one boat to another was done routinely to replace casualties, and I had volunteered this fellow because on one occasion he had too much to drink, leapt off the boat, and walked into a minefield. Whiting Shuford and I both jumped out of the boat to get him, and he took a swing at me when I tried to pull him back toward the boat.

Another time after he had drunk too much he wildly fired the 50 caliber machine gun into the river in the middle of the night. It scared the hell out of all of us. Given the uncertainty and danger of the situation we were in, I didn't want anyone on my boat capable of doing something like that. Because the south was considered high-risk, all swift boats that went there were assigned a full crew.

Whiting had befriended Harvey Miller, a member of Ken Norton's crew, and thought he would work well with our crew. Ken assured me that Harvey, who came from the Baltimore area, would prove a good man. He graciously agreed to let us take Harvey to bring our crew up to full strength.

Ken had decided to remain in the Da Nang area for the time being. He was a terrific guy to have had on my partner boat, and I knew I would miss him. We had become even closer friends, and he had paid me the ultimate compliment by naming his pet duck Elmo. The night before I left, we talked in the officers' quarters and vowed to meet again.

Before reporting to my new base, I first flew to Cam Ranh Bay to report to the commodore in charge of swift boats. The next morning, I had just finished shaving when I met another swift boat officer I knew from Da Nang. He asked if I had heard that Bob Crosby, the lieutenant who had trained me and my crew, had been killed. I was overwhelmed by the sheer horror of it. Bob had had only nine days left in Vietnam.

When I learned the circumstances under which he died, my horror only deepened. Bob had been killed when a 50 caliber machine gun round hit him in the back at point-blank range. The gun had been fired by a sailor on one of our own swift boats tied to the dock at Da Nang. They were a green crew, going through a series of checks. Bob apparently had been walking away from the boat when he was shot. He had been evacuated to a hospital in Saigon, where he died. Bob's death haunted me not only because of his premonition of death and my friendship with him, but for a more personal reason: The last crews to have patrolled with that swift boat before the new crew took over were mine.

Then, as now, I have wondered if I was in any way to blame for his death. Somehow, some way, an unspent shell was still in that machine gun. It had been Whiting Shuford's machine gun, and when I spoke to him later, he was absolutely certain he unloaded that gun when we brought the boat in after our final Da Nang patrol. Geoff Martin said he even witnessed Whiting tossing out the shell. I know them both to be honorable men.

But I have never been able to escape my feeling of responsibility in Bob's death. Officers-in-charge of swift boats were not required, or expected, to check every gun mount after patrol. I never did, and I never saw any other officer do it. Despite how irrational it may sound, I still feel that I should have checked those guns after our final patrol.

I have played and replayed the accident over in my mind. I know even if the worst is true, that my crew had left a live round in that gun, the new gunner still had to cock the gun and pull the trigger to fire it. At best, that would be grossly negligent. It is also possible that the ammunition linkage belts may have been left attached to the gun. If so, then this new gunner needed to cock the gun enough times to feed a shell into the chamber, which also would be grossly negligent.

I had sensed resentment from some Navy people ever since I first arrived in Vietnam. The Bob Crosby incident let some of that resentment come to the surface. My crew was still in Da Nang at the time of Bob's death. A member of another swift boat ran up to Geoff Martin and screamed that we had killed Bob. I think if the officer-in-charge of that boat had been anyone other than Admiral Zumwalt's son, no one would have made that accusation.

I left Cam Ranh Bay on my way south to An Thoi, but stopped first in Saigon to meet up with my crew. I would also talk with Dad. Although I was leery about meeting with him, I had a lot to tell him.

ADMIRAL:

Elmo came to see me at my headquarters in Saigon and I realized in very short order that something bothered him. When we had some time alone at my compound that night, he told me about the Bob Crosby incident. He said Bob's death caused him almost intolerable pain because in his own mind he felt in some way responsible. He explained why. I told him in wartime those tragedies happen, and I tried to convince him that he should not feel responsible because an entire intervening crew had been involved.

I recognized how difficult a burden he was carrying because of an episode that has haunted me for years. I had never told him before, but I thought this was the right time. It happened in 1945, when I was a brand-new executive officer aboard the destroyer *Saufley*. This incident occurred right after my marriage to Mouza, when we were based in Shanghai. We sailed out of Shanghai to help merchant ships coming into Shanghai navigate into the harbor. We brought the harbor pilots out to the merchant ships on the *Saufley*, and then transferred them to the merchant ships' lifeboats.

The first or second time we attempted to transfer a harbor pilot, the weather became rough. The wind whipped up huge waves, while a fierce nine-mile-an-hour current flowed. I recommended to the skipper that we stop sending pilots to the merchant ships and just instruct the merchant captains to anchor until the weather cleared. He overruled me and I argued with him, but he directed me to carry out his order. We began to launch a lifeboat to transfer a harbor pilot. Three sailors boarded the lifeboat. The normal procedure was to unhook the stern line and hold the lifeboat by the bow line. But somehow the bow line disconnected first, and the lifeboat swung around and swamped.

The three sailors were all wearing life jackets when they plunged into the water. Two drifted clear and we immediately retrieved them in another boat. But a line had caught around the ankle of the third fellow and the force of that current pushed him underwater. We threw over our grappling hook and caught his life jacket and began to pull him up. I stood at the gunnel with five other sailors, and we all reached for him as we hauled him up. He was no more than three inches from our grasp when his life jacket suddenly slid off over his head. At the same moment, the line wrapped around his ankle came off. He fell into the sea and was swept under. We never recovered his body.

I understood Elmo's torment, and I tried to tell him that to dwell on such events would not allow him to be fit and ready to carry out his wartime responsibilities. I think what I said registered with him, but it really did not ease the deep feelings he had about Bob's death.

The Navy convened a board of inquiry on the shooting, which is routine in such matters. I sent word to my superior, the Commander of the Pacific Fleet, that my son was involved. I requested that I be taken out of the normal chain of command. That meant that the board's inquiry would completely bypass me, and go directly to my superior. If there were even the appearance that I had influenced the board's decision, I knew the situation could become difficult for both of us, so I stayed completely out of it. Elmo fully supported my decision.

Both Elmo and I felt uneasy about visiting one another because Elmo never wanted to be perceived as someone who loitered around headquarters. He left for An Thoi early the next day, after we had talked much of the night. From a commander's perspective, it helped me to have someone in the rivers who told me exactly what he thought. Elmo had many ideas for improvements. For instance, he thought patrol boats should be painted green instead of gray to make them harder for the enemy to spot, and soon after we made that change.

We had also instituted other changes in our river patrol tactics to make them more effective, and less risky for our men. Instead of always waiting for the enemy to strike first, the patrol boats began positioning themselves along the riverbanks at night to ambush the enemy when he came to them. That was how we fought this river guerrilla war. We created new tactics as we went along.

We were still intercepting huge supplies of mostly Chinese and Russian arms infiltrating from Cambodia. We couldn't reach the source of the arms because the enemy took full advantage of the rules of limited war under which we operated. Because our coastal patrols had stopped the enemy from bringing their arms directly from North Vietnam into South Vietnam, they had made an end run around us by sending merchant ships laden with arms into the South China Sea around Vietnam over to Sihanoukville, Cambodia, where they docked. The weapons then were trucked overland to the border with South Vietnam, and then at night, sampans ferried them into South Vietnam.

We could not intercept these seagoing ships in international waters, but we knew our river patrols were making it harder for the enemy to smuggle arms along the rivers. They carried more and more of their weapons into South Vietnam by overland routes, often on their backs, which was much slower and harder. We could see the results in the pacification of the delta, the one area in Vietnam where the in-country Navy played a major role because of all the waterways.

Besides conducting the river war, I spent a considerable amount of time ensuring that the Navy people who served in-country in Vietnam were given proper credit. This would lead to their selection for promotion. I made certain the Navy would not ignore or downgrade their service just because many Navy traditionalists considered Vietnam some kind of banana war, not a "Navy" war. In one instance, I asked General Abrams to sign the fitness reports of all three of my task force commanders because I knew his signature carried a great deal of weight. I am pleased to say that Bob Salzer, commander of the mobile riverine flotilla; Art Price, commander of the PRBs; and Roy Hoffman, commander of the swift boat task force, all made admiral.

I spent most of my time on ACTOV, my acronym for Accelerated Turnover to Vietnam. Admiral Chon was my constant ally in ACTOV. Despite some misgivings within our command, Admiral Chon insisted the South Vietnamese could be rapidly trained to assume combat and command responsibilities.

Trained Vietnamese sailors were steadily replacing U.S. sailors on the river and coastal patrols, and by the fall of 1969, some of the patrol boats were fully manned by South Vietnamese crews. From the reports I received at headquarters, the Vietnamese boats did not operate differently from those run by American crews. Like ours, some sought out the enemy, and others played it safe. It was also clear from those operations reports that Elmo's was among the most aggressive boats.

Unannounced, I flew to the southern part of South Vietnam to accompany Elmo on a night patrol. I had always felt it important to go on combat missions with all the different Navy patrol crafts so I could understand better what the men went through. But when I arrived at Elmo's base, I discovered he had been called away because of a big firefight somewhere else. I arranged to ride on another swift boat that night. Before we left, the officer-in-charge, a lieutenant j.g., told me not to wear anything white or bright because it could be seen by the enemy. That evening we stopped and waited for hours along a riverbank. I remember thinking how nerve-wracking it must be for those crews to do this night after night. It made me realize what Elmo went through, the feeling that danger lurked all around.

At about two in the morning, my nose began to run and I absentmindedly took out my white handkerchief. The officer-in-charge damn nearly tackled me.

"Don't do that," he said.

I immediately put my handkerchief away and apologized because he was responsible for that boat, and had acted properly. Although there was some firing around us that night, we were not involved in any shooting. The next morning I returned to Saigon.

Back at headquarters, General Abrams sent for me. When I entered his office he looked directly at me and said, "I understand you're trying to be a goddamn hero."

I said, "No, sir."

"Then why are you riding in those goddam boats?" he asked.

I said, "General, because it's the only way I can fully understand what my men are going through out there."

I could see tears rolling down his cheeks. He handed me a message and said, "Look at this. Here's another goddam hero out to see the action."

The message reported that Colonel Donald Starry's helicopter had been shot down near the Cambodian border. He was one of Abrams's favorites, a real go-getter.

Abrams told me not to ride the boats anymore. I insisted it was important, so we agreed I would do it less, and would always tell him beforehand. Colonel Starry's story had a happy ending because we later learned he survived the helicopter downing. He went on to become a four-star general.

Several weeks after the Navy board of inquiry began looking into Bob Crosby's death, they issued their report. After asking many tough questions of Elmo and his crew, and examining the incident thoroughly, the board exonerated Elmo and his crew of responsibility in the shooting. The only one who has never exonerated Elmo is Elmo.

SIX

★

ELMO'S CREW

WHITING SHUFORD, AFTER GUNNER:

Elmo was a hard-assed commander, and he made a lot of bull-shit rules that annoyed the hell out of the crew. Behind his back we used to call him "Brass Brat III." I remember one time I wanted a cup of coffee when we stopped at a village. Elmo said no. Then he changed his mind and said he would get it, but as he was carrying the coffee back to the boat he tripped, of course. That was the end of my coffee. Elmo has a real good mind, but he's clumsy as hell. One time he fell off the boat when we were moving on a river, and another time he tripped carrying the pop flares—these were flares you could fire just by whacking them with your hand —and the whole damn box of them went off.

I finally had had enough of Elmo's rules when I put in my request to transfer off his boat, but deep down I knew I wouldn't accept it if it came through. I was smart enough to know that Elmo was a damned good officer, even if there were times I hated some of the things he did. At one point, when our nerves were taking a beating because of the constant tension and the living conditions on the boat, he gave us a pep talk. He told us he knew that what we had to put up with was difficult, but he said we were all in it together, and he was going to do his best to make sure we all got out of it together. That helped me, and I think it helped other members of the crew to have a better feeling about Elmo.

Elmo ran a tight ship. All the time we were in Vietnam, our guns never jammed, and our engines never failed. Not once. He was on our butts all the time about things like that. But he also has more guts than anyone I've ever known, with the exception of my father.

GEOFF MARTIN, TOP GUNNER:

When we had first arrived in Vietnam, Elmo told us all that we could all get into trouble once and he would bail us out, but that was it. Not more than a week later, I walked into town with another swift boat crew member, and we passed this whorehouse and we saw a girl out front advertising her wares. So we went in. A military police station was located about 50 yards away. These MPs apparently watched us walk into the whorehouse, and of course that was against regulations. We didn't even have time to get into trouble when these guys came charging in. They cuffed me, and brought me down to the MP station. The first thing Elmo says when he comes there is, "I can't believe you little fucks got into trouble already." Then he said we had used up our one chance. That's when we began calling ourselves "the little fucks."

I had already spent a year on riverboats in Vietnam, so I thought I'd have to babysit Elmo for a while. But he learned very quickly on the rivers, and it didn't take me long to realize that he was very serious about his mission over there. He could be a rigid, tough son of a bitch, and there were times when I got so damned mad at him I felt like shooting him, but we all realized he was a good officer. He sent us up rivers and canals no other patrol boats attempted. And when we saw a VC bunker along the side of the river, we would always try to blow it up. One time I threw plastic explosives into a bunker, and the VC there threw it back out. The fuse was still burning, so I tossed it on top of the bunker and ran. It blew up the bunker and whoever was in it.

We envied some of the other swift boats because they had a picnic compared to what Elmo put us through. We had many scary moments and I know Elmo was as scared as the rest of us, but he never showed fear.

BILLY NAIRMORE, DRIVER:

Elmo kept us alert all the time, and his stamina was unreal. I can't remember him ever taking much sleep. In my opinion, he was a hell of a swift boat officer. If we had intelligence about something and he didn't think it was right, he followed his own judgment, and 90 percent of the time he was right.

HARVEY MILLER, RADARMAN:

"You know how Pete Rose plays baseball? That's how Elmo ran our boat."

ELMO:

The canal wasn't much wider than our boat, and it was so shallow our screws kept churning up mud. At dusk we came to a spot near a bend, and pulled up to the bank and slipped under the over-hanging jungle growth. We cut down branches with our machetes, and draped them over the boat for camouflage. Then we waited in silence.

I knew we were a few hundred yards inside Cambodia. I also knew that just by crossing into Cambodia I was in violation of direct orders. But I disobeyed the orders because I knew the VC and the North Vietnamese were infiltrating along this particular river, even though Navy intelligence said they were not. I didn't always have the greatest faith in intelligence information, and I was pretty certain that the enemy was using this canal. I even told Dad, but he said he thought the intelligence was pretty good. It's one of the things on which we disagreed. I thought this would be the best way to prove my point, orders or no orders.

I knew other U.S. boats had ventured into Cambodia before so I wasn't the first one to do it. It was one of the best ways to stage an ambush because the enemy didn't expect us in there.

Within a few minutes, night fell and we were completely shrouded in darkness. I felt like I was in the middle of New York City when all the lights went out. Two of us kept watch while the other three crew members tried to sleep. Sleep was always hard to come by because of the heat and the constant feeling of danger.

We were near Ha Tien, a village at the southernmost point of the border between South Vietnam and Cambodia. The VC had heavily infiltrated this area and, given the nature of this war, we often did not know who was friendly and who would be out there at night trying to kill us.

Of all places I had been in Vietnam, the Ha Tien area was the most primitive. Besides the constant feeling of danger, we had to contend with impoverished conditions. On our patrols, we ate from C-rations and what food we could buy in the different Vietnamese villages. We were so far down on the supply line that no swift boat base had even been established yet. Supplies like toilet paper and soap were hard to find. When my complaints finally reached Dad, he sent a supply officer to Ha Tien for a couple of days, and the supplies began improving after that. But the living conditions remained miserable.

We suffered from dysentery much of the time. Once it got to be so awful we required intravenous fluids because we had become so dehydrated. We almost constantly suffered nausea and diarrhea. This is an intensely hot and humid part of the country infested with an ungodly number of mosquitoes. We carried huge cans of insect repellent and spread it on like shaving lotion when we went on patrol, but those damn mosquitoes would still be at us like bees on a hive.

Sometimes when we docked, rats scurried right onto our boat as if they owned it. One night when we were off patrol, we tied up at an old ferry landing and huge wharf rats crawled all over us. We couldn't fire at them because of the noise it would make, so I set a piece of cheese out on the landing and when the rats all clustered around it, I fired a flare gun at them at point-blank range. I thought it would frighten them, but one of the rats, about the size of a small dog, just looked up at me as if to say, "Who do you think you're trying to scare?" and finished off the cheese.

Most of the time we lived in our own sweat. Even at night, the temperature would hover around 80 degrees with high humidity. Daytime temperatures soared to 110 degrees. You couldn't stand your own smell after a while. The only way to clean up was to jump in the river, but the rivers were as dirty as we were.

That night in Cambodia we waited under the cover of camouflage for several hours before we heard noises coming down the river toward our boat. First we heard the movement of their boats in the water, then the sound of voices. The Vietnamese had been warned not to be on the rivers at night, so if we saw a boat, we could be pretty damn sure it was the enemy. Everything and everyone on our boat was stone-silent, and ready.

I had a signal for my crew. Nobody fired until I shot my M-16. By the time the other boats came into view, I realized it was a convoy of sampans. They drew to within twenty or thirty feet of us, and before they had a chance to see us, I opened fire. Geoff and Whiting let go with the machine guns. It was my thought that if one shot were fired at us, we should return ten thousand, so I sacrificed some speed on our boat by loading us down with extra ammunition. But we never ran out.

Geoff and Whiting pumped thousands of rounds into those sampans. It sounded like all hell breaking loose. At first, we took some return fire and then their firing stopped. I ordered us to cease fire and jumped out of our boat into the canal. I shot some pop flares into the air toward the sampans. The flares gave off a brilliant white light, and dropped slowly because small parachutes opened as they fell to earth. I knew they would illuminate us as well, but I thought whoever was on those boats, if they were still alive, were lying low right now.

I began wading toward the sampans. The water was neck-deep. Harvey Miller jumped off our boat and we waded in together. When we reached their boats, we found them loaded with weapons, along with some medical supplies from Sweden. There was no question we had found a VC convoy. When we opened fire on them, they had enough presence of mind to sink some of their boats. They sank them in order to hide their weapons from us. I realized other VC would come back the next day to retrieve the submerged weapons and start using them against us. So we immediately began to unload their weapons onto our boat. There were AK-47s, mortars, all kinds of weapons. I was damn sure I would let naval intelligence know that the VC was shipping weapons and supplies down this canal.

As we removed the weapons, I heard noises from the riverbank and ordered Geoff Martin to open fire. Geoff yelled back that I was too close to his line of fire. I told him I would duck underwater, and for him to fire over me. I went under and he fired another machine-gun burst. When I think about what I did, the whole episode strikes me as unbelievable. I had ordered my gunner to shoot his 50 caliber machine gun right near me. Just one round from a 50 caliber, which is about as thick as a thumb and about three and a half inches long, would have blown my head off.

Geoff sprayed the bank, chewing up trees and bushes and whoever the hell was out there. The noises stopped, and we went back to loading as many of their weapons onto our boat as we could. At one point, I felt I was standing on something. I called for a waterproof flashlight, and when I looked into the water, I realized it was a dead VC. After we loaded all the weapons, we got the hell out of there. An army patrol went into that area the next day and reported they found four bodies that had not been carried away by the VC.

HARVEY MILLER:

All the guys on the boat knew I have this dread fear of snakes. So after Elmo and I jumped into the water and started to wade toward these sampans, Elmo turned to me and said, "Lookout, Harvey, there's a snake over there." I jumped and he started laughing. I mean, I couldn't believe he would pull a joke then.

The other thing I remember is when Elmo threw all those enemy weapons into our boat, he kept repeating, "Now I can show my father all the goddamned weapons that Navy intelligence said weren't coming down this goddamned canal."

GEOFF MARTIN:

I filled out a commendation form and sent it on to headquarters. I thought what Elmo had done in that ambush was above and beyond the call. Most officers would have ordered someone else to wade over to those sampans, because we didn't know what the hell was on them. There could have been some VC still alive there, just waiting to pop the first guy they saw, and that would have been Elmo. He never asked us to take any risks he wouldn't take himself.

ELMO:

Because most of the war was fought in and around villages where people worked and lived, we couldn't just fire at will at anything that looked suspicious. I know I made mistakes in the beginning. I ordered us to fire when, in hindsight, I really should not have done so. I don't think I was reckless, but just reacting to a dangerous situation. The decision to fire often proved treacherous. If I did not give the order to fire, I might have left us open to attack. If I did give the order, I could have placed innocent civilians under fire.

One time when we waited along a riverbank at night, we could see a sampan drifting down the river toward us. We heard people talking. Whiting, who had the boat in his sights, cocked his gun. Civilians were not supposed to be on the rivers at night, but for some unknown reason we did not fire. To this day I'm not sure why. When the sampan pulled close to us, we found a woman with a young child and a baby. We took them on board for the rest of the night because I did not know if she would go downriver and tell the VC where we were.

Another time during a cease-fire we were ordered to pick up a Navy lieutenant who had been drinking. The lieutenant asked us to take him back to his base. We had to navigate through places where we had constantly run into the enemy. It was dark and we moved slowly. Through our starlight scope we saw a cigarette burning at one of the VC ambush sites. I told my crew we were going to run past that ambush site with our machine guns firing, cease-fire or no cease-fire. We became one of two units in Vietnam to violate the cease-fire, but I put the safety of my crew first.

The one time when I knew absolutely it would be them or us occurred on a river patrol during the day south of Da Nang. No one had ventured up this particular river because of the treacherous tides. Boats could get in and out of the river for only one hour a day. At any other time, they would go aground because the water dropped so low. My partner boat decided not to go up with us.

The riverbanks were so high that only our forward 50 caliber machine-gun mount rose above them. The banks also baffled the engine sounds of our boat. I stood on the forward-gun mount looking through a pair of binoculars when I spotted about a dozen soldiers standing under a tree. They appeared to be North Vietnamese army regulars, apparently listening to their company commander, who had his back to us. We drew closer to them but they still did not see us. I needed to make a fast decision. I could not be absolutely sure they were not South Korean troops, but I knew if I called the base to find out, they could shoot us and we would all be dead before we finished checking.

We came abeam of them and I will never know why they failed to see us. Just thirty yards away I made the decision to fire. We killed all of them and we left at full throttle. But later I held my breath when I checked with the base, and breathed a sigh of relief when I learned they were not a South Vietnamese or South Korean unit. Those were the kinds of judgment calls we had to make in that war.

We became numbed by the killing. We operated on an animalistic level of kill or be killed. One of the Navy SEALS working with us told me about the dismembered body of one of our people, a reminder from the enemy of the horrors that might lie in wait for us. There were hundreds of signs all along the riverbanks saying, "You Die." One member of a swift boat crew took a direct rocket hit, and the only thing they brought back was his leg. A classmate of mine at North Carolina, Shelton White, was also a swift boat officer and had run into a river ambush. One man was decapitated and Shelton had been sprayed all over his body with shrapnel. My own boat had taken plenty of hits from snipers, and some put holes right through the side. Death surrounded us every day.

However, nothing could have softened the impact of the news I received from a fellow swift boat officer. My friend and former roommate Ken Norton had been killed in a firefight in the Da Nang area. He was shot in the chest in an enemy ambush. He was the only member of his crew to be hit. He was twenty-five.

Of all the people I met in Vietnam, only two had told me of a premonition of death, and both had been fulfilled.

ADMIRAL:

When someone disobeys orders the way Elmo did when he ventured into Cambodia, but also succeeds in his mission, you don't know whether to give him a medal or a court-martial. Technically, his violation should have been reported up the chain of command, but on the operating level we realized it was done with some frequency both by our boats and aviators. No serious thought was given to court-martialing Elmo, and personally, I was not the least bit angry at him. If the truth be known, I was proud of him, but I didn't show my pride as much as I wanted to because my job was to enforce the rules of engagement.

I routinely flew down to Ha Tien because it was such a hot combat area, and just after Elmo's Cambodian ambush I saw him there. Elmo seemed more comfortable when I appeared on his turf than when he came to Saigon. He complained to me that the rules of engagement were too restrictive, and if he were running things he would go all the way to Phnom Penh in Cambodia. I tried to

cool him down a bit. He had already been across the border once
and I did not want him up there again. I kidded him that in every
naval officer's career there came a time when as a matter of con-
science, you had to disobey orders and stand up for your beliefs.

"The trouble with you, Elmo," I said, "is that you do that about
three times a week."

Later, when Geoff Martin's commendation request for Elmo
came to my desk, and I learned details of the ambush, I was not
the least bit surprised at what Elmo had done. I thought he demonstrated his courage and selflessness, qualities I had seen in him
since he had been a very small boy, and which always made me
proud of him.

Normally, I would have made the decision on what commendation to award, but I couldn't in his case, so I forwarded the request
to fleet command. They reported back and awarded Elmo the
Bronze Star for bravery. I think it was one of those times when the
fact that Elmo was my son worked against him. In my judgment,
his actions warranted the Silver Star, but I think the brass felt that
a Silver Star would be perceived as favoritism.

Unlike some officers, I knew Elmo had not tried to win a medal
to enhance his career. He didn't even know how medals were
awarded until Geoff Martin wrote up the request. After Elmo
learned he had been awarded the Bronze Star he thought it was
unfair that his crew did not receive any recognition. He felt they
were exposed to the same risks, so he officially requested that all of
them be given Bronze Stars.

Elmo had proved by his ambush that he had been right, and our
intelligence had been wrong. The enemy used that canal to bring
down very substantial amounts of arms and he had interrupted one
hell of a big load of weapons. I told naval intelligence in our daily
meeting and they were embarrassed by the fact that they were so
wrong.

I was accustomed to differences of opinion regarding our intelligence information. We had had a running battle with the CIA
because they became convinced that infiltration into the southern
part of South Vietnam occurred along an extension of the Ho Chi

Minh Trail, which we knew served as the major infiltration route into the northern part of the country. I suspect the CIA was too proud to admit its mistake, because it had taken us a long time to convince them that the enemy used sampans on the rivers to infiltrate the southern part of the country, with supplies coming by sea to Sihanoukville.

Elmo's ambush provided a valuable lesson. He demonstrated that the intelligence we received from our agents who had penetrated the Cambodian weapons supply system gave us only part of the story. They had identified the infiltration routes along the major rivers, but the Viet Cong and the North Vietnamese were clever enough to smuggle supplies along these lesser routes. So largely as a result of his ambush, our thinking changed and I ordered our riverboats into the mouths of the smaller canals and creeks.

At Christmastime 1969, I had planned to fly back to Clark Air Base in the Philippines to see Mouza and our daughters. Elmo took the R and R that each serviceman was granted during his Vietnam tour and we flew back together. It was the first time Elmo had left the combat zone for an extended time since his arrival in Vietnam in August. He had been promoted to lieutenant j.g. and had more than earned his battle spurs. On the flight over, I told him that I needed a new flag lieutenant in Saigon, and I really wanted him to take the job. I said he had nothing more to prove in combat. He had won a Bronze Star, and had the respect of his crew and the other swift boat commanders. I told him he could gain a valuable perspective on the war from command headquarters.

I explained that the sons of many generals and admirals served their fathers' staffs. I convinced him that it would not be a cushy job. He would really work and there would be almost daily helicopter flights to the scenes of firefights, so he could find enough adventure. Elmo said the idea tempted him and that he would consider it.

We met Mouza, Ann, and Mouzetta, who were living at Clark, and Jimmy flew in from North Carolina, so for the first time in more than a year our entire family came together. Kathy Counselman, Elmo's girlfriend, had also flown to the Philippines and was a delightful addition. She and Elmo had not seen one another in five months.

I worked on both Kathy and Mouza to help me convince Elmo to become my aide in Saigon. Elmo had even told me that being away from the war was in some ways more frightening than being in it because it heightened his sense of danger. I understood what he meant. Men at war become desensitized to the fact that people are out there trying to kill us, and we begin to accept the danger as a fact of life. But when we reenter civilized society, we realize that's not the way life is supposed to be, and it makes combat all the more terrifying.

After Kathy, Mouza, and I had worked on Elmo for nearly two solid days to persuade him to be my aide, he finally consented. All of us were elated. I also knew that by persuading Elmo to join me, I would be getting a hard-working, independent-minded officer who would tell me exactly what he thought, precisely the kind of aide I had in Lew Glenn, whom I needed to replace.

It also gave me peace of mind because I continued to fear that Elmo would not survive the war. While he would not be completely safe as my aide, it would be a far safer place than the swift boats. I immediately called Saigon and reported Elmo's change of duties, and began the necessary paperwork in order to have him with me as soon as we returned.

We had a wonderful Christmas together. Seeing Ann and Mouzetta after long stretches of time away made me realize how quickly they were growing into beautiful young women. Mouza was still spending long hours at the Air Force hospital with many of the young men who had been wounded in the war. Jimmy, who had given me gray hairs because of his high school study habits, had turned into a good student at the University of North Carolina. Like Elmo, he was also in NROTC and would graduate next June as an ensign.

Kathy and Elmo spent a lot of time together. They went out horseback riding, and sunned at one of the beaches. I knew how much Elmo loved Kathy, and it was clear she loved him too. I thought she would make Elmo a wonderful wife.

We were in the Philippines for about a week, and the night before Elmo and I were scheduled to leave, we had a big family dinner. It went beautifully until Elmo shocked us all by announcing he had changed his mind. He was not going to join me in Saigon.

"Dad," he said, "I've given it a lot of thought, and as much as I'd like to be with you, I just can't leave my crew."

He told us he really thought they were a special group, and they were bound together now like blood brothers. He said if he went to Saigon, it would be unfair to leave them with an untested boat officer. We all tried to talk him out of it until I finally asked him if he were completely certain of his decision. He said yes. I knew Elmo well enough to know that when his mind was made up, it was made up for good. I reluctantly accepted his decision and called Saigon to tell them that there had been another change of plans.

When we arrived back in Vietnam, Elmo went south to Sea Float and discovered that the commander there had assigned him to a new crew. I guess he had been annoyed at the change of plans. That was the one time that I really leaned on the system for Elmo. I told this commander Elmo had agreed to leave the swift boats only because I had pressured him into joining me in Saigon. I added that he had decided to stay on the swift boat out of loyalty to his crew, so the least he could do was give him his crew back. Elmo was then assigned back to PCF 35, his old boat and crew. More than any other time that he had gone into the combat zone, I felt as though Elmo had pressed his luck once too often.

KATHY COUNSELMAN ZUMWALT:

I enjoy the taste of beer, and when I returned to college that fall, I gave it up completely. I knew Elmo faced danger. Giving up beer was sort of my sacrifice so that Elmo might come home alive.

I had even worried that his own crew might do him in because I knew how hardheaded Elmo could be at times.

He had asked me to date other men while he was in Vietnam. I did a little, enough to know that I loved Elmo, and when we were together again in the Philippines, I became certain I wanted to marry him. I had never met anyone like him. His strength of character caused him to remain with his crew in the face of all our pleading, and his strong character is why I loved him.

We talked about marriage during that visit, but Elmo did not ask me to marry him. Just after I returned to college, Elmo called me from Vietnam and proposed. Knowing Elmo, I guess he just wanted to think about it a little more. I had no hesitation about marrying Elmo, and I accepted right there on the hall phone in my dormitory. He said he was going to call my parents to ask their permission. My dad really liked Elmo. He had even told me that if he had to pick out a husband for me, it would have been Elmo. But he thought I was too young to get married, and he wanted me to finish college. I also knew Elmo, so I was pretty sure Dad would yield and give his permission. Even if Dad had wanted me to wait, I would have, because Elmo was someone worth waiting for.

JIM ZUMWALT:

Elmo has a great capacity to look at himself objectively to see if what he is doing is fair to other people, so I wasn't at all surprised when he turned down Dad's offer. I think Elmo felt that if others were fighting, he couldn't take advantage of being Admiral Zumwalt's son and avoid danger.

Elmo and I exchanged taped messages regularly while he served in Vietnam, so I knew how much he cared for his crew. I also knew from experience how loyal he could be. I had been on the college wrestling team and the coach selected an honorary captain for each meet according to how well each of us performed in practice. Before one particular meet, I practiced as hard as I could and I believed I had earned the captaincy.

But the coach selected someone else. I told Elmo how disappointed I felt. At the next meet, the coach selected me as honorary captain. I didn't learn until much later that after Elmo had received my tape, he had written to the wrestling coach, whom he knew, to ask him if he would name me captain. That's the way Elmo is. If somebody he cares about needs something, he just charges in there and does something about it.

SEVEN

★

ELMO:

The helicopter swayed in the crosswinds as we flew south from Saigon over the dense jungle terrain, crisscrossed by hundreds of small waterways, and then over the big, winding Cua Lon River. We were deep within the Ca Mau Peninsula at the southernmost point in South Vietnam. In the distance, appearing as a huge raft in the river, was the strange-looking sight of Sea Float. This was the man-made Navy island that Dad had conceived to bring a U.S. presence into this part of the country. Two hundred men were stationed on Sea Float. They included logistics people, psychological warfare teams, Vietnamese Montagnard troops, and other vital elements of antiguerrilla warfare. As we drew closer, I could see the Sea Wolf helicopter gunships on the deck, and the river patrol boats docked alongside. I had been to Sea Float before in my swift boat because it served as a base of operations in that part of the country, but I had never seen it from the air.

As I climbed out of the helicopter, I saw the dead body of a Navy chief petty officer lying on the Sea Float deck. He had been decapitated in a vicious firefight and they were preparing to fly his body out. I wondered to myself what I was getting back into. I had passed up my opportunity to avoid returning to these rivers. I realized the enemy surrounded the area around Sea Float, which only added to my sense of unease. I wondered if I had pressed my luck a little too far. I had been in scores of firefights and I had been shot at many times already. One bullet that had missed me sounded like it passed only inches away from my head.

At Sea Float, there were almost daily reminders of the danger of combat. Riverboats returned from patrols with crew members either killed or wounded in ambushes. Navy SEALS would penetrate into the jungle and sometimes not come back. The sense of adventure and self-testing that had first drawn me to Vietnam had long since gone. Now I just wanted to get out alive and marry Kathy. I also remember telling myself that if I did make it, I would not take life so much for granted.

When I returned to Sea Float I was also struck by my aerial view of the defoliation. It appeared as if a huge circle had been etched out of the jungle cover along the surrounding riverbanks, as if a massive forest fire had swept through. I had seen Agent Orange defoliation in the Da Nang area, and nearly every place else where we had patrolled, but this defoliation was much more extensive. I saw it everywhere. Trees were stripped of leaves, thick jungle growth reduced to twigs, the ground barren of grass.

I had often walked around in these defoliated areas and washed and waded in the rivers and canals into which Agent Orange had drained. I tied a line to Sea Float and jumped in the Cua Lon River because the nine-mile-an-hour current was so swift that I was washed clean as it swept past. We ate fruits and vegetables we bought from the local Vietnamese, which I suspect were doused with Agent Orange.

I remember having a skin rash while I was stationed at Sea Float area. I thought it might have been caused by the sun, but I have since learned that one of the effects of Agent Orange exposure is a skin rash. But at the time, I was thankful for the defoliation. It meant the enemy could not attack Sea Float without great cost to itself.

Despite my apprehensions about going back on the rivers, I felt exhilarated to be reunited with my crew again. They had gone on one or two patrols with a new officer-in-charge, and told me they were greatly relieved when they found I was coming back to the 35 boat. I knew that I could never have abandoned them. Billy Nairmore's wife, Alice, had given birth to a daughter, Tara, which gave me, and all the crew, even a stronger sense that we had to stay together and survive.

The five of us had become more relaxed with one another. We kidded and joked easily. I once told them none of us would ever have another relationship as close as the one we developed among ourselves, not even with our wives. We lived with one another around the clock, sometimes patrolling for days at a time on our 55-foot boat, under conditions of fatigue and fear, anger and frustration. We knew each other's strengths and weaknesses intimately, and I had the deepest respect for each of my crew.

We had evening briefings on Sea Float from the operations officer, Lieutenant Dave Halperin. He would describe the events of the day, tell us where the ambushes had occurred, and explain the operations planned for that night. Dave was an extremely articulate and capable officer, and he and I soon became friends. Besides his intelligence, Dave had an easy sense of humor that helped relieve some of our tensions. At Sea Float we all felt fatigued and anxious.

The Dam Doi River ran near Sea Float, and had become notorious for savage ambushes against our boats. North Vietnamese regulars patrolled there, and they were much tougher foes than the Viet Cong.

The VC were more like a mom-and-pop operation. They would usually hide in a tree or mud bunker along the riverbank and fire a round or two at us and flee. It could be nerve-wracking as hell because you could not tell where the shots came from. Many times they would begin firing near a friendly village, so we could not respond with much, if any, firepower. They also set up river booby traps using homemade claymore mines that exploded shrapnel. Sometimes they used command-detonated mines powerful enough to blow a riverboat out of the water. The VC were certainly deadly, but in my experience the North Vietnamese soldiers were more willing and able to fight us head-on, and when they dug in they were damn tough. That's what they were doing along the Dam Doi, digging in and blasting our riverboats.

During one of our evening briefings at Sea Float, it was agreed that my boat, and another commanded by Lieutenant John O'Neill, would go up the Dam Doi that evening. I knew John O'Neill from Ha Tien as a good swift boat officer. It was unusual to put two senior officers together on the same patrol—because of my experience I was now considered a senior swift boat officer—but we did it because of the special hazards along the Dam Doi. We set out at dusk, several hours earlier than our usual patrols along that river.

As night fell, we moved slowly up the river, which is about seventy-five yards wide. I was tense, and so was everyone in our boats. We remained silent as we neared one of the sites where a horrendous ambush had taken place just a day or two earlier. As John O'Neill looked through his binoculars, he suddenly stopped his boat dead in the water. Up about two hundred yards on the riverbank, he had seen what looked like a campfire and some North Vietnamese regulars near it. We didn't know whether it was a trap, or if they were completely unprepared for us at this time of night. I was damn sick and tired at what they had done to our other boats, and I wanted to take the risk of attacking them by firing everything we had to give them a taste of what they had been giving us. I thought we could surprise them.

John, who was senior to me, agreed. Geoff and Whiting turned their machine guns to that side of the river. Harvey aimed his M-60 hand-held machine gun in the same direction, and I had a full clip in my M-16 as both boats took off firing. A round from a 50 caliber machine gun has an effective range of nearly a mile, so we were plenty close enough to inflict damage. I don't know how many rounds we fired, but it was a lot. The spent shells popped out of our weapons in a blur.

Once we were beyond their position, Billy Nairmore, a great driver, spun our boat around in a tight circle and we headed back past them still firing with everything we had. I hoped they didn't have a mine set up or some other way to nail us. I didn't see any return fire either time we shot and we made it out safely.

In a situation like that, the adrenaline pumped so fast I never felt fear. I concentrated so much on staying alive, and keeping my crew alive, that there was no time to be scared, even when I heard bullets ricocheting near me. Fear set in when the shooting stopped.

After our firing run, John O'Neill said that was the only time in Vietnam that he was sure he was going to be killed. He felt absolutely certain the North Vietnamese were going to open up on us and get us all. I didn't feel that way, but as I told John, it may have been because I lacked imagination. I think we hit them with so much so fast that they got out of the way as quickly as they could. That didn't make the Dam Doi River safe for our swift boats, but it did seem to diminish the frequency and ferocity of their ambushes against us.

We also regularly "inserted" Navy SEALS or South Vietnamese troops into different areas around Sea Float. The SEALS were a group unto themselves. They were usually loners and tough as hell. They'd slip into enemy areas to set up mines or lay traps, or make contact with friendlies.

One time we carried about seventy-five South Vietnamese militia to a place near the Cambodian border. I had respect for the fighting abilities of the South Vietnamese regular troops. I think they earned a bad reputation early in the war, perhaps deservedly. But most of the ARVN troops I saw when I was there were well-trained fighters.

The militia we inserted, however, had a reputation for stealing from Americans. As we headed upriver, I heard the South Vietnamese laughing. At about the same time, I saw Harvey Miller looking as mad as I've ever seen him. His favorite knife was missing, and he knew one of the South Vietnamese had stolen it. I told him to forget about it because it was not worth getting that upset over, and he quieted down.

The next night, we went back and picked up these same troops. Suddenly a big commotion erupted. Their commander told me that one of his men was missing his M-16 rifle. I asked Harvey if he knew anything about it, but he said no. Everyone calmed down, but when we picked these same troops up the next morning to insert them into another area, I heard the unmistakable sounds of rifles being loaded and cocked as we rode on the river. I looked back and saw Harvey surrounded by the South Vietnamese, his hands in the air, and several automatic weapons at his back. I asked what the hell was going on, and the South Vietnamese commander told me that after thinking it over that night, they became convinced that Harvey had stolen the rifle.

I radioed my partner boat, commanded by Lieutenant Luther Ellingston, to pull alongside and train his machine guns at my boat. That convinced the South Vietnamese to remove their weapons from Harvey's back. Then I told Harvey to return the missing M-16. He did and the incident ended without injury. But Harvey never got his knife back. I think the entire episode reflected the tension and suspicion we all felt in that war.

In April 1970, Captain Charles F. Rauch, Jr., a former ballistic missile submarine skipper and one of the analysts Dad had brought to Vietnam, asked me if I would carry out a study of the overall effectiveness and efficiency of the river patrol operations. At that point, I had been on the rivers for about nine months and this new assignment would take me out of the combat area. I recognized the need for such a study, and thought I could make a contribution to it.

My tour of duty was theoretically for one year on the boats, but as a practical matter not many of the swift boat officers did a full year in combat. If you were caught in a bad firefight and took casualties, usually you were taken off the boats and given an administrative job.

That's what had happened to Jeff Jones, the third swift boat officer who had trained with Ken Norton and me in San Diego. Jeff's boat was hit hard soon after he arrived in Vietnam. If you were badly chewed up in a firefight, you often lost your effectiveness. I particularly remember one swift boat officer who lost a crew member in a firefight; he trembled visibly whenever he rode on the rivers.

By this time the South Vietnamese Navy played a much greater role in the river patrols. This change grew out of Dad's accelerated program to turn the river war over to the Vietnamese. We now had a surplus of American patrol boat officers.

I still felt loyal to my crew, and I told Captain Rauch, and Dad, that I would not leave my boat unless my crew left with me. Dad agreed to bring Whiting and Billy to Saigon to serve as military policemen in charge of guarding him, and Geoff and Harvey both had leave coming.

When that issue was settled, I accepted Captain Rauch's offer with one important provision: I did not want to head the study. I thought it would prove impractical, given my name. I would be talking to officers all over Vietnam, a large number of them senior to me. I knew from experience that many of these officers had difficulty dealing with me. Some tried to curry favor. One captain had come to Ha Tien specifically to ride on my boat. It was very unusual for a captain to do that, but I knew the reason. So did Dad. Others, like the commander who wanted to assign me to another crew after I had come back from the Philippines, tried to give me a hard time.

For these reasons, I told Captain Rauch that I thought another officer should head the study. He asked for a recommendation and I immediately thought of Dave Halperin, the operations officer on Sea Float. Besides liking Dave, I thought we would be a good combination. I had the river experience, and he had a broader operations perspective, as well as a first-rate analytical mind. Arrangements for our study were set in motion.

I still had a few more river patrols to go on before leaving the boat, and the closer it got to my last mission the more worried I became. When I finally set out on my final patrol, I was more afraid than I had been on any other mission, even more than on my first patrol. I had heard so many stories about people not surviving their last patrol that I couldn't help but dwell on the irony of getting killed my last time out. We had made it this far without a casualty of any kind.

My last patrol took place in the daytime in the Ha Tien area. A junior officer who had been in Vietnam for a few weeks commanded my partner boat. As we moved down a narrow river, my partner boat hit a wire that triggered a claymore mine. I heard the explosion and immediately turned and raced toward him. When I pulled alongside, I realized they had taken only minor damage to their boat. I kidded them that Billy Nairmore was such a good driver we had never hit a mine during our time in Vietnam.

Just at that moment, I spotted a sampan with one person on board move out from a small inlet downriver. I wanted to know what that sampan was doing there. I ordered my boat to head right at him at full throttle. Billy turned our boat and we took off.

We had reached full speed when, all of a sudden, a mine exploded near the bow of our boat. At the same instant, another exploded near our stern. Our boat heeled over 45 degrees on its side, with the engines still at full bore. Everyone on the boat was knocked down.

I was in the forward gun tub with Geoff Martin. I started to slide off the boat. I grabbed the sides to hold on. I was certain the boat would flip over. I hoped we could maneuver ourselves from under the boat and swim free.

Just then, our swift boat began to right itself and I realized we weren't going to turn over. A towering gusher of water soared hundreds of feet into the air and enveloped us. When it crashed down, we were knocked off our feet again. My mind raced. I knew the VC sometimes first hit patrol boats with a mine to disorient the crew, and then attacked from the shore with automatic weapons. I screamed for Geoff and Whiting to open fire.

"At what?" Geoff yelled.

"I don't give a damn. Just rake those riverbanks," I yelled back.

Geoff and Whiting both began firing. I called in helicopters and they responded quickly, strafing the bank with machine guns and rockets. My partner came to help, and in a few minutes the situation calmed down. There was no ambush. The other boat officer told me that he saw our boat disappear in a huge geyser of water and thought to himself that no one would survive. But just before the water cleared, he heard our machine guns firing.

Our rudder and screws were damaged, which disabled our boat. We could return our boat to base, but we had to come off patrol. Before we left for the base, we banked our boat on the shore where Geoff Martin found a trip wire buried in the sand. It led into the river, and back into the jungle cover. We realized this wire had been used to detonate the mines. Geoff followed the wire into the woods for about one hundred yards to where it ended, a place near a tree where someone had waited. Geoff sighted down the wire, and saw two sticks stuck in the ground. They had been the mine's sights. When our boat moved in between those two sticks, we were like a target in the cross-hairs of a telescopic sight. The triggerman yanked the trip wire, and the mines exploded.

The VC had laid a perfect trap for us, which was typical of their cleverness. They understood human psychology well enough to set traps in which we ensnared ourselves. One tactic was to set a mine in the river. A boat might hit it at a slow speed, and when we did, our impulse was to escape by going full speed ahead. But a little farther upriver they would have set a number of mines and by now we would be going so fast we would trip a whole series that could destroy our boat and crew.

This had been a slightly more sophisticated booby trap. The first mine was the setup, and the sampan was the bait. They figured one of our boats would take off after the sampan, and when we did, we moved directly into the sights of their command-detonated mines, which the VC triggered onshore. Dad always thought the VC had set that trap specifically for me and my boat. I'm not sure they did, but it made one hell of a dramatic ending for my swift boat command.

Dave Halperin and I then toured much of the delta, analyzing the operations reports, talking to the boat officers, crew members, and the whole chain of command involved in the river operations. We tried to provide criteria for a successful mission, and establish which part of our river forces was best suited for specific operations. During this time, I went up to Saigon once or twice and met with Dad. He knew he would soon be offered a new command, and it appeared that it would be a very significant one. Neither of us realized at the time that he would be appointed Chief of Naval Operations, the Navy's top job.

ADMIRAL:

I was eating breakfast at headquarters in Saigon with Vice Admiral Walter "Red" Baumberger, the Deputy Commander of the Pacific Fleet, and members of my staff, when a messenger ran in from the communications office to tell me I had a telephone call from Secretary of the Navy John Chafee. Just a month earlier, in March, I had been summoned to Washington for an interview with Secretary Chafee regarding my next assignment, which still remained a mystery to me. I hoped it would be a command of one of our numbered fleets, perhaps the Sixth Fleet in the Mediterranean, or the Seventh Fleet in the Pacific. Those are the real plums in the Navy, but they had been traditionally commanded by aviators, a source of hard feelings among many surface sailors, myself included.

As I left the table to take Secretary Chafee's call, Red Baumberger said, "Bud, my guess is that that's your summons to the top job in the Navy."

I offered to bet him he was wrong, that being the kind of bet I was happy to lose. In truth, I did not honestly think that I would be offered the post of Chief of Naval Operations. I had jumped over 130 other flag officers to become a vice admiral. I was only forty-nine at the time, and I figured I was too young for the CNO job. So, for these reasons, I was fairly sure I would remain at my rank for some time to come.

Secretary Chafee instructed me to take the next commercial flight to Washington, dressed in civilian clothes. I was not to tell anyone. I did not know why he wanted me to return to Washington so soon after my last trip, and so secretly, but I told him it was impossible for me to leave a wartime post without checking with the theater commander, General Abrams, and my Navy boss, the Commander of the Pacific fleet. He agreed and I drove out that morning to see General Abrams.

I had hoped and expected to remain in Vietnam until the summer of 1971, which was more than a year away, because I wanted to see the ACTOV—the Vietnamization of the in-country naval war—move into its final phase. I asked Abe if I could quote him as saying he wanted me to stay in Vietnam for another year.

Abe thought for a moment and said, "Sure, Bud, you can tell them that. But first listen to what they have to say. You never know when those civilian fellows are in trouble and might decide you're the only man who can do a certain job for them."

I thought that was sound advice, and told Abe I would follow it. We shook hands, and I headed off to Washington wondering along the way what was in store for me.

I met with Secretary Chafee, a man of great warmth and charm, in his Pentagon office. He asked me several questions, among them what I perceived as the Navy's problems and how I thought they should be dealt with. I told him we had serious morale problems that were reflected in our low re-enlistment rate, and I offered my ideas to increase re-enlistments.

When we finished, he said his boss, Defense Secretary Melvin Laird, wanted to see me the next day. I saw Laird, whom I'd met a year earlier in Vietnam, and briefed him on Vietnam. Laird acted cordially, but I still wasn't sure why these fellows had summoned me back to Washington.

Laird sent me to see Henry Kissinger, who at that time was the presidential assistant for national security affairs. In his outer office, I met Colonel Alexander Haig, Kissinger's deputy, whom I had known since we had served together as junior members of the task force that handled Cuban affairs after the missile crisis of 1962.

I was ushered into Kissinger's office. My meeting with him was brief and, to my mind, inconsequential since he spent most of the time talking to someone on the telephone. He appeared affable and charming, and I suspected he was talking to a news reporter.

Navy Secretary Chafee revealed the reason for all these meetings the next day when he met with me and said, "Bud, you are the one

Mel Laird and I have nominated to the President to relieve Tom Moorer as Chief of Naval Operations."

Although I had prepared myself for this possibility, it was stunning to hear the words actually spoken. It was not an offer I could turn down, despite my regrets about not completing my Vietnam tour. I felt very deeply that significant changes were needed within the Navy, and this was the one way I could effect those changes.

Secretary Chafee told me he wanted me to bring the Navy "into the modern age." He also said I had not been Tom Moorer's first choice, which didn't surprise me a bit. In fact, I later heard that after Chafee told Moorer about my appointment, Moorer returned to his office and kicked his wastepaper basket across the room.

Two days later, I was taken back to Mel Laird's office where he congratulated me. Probably more than anyone, Laird was responsible for my appointment, apparently because of the favorable impression I had made when he came to Vietnam a year earlier, and the strong endorsement of me he had received from General Abrams.

Laird introduced me to President Nixon, who was in Laird's office. The President congratulated me and said the official announcement would take place the next morning. He went on to say that he knew I was young for the job, but he personally considered my age an asset. He asked me where I came from, and I told him that I had grown up in Tulare, in the San Joaquin Valley.

He brightened a bit and said, "Oh, yes, I know where that is. I picked lemons right near there at Lindsay one summer when I was a kid. It's very hot."

I agreed. We talked of the growing Soviet naval threat and some other issues, and then parted. My official duties as CNO, which is a four-year term, would begin in two and a half months, on July 1, 1970.

I was asked to wait until the next morning to break the news to my family. I obeyed, and when I called Mouza at Clark Air Base, she shrieked with delight. Then with her second breath, she said, "My God, in four years, you will have to retire."

I next called my Dad, who was then seventy-eight. Several years after my mother's death, Dad had returned to the U.S. Army for World War II service. While stationed at Ft. Lewis, Washington, he met and married a Seattle woman. They returned to Tulare after the war, where Dad practiced until 1962. On retirement at age seventy, he and his wife Doris left Tulare and moved to Indianola, Washington. Given the demands of my career and family, I had not seen very much of him over the past several years. A few years earlier, when I had commanded the *Dewey,* he had accompanied me when I took that ship to visit ports of call in Scandinavia.

Soon after Dad had retired from medicine, he developed a stomach ulcer. He diagnosed the cause as inactivity. At about that time, I learned that the Naval Ordnance Test Station at China Lake, which is in the California desert some one hundred miles from Tulare, needed someone to head up the industrial medicine department. I suggested Dad, and they offered him the job. It had proved of great benefit for both Dad and China Lake. Dad had become so popular that when I was named rear admiral in 1965, the local paper headlined: "Dr. Zumwalt's Son Selected for Rear Admiral."

When I told Dad I had been named CNO, he was happy for me and very proud. I reminded him of the time I telephoned him soon after I had arrived in Annapolis for my plebe year at the Naval Academy. I felt lost and alone, and terribly homesick. I also was not sure I could do the work. When I told Dad I wanted to return home, he said, "All right, son, if that's what you want to do, come on home." But I heard the tears in his voice as he said it, and they had persuaded me to stick it out.

I later made one other call, to General Abrams in Saigon, just to let him know that I would be back on Saturday morning. I assumed that Abe had heard of my appointment, and I was hurt when he did not offer his congratulations. I said nothing about the appointment, however.

But the next day I received a message from him that has always meant a great deal to me. He said when we had talked the day before, he had been unaware of my appointment as CNO. He later learned of it, and he said headquarters buzzed with the news. In his message to me, Abe said: "The atmosphere was like a small town where the news has come that one of 'their boys' has made good. I join with your many friends in acclaiming this selection. More than this, I am aware of the awesome burden of leadership that will soon be yours. For this I pray that God will bless you with the health, the patience, and the wisdom you will need to fulfill this responsibility."

I flew back to Saigon to continue pressing the war and begin the transition of command to Admiral King, who was to be my successor. I was scheduled to leave Vietnam in mid-May, a year and a half after I had arrived.

Although, in my own view, I had not finished my job in Vietnam, on balance I felt good about leaving. Our forces were performing well militarily, and the naval component was doing an exceedingly fine job. The delta had been taken from the enemy and became a friendly area with only a few unfriendly pockets. The VC in the delta had broken themselves into still smaller groups, and now didn't even have company-sized units. I also thought that the training and organization we helped provide the South Vietnamese military forces were showing results.

I always thought the Vietnamese were courageous fighters. During the early part of the war, only the Viet Cong and the North Vietnamese fought that way because they had the organization, training, and esprit. Now many of the South Vietnamese troops showed the same kind of courage, although I don't think the American public perceived the South Vietnamese in that fashion. Admiral Chon had quickly and skillfully taken command so that the South Vietnamese now waged the naval war pretty much on their own. And in my view, and in the view of others, one of the finest division commanders in the history of warfare was General Truong. Truong commanded the first ARVN division, which led the liberation of Hue. Like us, the South Vietnamese had their share of mediocre leaders, but on the whole they were turning into a good fighting force.

I was able to see Elmo from time to time, now that he was no longer on river patrols. I also grew to know Dave Halperin better. Dave had first impressed me by the thoroughness and scope of his briefings when I visited Sea Float. Elmo had also spoken very highly of his ability. In fact, Elmo suggested that I try to persuade Dave to remain in the Navy and take him with me to Washington to be on my CNO staff.

Dave had graduated from Columbia University and did not intend to make a career of the Navy. He was planning to attend Harvard Law School. I asked him if he would consider coming to Washington with me and delay law school for a little while. I told him I was anxious to find ways to increase our re-enlistment rate, and I thought he could be very helpful. He agreed to come.

I had set everything in motion for my departure, and the change-of-command ceremony was held on an LST in Saigon Harbor on May 15. Mouza and our daughters, Ann and Mouzetta, had flown in from the Philippines. My close friend Admiral Chon was there. He thanked me for helping his country, and for being his friend. I embraced him and we wept.

Elmo also came to the ceremony. I had last met with him when I proudly presented him with his second Bronze Star. This was awarded for his consistently heroic conduct throughout his tour. Elmo joked that every patrol boat officer received a Bronze Star if he had not embarrassed the Navy during this tour, but we both knew that wasn't true. With the addition of the other Bronze Stars and the Vietnamese Cross of Gallantry, which had been awarded earlier to Elmo and his crew for their heroism in Cambodia, Elmo's swift boat became very highly decorated.

Before I departed for home, I asked Elmo not to take any more chances. We hugged one another and bid goodbye. I knew he would be out in a few weeks, but I worried until that final moment when I was notified that he had left Vietnam for home.

Mouza, the girls, and I flew back to North Carolina to attend Jim's graduation. Next we flew to Washington. Mouza was thrilled with our new living quarters on the spacious grounds of the Naval Observatory, off Embassy Row on Massachusetts Avenue in Washington. It is a graceful Victorian mansion that has since become the home of the Vice President, and was far more luxurious than any home we had ever dreamed we would live in.

I began to assemble my staff and create a detailed agenda for modernizing the Navy. I had only four short years, and so much I wanted to accomplish.

ELMO:

I have always felt Dad has unusual gifts and talents, and I was tremendously proud that he had been named Chief of Naval Operations, but I can honestly say I was not surprised, nor were other people who had known him. We were only surprised that he had made it to the top so fast, becoming the youngest CNO in the history of the Navy.

Our Vietnam tours wound down at about the same time. I was due to return to the States at the end of June, about six weeks after Dad. When I left the swift boats, Dad had asked me to stay out of harm's way, but when Dave Halperin and I completed our river patrol study, I volunteered to command the lead boat for the incursion into Cambodia.

I realize that invasion was, and continues to be, highly controversial, but for those of us who served in Vietnam, it was long overdue. In Ha Tien, I had seen with my own eyes trucks drive up to the Cambodia–South Vietnam border to unload weapons for infiltration into South Vietnam. Our men, and the South Vietnamese, were being killed every day with those weapons and I thought this activity inside Cambodia should not go unpunished. It was a bad way to fight a war.

I was assigned to be the naval liaison during the invasion. I did not penetrate far into Cambodia but remained at a base camp, which normally would have been relatively safe, but in this case turned out not to be. The first night we were there, we were hit hard with rocket fire, and I remember thinking that I would much rather be on my boat where we could at least take off when we were under attack. Instead, we had to stay there and slug it out and hope like hell one of those incoming rounds that were explod-

ing all over the place didn't hit us. It gave me an appreciation of
the hell the ground forces faced. Fortunately, I made it out of
there without injury.

My days in Vietnam were growing short and I began preparations to leave. I planned to marry Kathy after I returned home.
Our wedding date was set for July 11. I had also intended to
remain in the Navy. For the third and final year I hoped to be
assigned as special assistant to the military assistant to the U.S.
Ambassador to the United Nations. That would put me close to
Kathy's college in Tarrytown, New York. Kathy's father had given
his permission for us to marry only after I promised him that
Kathy would finish college. I also thought the U.N. would be an
interesting experience, with the added benefit that it would provide a steady income for us during our first year of marriage. I had
applied to law schools and had been accepted at two, including the
University of North Carolina. I planned to defer my acceptance for
one year.

My plans were abruptly changed when the Navy informed me
that, because of budget restrictions, I and other NROTC officers
would not be allowed to serve our promised third year. We had the
option of signing for an additional year, which I didn't want, or
leaving right away. I thought this was a lousy way to treat the men
who fought in Vietnam, and before Dad left Vietnam I told him
so. He agreed with me, but he said he did not think it was fair for
him to lean on the system to make an exception for me. I told him
I didn't want him to do that, but I did tell him what I felt like
doing with his Navy. I called Kathy and apprised her of the
change. I told her I wanted to go to law school in the fall, but it
would not preclude my promise to her dad that she finish college.

During those final weeks in Vietnam, I did not see much of my
old crew, now that we were in different areas, so we did not have
an opportunity to say goodbye. I did learn that Harvey Miller and
Geoff Martin had volunteered to go back on the river patrols. I
heard that Harvey's boat got caught in a bad firefight, and one of
the other crew members had been killed. Before I left, I knew they

had come off the boats, and we were all leaving at around the same time.

Being away from them made me appreciate them more, as well as the camaraderie we had on our boat. I know Dad has many long-time friends from the days he served in World War II and Korea. They held reunions and Dad always spoke warmly of those men. I began to understand what he felt. I loved my crew members like brothers.

As my departure from Vietnam drew close, I felt more than ready to get out of that country, and the Navy. I remember meeting another officer as I was signing some papers in Saigon. When he noticed my name, he asked me if I wanted to become an admiral like my dad.

"Not unless they can do it in the next three weeks," I said.

I had come to Vietnam to test myself. After more than nine months as a swift boat officer, after firefights and ambushes too numerous to count, after being scared, sick, exhausted, angry, frustrated, saddened, and challenged in ways I never imagined before I arrived, I found I could cope with everything that had been thrown at me and still perform. I have always believed that you need a lot of luck in life, and I had been very lucky in Vietnam. Other good officers, like Ken Norton and Bob Crosby, had been killed, so I have never been presumptuous enough to think I alone was responsible for getting myself and my crew out alive.

I also realized that I absolutely hated combat. There was nothing about it that appealed to me. The fear, the horrendous living conditions, and all the killing were not experiences I ever wanted to repeat. I was more certain than ever that I did not want to make the Navy, or any other military service, my career. I wanted out.

At the end of June, when I finally boarded the plane at Ton Son Nhut Airport to leave Vietnam, I had an indescribable feeling of exhilaration and relief knowing I was really getting out, and that my crew was leaving too.

Lt. Elmo "Bud" Zumwalt, Jr., later to become the youngest Chief of Naval Operations, on the deck of the USS *Robinson* in the South Pacific, just before the end of World War II. *(Courtesy of Mouzetta Weathers)*

Mouza Zumwalt and Elmo R. Zumwalt III, in Tulare, California, a few days after Elmo's birth on July 30, 1948. *(Courtesy of Ann Coppola)*

The Russian Orthodox wedding of young Bud Zumwalt and Mouza Coutelais-du-Roche in Shanghai, China, October 22, 1945. *(Courtesy of Ann Coppola)*

Elmo and General George C. Marshall in 1949 during the Zumwalts' visit to Marshall's summer home in Pinehurst. On this visit, Marshall, whom Bud Zumwalt called "one of the greatest Americans who ever served this country," convinced the young officer to stay with the Navy. *(Courtesy of Ann Coppola)*

Elmo on the day of his college graduation and NROTC commission at the University of North Carolina, June 1964. *(Courtesy of Ann Coppola)*

From left: Elmo, his brother Jim, and Admiral Zumwalt at the swift boat base in Da Nang, South Vietnam, in 1969. Jim, then an NROTC midshipman, was in Vietnam as part of a summer training cruise. *(Courtesy of Ann Coppola)*

Elmo's swift boat crew at Ha Tien, South Vietnam, in 1969. From left to right are Al Lund, Elmo, Geoff Martin, Harvey Miller, Dave Collins, Whiting Shuford, and Billy Nairmore. Lund and Collins had gone on a patrol with Elmo's boat. *(Courtesy of C. W. Nairmore)*

Elmo's swift boat, the PCF 35. *(Courtesy of C. W. Nairmore)*

Sea Float, a floating naval base placed in the middle of the Cua Lon River at the southernmost part of South Vietnam. Sea Float was Admiral Zumwalt's idea to secure the Ca Mau Peninsula, long a Viet Cong stronghold. Though the river was only 400 yards wide, Sea Float worked. The quonset huts to the right housed storage and sleeping facilities, and the pad at the left is where helicopters landed. Tied to the sides are river patrol boats.

The effects of defoliation can be seen by comparing the top photo, which is an unsprayed mangrove forest near Saigon, with the bottom photo, which is another mangrove forest, five years after it was first sprayed. The dark spots are some surviving trees. *(Associated Press/Wide World Photos)*

Admiral Zumwalt and his close friend Admiral Tran van Chon, Commander of the South Vietnamese Navy, signing over the first major transfer of U.S. Navy ships to the South Vietnamese Navy on October 10, 1969. *(Courtesy of Ann Coppola)*

The Saturday morning intelligence update at command headquarters in Saigon. General Creighton Abrams, theater supreme commander, sits at the head of the table. Admiral Zumwalt is third from the left. Second from the right in the foreground is William Colby, who later became director of the Central Intelligence Agency. *(U.S. Army photograph)*

Admiral Zumwalt dances with his daughter Ann, who was then sixteen, at the Navy Ball in 1970, the first year he was Chief of Naval Operations. *(Courtesy of Ann Coppola)*

Elmo's sister Mouzetta with his son, Russell, and his daughter, Maya, in March 1985. *(Courtesy of Mouzetta Weathers)*

Bud and Mouza Zumwalt at their daughter Mouzetta's wedding in December 1984. *(Courtesy of Mouzetta Weathers)*

Elmo's wife, Kathy, riding her horse Egypt in 1968, the year she and Elmo met. *(Courtesy of Ann Coppola)*

Elmo's crewmate Whiting Shuford asked Elmo and Kathy to be godparents to his daughter, Adrienne. Here they hold Adrienne after her christening in Hickory, North Carolina, in December 1985. *(Courtesy of A. Whiting Shuford)*

Elmo's swift boat crew reunited at Harvey Miller's wedding reception at Harvey's home in Baltimore in August 1985. From left to right are Harvey, Whiting Shuford, Elmo, Geoff Martin, and Billy Nairmore. *(Courtesy of Harvey Miller)*

Elmo Russell Zumwalt IV getting a swing from his father and grandfather at their vacation home in Pinehurst, North Carolina, during Thanksgiving 1985, just two months before Elmo entered the Fred Hutchinson Cancer Research Center in Seattle to undergo a bone marrow transplant. *(Lynn Johnson)*

Dave Halperin:

There is something about battle that strips us of all pretense and brings forth what is inside us. Those were the conditions at Sea Float under which I first grew to know Elmo.

My earliest impression gave me the feeling Elmo was willing to assume enormous risks by going on the patrols we knew to be the most hazardous, the patrols the other boat officers would avoid. It would have been much easier not to volunteer for some of the missions he undertook. Perhaps he did it because his father is such a giant, and he wanted to measure up. I don't know. I do think Elmo wanted to be absolutely sure not to permit himself any special favors so he would not be vulnerable to criticism.

I don't think it was criticism of others that concerned him so much but criticism from himself, because Elmo is a very tough judge of Elmo. I think he felt as the admiral's son he must demonstrate his courage. And he was as brave and as fearless as anyone I ever encountered in Vietnam. Elmo was tough on his crew. He drove them because he drove himself. But he also loved them, and I know they loved him.

Besides his courage, what affected me most about Elmo were the times he talked about his father, and how openly he expressed his love for him. In this life, one doesn't often encounter something as simple, as direct, and as uncomplicated as the love and respect Elmo feels for his Dad. And I came to learn that the admiral was proud and honored by Elmo's courage and determination.

It was largely through Elmo that I first began to know the admiral. Although I had briefed him many times at Sea Float, and I had known him in Saigon when I had been an aide to his deputy there, the admiral is a private man whose inner thoughts are not easily known. In Saigon, his day would begin before dawn with a three-mile run, a briefing at 6:30 AM, and he would go all day long, often into the field, exposing himself to as many, or more, risks than anyone in the senior command.

But what I remember most vividly was that late at night, sometimes until two in the morning, he would be on the phone to the Pentagon discussing the fates and futures of literally hundreds of people who had worked for him in Vietnam, and before. These were people he continued to look after and protect. He fought for them so that they were recognized properly for their Vietnam service, or were given assignments that would put them on track for promotion.

He gave those of us who worked under him that same feeling of protection. I remember the time he came down to Sea Float once and told the story of when he had commanded his first ship. When his younger officers first took responsibility for navigating his ship, he would tell them not to worry because he could get them out of any problem they got the ship into. He made me feel the same way, on a professional level and, as I grew to know him better, personally as well.

The admiral has an extraordinary intellect. At every meeting where he was present and I attended, in Vietnam and Washington, he was conspicuously the brightest person there. Looking back, I honestly think I learned more from him than I did at Harvard Law School, and that is not an exaggeration. But along with his intellect he also has wisdom and compassion, which I think is a very rare blend. He's at peace with himself, and I think one needs that kind of personal equilibrium to be wise.

The admiral and Elmo have divergences of personality and temperament. Elmo is more emotional, more a man of the heart, whereas the admiral is in some ways an intellectual, a reflective, analytical person. Elmo is open and expressive about his feelings and thoughts, while the admiral is more private.

It is on the level of character that you see their similarities. They both have a stubborn tenacity, a toughness of spirit, a belief that anything is doable, and an unshakable loyalty to friends and family. Their other common denominators are their moral courage, and their love for one another.

--- ★ ---

BACK
HOME

EIGHT

★

ADMIRAL:

Shortly after World War II, I served as executive officer aboard the destroyer *Robinson*. A Filipino steward on board wanted to be an electrician's mate. He was very able, so I sent his request up the chain of command, strongly recommending that it be approved. Every time it reached a new level, I had to fight for a favorable recommendation. After the request arrived at the Bureau of Naval Personnel, I had to call five different departments to gain approval, which was finally granted but only as a special exception.

That episode taught me a healthy contempt for bureaucracy and for the institutional racism in the Navy. President Truman had ordered the armed services to integrate in 1947. Moreover, there were written policy directives within the Navy prohibiting discrimination. However, when I became Chief of Naval Operations on July 1, 1970, racism and sexism were still an integral part of the Navy tradition. For years, white men from the South in large measure ran the Navy while it lagged far behind the other services, and the country, in its racial attitudes and policies.

I can still recall the briefing reports received when I reported for duty as a detailer in the Office of Naval Personnel. If you were assigned a black officer, which was rare, we were supposed to order him to become a recruiter, considered to be the least desirable type of duty. When he finished two years, his posting was extended an additional year. If he was promoted, we sent him to sea but put him on the worst ship for professional experience you could find, either a tanker or an auxiliary ship. By that time, he was bound to be passed over for promotion and you were rid of him. I never carried out those verbal orders, but they were obeyed by detailers many times, and in effect became a Navy policy. This discriminatory policy successfully prevented the rise of black officers because, when I became CNO, there had yet to be a black admiral in the entire history of the Navy.

Although I recognized intellectually that the Navy had a race problem, I never had a gut feeling for it until Lieutenant Commander William Norman, a black flight officer, agreed to become my special assistant for minority affairs. I had brought Lieutenant Dave Halperin to Washington to serve as my special assistant in the personnel field. Bill had come to Dave's attention because of his strong and continuing advocacy of equal treatment for minorities in the Navy. Although Bill had a distinguished record, and had moved up in rank, he wanted to put an end to the constant strain of being a black officer in a white Navy, and had just submitted his resignation when we located him.

Lieutenant Commander Norman reluctantly came to Washington for our first interview, highly skeptical of my motives, but willing to hear me out. When he walked into my office, he offered no pleasantries, and placed a one-page checklist on my desk. He wanted me to agree to it. If not, I later learned, he would resign. So he really meant to test me. Direct, weekly access to me was high on Bill's list. I readily agreed to it.

Bill turned into a superb addition to my staff. Not only was he a model of managerial efficiency, but we became close friends. He taught me a sense of what his life was like in the Navy. I learned that as a young black officer he had seldom received a voluntary salute. He told of the time he returned to his ship in civilian clothes and the officer of the deck told him the enlisted men's gangplank stood at the other end of the ship. He recounted an experience in Japan when he intervened to prevent a white chief petty officer from abusing a Japanese, and the chief called him a "goddam nigger" and punched him. But the captain of the ship refused to punish the chief because he had a "perfect record."

In December 1970, I sent out Z-66, one of my "Z-grams" as they were called. These were directives to the entire Navy, and I considered this particular message the most important, and certainly the most heartfelt, of all the 121 Z-grams I issued as CNO. It was called "Equal Opportunity in the Navy."

I said we needed to open up lines of communication for black sailors and their families, and directed a specific, point-by-point program to remove the stigma of racism from the Navy. The policy was to be in place by January 15, 1971.

Among its provisions was the requirement that the commanding officer of every ship, base, or aircraft squadron appoint a minority member as his special assistant for minority affairs; that the Navy give its full and immediate support to end housing discrimination against black sailors and their families in the cities in which they are based. I directed that every naval base and station employ a qualified black barber or beautician in major barber shops, and that suitable cosmetics, foods, and other products for black personnel be stocked in Navy exchanges. I also required that books, magazines, and records by and about black Americans be made available in Navy libraries, clubs, wardrooms, and other areas. The final sentence read: "There is no black Navy, no white Navy—just one Navy—the United States Navy."

Although my directive seemed to me to be eminently reasonable and fair, and had the unqualified support of Secretaries Laird and Chafee, it received considerable opposition, both overt and covert. I had realized this would happen. I knew I couldn't change a lily-white Navy into a representative Navy without offending the people who made it that way. I found some of the opposition especially contemptible, such as that from Tom Moorer, my predecessor as CNO. When I had become CNO, Moorer became the Chairman of the Joint Chiefs of Staff, because it was the Navy's turn to assume that post. As the Navy's chief of staff, I often met with Moorer and the other joint chiefs. Moorer, who is from Alabama, wasted few opportunities to comment sarcastically on my "blackening" of the Navy.

Just as in the other military services when they had integrated years ago, long-simmering racial tensions erupted as we integrated the Navy. The opposition to an integrated Navy grew more heated when racial fights erupted aboard the carrier *Kitty Hawk* and an oiler in Subic Bay. In addition, we also had 100 blacks and 20 whites stage a sitdown strike aboard the carrier *Constellation*. Many retired admirals alleged these disturbances were the result of my "permissiveness." They were not alone. President Nixon became livid about the situation, and apparently with me as well. At one point he had Henry Kissinger call me. Kissinger was highly agitated and just about shrieked that the President wanted all the sailors involved in the *Constellation* protest to be given dishonorable discharges immediately, something I would not have done even if it were legal. Mel Laird backed me and was able to call off Nixon's dogs.

This eventually led to an investigation by the House Armed Services Subcommittee into "disciplinary problems in the U.S. Navy." That subcommittee looked very closely at both me and my policies. Most of the media across the country came strongly to my support. The politicians on the subcommittee, torn between racist and liberal pressures, cooked up a compromise report that was ignored by the administration.

I firmly believe if I had not set the racial and personnel reforms in motion, the racial explosions in the Navy would have become far more severe. I am very proud that the first of several black admirals was selected when I was CNO, and the Navy today is totally integrated.

Another personnel problem that I had to face head-on was our plummeting re-enlistment rate. For many years the Navy had a 35 percent re-enlistment goal after the first hitch. By the time I became CNO, that figure had dropped to 9.5 percent, with little prospect for improvement. That meant we were almost constantly training people for their jobs rather than keeping those with training and experience.

During my command in Vietnam my misgivings about many Navy personnel regulations came to a boil. I had always believed that you treated subordinates with consideration and respect. I had never believed that a "tight" ship had to be an "uptight ship."

In Vietnam, I spent much of my time talking with young fighting men. These sailors did not complain about risking their lives, or living in often deplorable conditions, or being away from home. Above all else they resented the "Mickey Mouse" restrictions the Navy imposed on their personal lives. These restrictions included everything from the length of their hair, to the kind of clothes they could wear. The sailors were so demoralized that I thought the Navy's future success could well hinge on the issue of these restrictions.

I established what we called "retention study groups," in which we brought in a variety of Navy people to give us a broad view of the Navy, and how to improve it. We included aviators, blue water sailors, submariners, administrative people, officers, and enlisted men.

Through these groups we gained the detailed information we needed to make new policies, and I sent a series of Z-grams to announce them. One of the Z-grams permitted women to serve on the one ship on which they could be legally assigned. We called another "Demeaning and Abrasive Regulations, Elimination of." I had originally wanted to give it the title "Mickey Mouse, Elimination of," but decided that name sounded too flippant.

This policy change permitted sailors to wear beards, sideburns, and longer hair styles, dress in civilian clothes when off duty, and ride motorcycles. It also authorized overnight liberty for junior ratings, and instituted a number of other changes. I thought these and other changes were needed to humanize the Navy, and to increase the esprit of the men and women who served. Predictably, many, but not all, of the Navy's old guard attacked both these new policies and me. They said they would undermine discipline, and accused me of being a "Popularity Jack," someone who tries to curry favor with enlisted men. About 15 percent of middle-level officers regarded many of these changes as a personal affront, and found them difficult to cope with. For some of them, the old, rigid regulations had served as a way to exercise control, a poor substitute for leadership. I had to remind them that our naval forebears wore beards and sideburns, and *they* were a sturdy, disciplined group.

We must have done something right, because in my four years our re-enlistment rate for first-tour sailors rose to 30 percent, more than three times what it had been when I had become CNO. Moreover, the re-enlistment rate for career Navy people increased by about 10 percent.

Although I was usually depicted by the press and public as the admiral who wore sideburns and let his sailors grow beards, I spent at least 90 percent of my time as CNO working to restructure and rebuild the Navy's fleet in response to the Soviet threat. I pushed very hard for a fourth nuclear-powered aircraft carrier and the immediate development of the Trident submarine and missile system because of my genuine fear that the Soviet Union was fast becoming the world's strongest naval and strategic nuclear power. I thought such a situation would leave this country in an untenable position.

I never hesitated to state my views on the issues, which caused uncertainty among many about whether I was a bleeding-heart liberal or a war-mongering militarist. I never thought I was either. I analyzed problems as I saw them, and acted to correct them as best I could.

CAPTAIN WILLIAM NORMAN, USNR:

Before he became NCO, Admiral Zumwalt was perceived within the Navy as a bright young officer and a forward-thinking military strategist, clearly a superstar. He was not known for his human sensitivity, or as a man determined to right wrongs. He should have been seen that way, because that is the side of him I came to know.

Before I met with him in his office the first time, someone told me beforehand that I had only fourteen minutes with him—that's all the time he ever gave for a meeting—I thought I had to know then and there if we had a basis for working together. That is why I presented him with my request list. I realized the Navy had fallen far behind society at large in redressing the wrongs inflicted on minorities, and that racial tensions within the Navy had reached a dangerous level. I was not about to accept something I regarded as tokenism. But I soon realized he meant what he said, and in all my time with the admiral, I never had to go back and show him that list to remind him of his commitments, despite all the heat he took.

As I grew to know him better, I began to see many of his human qualities, his sense of humor, and his extraordinary sensitivity and candor. He also has a relentless tenacity once he's committed to a cause, and that was evident as he followed up his directives to make certain they were implemented. He insisted on fast results and hard numbers from people. He pushed the Naval Academy to increase black enrollment. At the time, the Academy had only 6 or 8 black midshipmen out of a total student body of approximately 4,000, a far smaller percentage than even the most prestigious universities in the country.

He said he wanted 50 black midshipmen in the incoming class. When he was told that would be next to impossible, he said if he had to, he would expand ROTC programs into black colleges and universities because he was determined to significantly increase the number of black officers in the Navy. In his last year as CNO, the Naval Academy took in more than 100 blacks in its incoming freshman class of 1,200.

Certainly in terms of the Navy's attitudes and policies in the early 1970s, and what he accomplished as CNO, Admiral Zumwalt was a revolutionary, and that is why he remains controversial to this day. In fact, he dramatically and permanently reshaped the Navy into a more humane and just institution for everyone in it.

ADMIRAL:

The CNO's job became all-consuming. Virtually every night of my four years there I arrived home with two to four bulging briefcases and worked until 1 or 2 AM. In the morning, Mouza would lay out my uniform, but I was so preoccupied that one time I just reached for a tie and put it on, discovering later at my office that it was a civilian tie. I even began reading my briefing papers at breakfast until Mouza kissed me one morning as I read at the table and said, "See you in four years."

I spent considerable time travelling around the country speaking to civilian gatherings about the state of U.S. and Soviet seapower. I also spoke at different military functions. On one such trip to Houston I stayed at the home of Paul Howell, a rear admiral in the Naval Reserve. We arrived late at night and early the next morning, while it was still dark, I took my usual three-mile run. I counted out the paces on my fingers as I always did, while absorbed with the problems of the day. As I ran from the house, I forgot to note my host's street address, and I was so wrapped up in what I was thinking I didn't pay careful enough attention to the street signs. I reached the halfway point and ran back a mile and a half, and realized I was lost. I didn't have any coins to make a telephone call, so I went into a circular search pattern.

I happened upon a construction foreman seated in a panel truck and asked him if he knew where my host lived. He was a contractor from the other side of town and had no idea. He offered to let me come into his construction shack to look up the address in his phone book. I couldn't read without my glasses, so I had to ask him to look it up. It wasn't listed. Then a stroke of genius struck me. I picked up his office phone and called my Pentagon office collect. When they answered, I said I wanted no wisecracks, just tell me where I spent last night. After they told me, the foreman kindly offered to drive me there, and on the way he asked me what I did for a living.

"I run the Navy," I said.

"Huh," he replied, "you don't know where you live and you can't read, and you expect me to buy that?"

By the time I arrived in Washington, my beloved aides had spread the story all over the Pentagon, so I took a lot of ribbing everywhere I went.

Mouzetta and Ann were living with us at the CNO's home, while Elmo was in law school in North Carolina and Jim served as an ensign in the Navy. Jim had expressed some concern in his calls and letters about my job pressures. When he had accumulated some leave time, he headed home. It was to be the first time I had seen him since my installation as CNO.

Before we drove out to the airport to meet him, Mouza, Ann, and Mouzetta put all kinds of makeup on me so I would appear older. They used eye shadow to create dark circles under my eyes and sprinkled talcum powder in my hair so it was almost snow-white.

When Jim first spotted me at the terminal, his jaw literally dropped, but he said nothing about how terrible I looked. On the ride home, he spoke quietly to the girls and Mouza about how old I appeared. They said the job was aging me so fast they didn't know how long I could hold up.

After we arrived home, I excused myself while Mouza and the girls told Jim how worried they were about me. I took a shower, washing away all the makeup and powder, and then went back downstairs. Jim looked at me with a startled expression. He knew he had been had.

As CNO, I no longer involved myself in the day-to-day conduct of the Vietnam War, but I kept close watch on the course of the war, particularly the progress of Vietnamization. In early 1972, I returned to Vietnam for the first time in nearly two years. I met with my old friend Admiral Chon and learned firsthand that we had turned over to the Vietnamese Navy about 1,000 craft of various kinds. As a result, the Vietnamese Navy had grown from a force of 17,000 to 40,000, which put the program right on sched-ule. Admiral Chon proved to be as good as his word.

I had to attend to another important piece of business. From my conversation with Elmo, I had realized how sorry he felt over the death of his good friend Ken Norton. Soon after I became CNO, I learned from Ken Norton's father, retired Commander Leroy Norton, that Ken's brother Charles had named his newborn son after Ken. I then placed in the files a letter I had written to the Chief of Naval Operations for the year 1987, a copy of which I also sent to young Ken's parents. In the letter I wrote of Ken Norton's tragic and heroic death, and asked for a special consideration on behalf of young Ken if and when he applied to the Naval Academy. I concluded by saying, "It would be most fitting if young Kenneth could follow in his uncle's footsteps."

Kathy Counselman Zumwalt:

Elmo and I were married on July 11, 1970, eleven days after his dad had been installed as Chief of Naval Operations. I am Catholic so we were married in St. Anthony's Catholic Church in Falls Church, Virginia, a suburb of Washington, D.C.

My mother had asked us to hold the wedding in December, but Elmo wanted to get married as soon as possible, so he convinced her that the winter weather could be bad enough to prevent many out-of-town guests from attending.

We had more than two hundred guests at the wedding and reception. My dad invited many of his professional colleagues, and quite a few people who came to Washington for the CNO installation ceremony for Elmo's dad stayed for the wedding. I remember Elmo's grandfather attended.

Our reception was held at the Washington Golf and Country Club in Arlington. The champagne flowed and people had a great time. Elmo and I left early to go on our honeymoon in Puerto Rico. We drove to my parents' home to pick up my suitcases but before we left town, Elmo stopped at a phone booth and called my dad at the reception. I stood next to Elmo.

When Dad got on the phone, Elmo asked him, "Do you know where Kathy is?"

"I thought she was with you, Elmo," Dad answered.

"No, she's not with me," Elmo said. "I've looked all over for her. You don't think she's ducked at this late date, do you?"

My dad had drunk some champagne, and he fell for Elmo's story. Knowing Dad, I'm sure he thought, My God, this wedding cost me a fortune and she's left him already.

Elmo could not contain himself any longer and burst out laughing.

After he hung up, Elmo could hardly talk because he was laughing so hard. "Your dad said, 'Elmo, you son of a bitch.'"

Elmo entered the University of North Carolina Law School later that summer. The first year was a terrible experience for me. Elmo studied all the time and paid little attention to anything else. I did not know how to cook, but I attempted to learn. I spent hours preparing a good meal and Elmo would take a break, gulp down his food in five minutes, and go back to his books.

Elmo studied in the closet, an old habit he brought from high school. He said the confines of the closet kept out distractions and helped him concentrate.

Saturday was the only night Elmo relaxed. We usually barbecued steaks on the backyard grill and I looked forward to that night like it was a trip to Europe.

I think Elmo went through some changes resulting from his Vietnam experience. He had become more emotional, which I realized was unusual. I remember he broke down a couple of times when talking about Bob Crosby's death. Another time we had an argument and he became quite angry over something trivial. He also withdrew from me and at times I wondered if he loved me. But the war also made him appreciate life more.

He once said to me, "You know, Kathy, it's just incredible what we take for granted. Just having a decent place to live, clean water, and a bathroom is luxury compared to Vietnam. In some ways I want to remember my Vietnam experience so I won't forget how lucky I am."

ELMO:

In the summer between my second and third years of law school at the University of North Carolina, John O'Neill, one of my old swift boat partners in Vietnam, asked me if I would volunteer to help him with Democrats for Nixon, an organization in which John had assumed a leadership role. I did what I could, and later that summer John was asked to give one of President Nixon's seconding speeches at the 1972 Republican National Convention in Miami. He invited me to come along. My recollection of the convention is not all that clear, but I will never forget an incident that occurred one evening as John and I walked toward the convention center.

Just outside the entrance, we confronted a group of Vietnam War protesters burning an American flag and waving a Viet Cong flag. The incident outraged me beyond words. Even to this day its memory arouses emotions in me. I realized people hated that war. I probably hated the war more than most. But I could never despise the war enough to turn away from my country and support the enemy. The realization that the Viet Cong had been responsible for the death of many people I knew, including my friend Ken Norton, made that protest all the more unbearable. I hurried past them into the convention center, unable to speak.

My reaction to that protest made me realize the depth of my emotions over Vietnam. I was surprised because until then I had not fully appreciated how strong they were. I experienced some aftereffects from the war. For instance, every time I heard a helicopter my mind went back to Sea Float, where helicopters landed twenty-four hours a day. At night, I would be disturbed in my sleep by even the slightest noise in the house, like a faucet dripping in a distant room. My ears had been so attuned in Vietnam to picking up sounds as we waited along riverbanks at night that I heard everything.

I certainly do not believe my combat experiences in Vietnam, and those experienced by the thousands of other fighting men, were any more searing than those experiences men had in other wars. But in the other wars, the sacrifices of the returning veterans were rightly recognized and applauded. I think that helped validate what they had been through and made them feel proud of their military service, and what they had accomplished for their country. I also think the warm welcome the veterans received helped heal some of the psychological wounds they suffered in those wars. The Vietnam veteran was given no support from his countrymen. Significant numbers of Americans actively supported the enemy, which made what we went through in Vietnam all the more wrenching. When we were not shunned, we were reviled as war criminals or baby killers.

These attitudes opened new wounds, and placed brutally unfair burdens on the people who fought in Vietnam. One quarter of the men who served there had been drafted. This wasn't a war they had chosen. But they did their duty and served. Many were from low-income families and had little education or opportunity. Their average age was nineteen, younger by seven years than their fathers who fought in World War II. At that age, they witnessed horrors most people never see in a lifetime. They saw their friends maimed and killed, they lived under constant tension and fear that was different from other wars, and they saw the unspeakable devastation war inflicts on a country and its people.

When they returned home, the Vietnam veterans were somehow made to feel ashamed and responsible. The warrior was blamed for the war. I think the veterans, and the military in general, became an easy target because we were more visible, which made it all the more unfair. What this country often forgot is that the Vietnam War was largely conceived by civilians.

There was one universal aspect of being a Vietnam veteran that I shared with all the others: our silence about serving in that war. Because of how we were perceived at home, we kept to ourselves our anger, grief, fear, confusion, guilt—the whole range of emotions we have experienced.

In isolated instances, Vietnam veterans have exploded in violence. I have long believed that the cause of at least some of those incidents is the unexpressed emotion they held in about Vietnam.

These stories of violence often made the headlines, but thousands more veterans have suffered quietly. They divorce, turn to alcohol or drugs, and have significantly higher rates of emotional problems than the rest of the population. Depression, anxiety, and even suicide became so widespread among Vietnam veterans that the term *post-traumatic stress disorder* became a familiar part of our language.

The psychological problems I experienced as a returning veteran were small by comparison, and that is because I am privileged. I belong to a supportive family that had a very clear understanding of what I had been through. I also had had some successes in life. So if I still carry scars from my Vietnam experiences, I can only imagine how much so many of the other Vietnam veterans have suffered. I feel deeply for all of them.

I think my marriage to Kathy was also an important factor in the ease with which I adjusted to civilian life again. She is a loving, understanding woman whom I also love very deeply.

While I attended law school, Kathy went to Meredith College in Raleigh for her senior year, completing the requirements for her B.A. degree. Academics came easily to her and she did very well there. She also worked for a local veterinarian, which supplemented the small amount of money we received from the GI Bill. My traditional Christmas gift to her for those first few years of our marriage consisted of a bottle of Jean Naté bubble bath.

Kathy met and enjoyed our old friends, Dr. and Mrs. Caldwell. Dr. Caldwell was still a professor of history at Carolina, and had become one of the truly revered teachers there. Their invitations to dinner were among the few times I broke my study routine.

Kathy and I returned to the Washington area during the summers. To save what little money we had, we stayed part of the summer with her parents, and the other part with mine. I worked as an intern for the General Services Administration and saved my salary. We met with old friends from Vietnam and high school. Mom and Dad held "surprise" birthday parties for me at the CNO's residence in July and invited our friends. After the second or third party a friend asked me what it would take to surprise me the next year.

My brother Jim had been granted an inter-service transfer from the Navy to become a Marine lieutenant. He also spent part of one summer in Washington. Jim had become the third Zumwalt to fight in the Vietnam theater. He served offshore for six months as a platoon and company commander, and later as an executive officer of a military police command. He had left the Navy because tests revealed he was color-blind, and under Navy regulations being color-blind prevented him from commanding a ship, which is the only way to advance in the Navy. Dad probably could have bent the rules for Jim, but he didn't. So Jim went to the Marines, where being color-blind would not interfere with his advancement. At that time, he wanted to be a career military officer.

I once asked him how he felt about being a Zumwalt in the Navy. He told me he had no problems. "I asked my commanding officer to treat me just like he'd treat any other CNO's son," he said. Knowing Jim, I'm sure that's exactly what he said.

When Jim and I visited Mom and Dad at the CNO's residence, we realized how much the upbringing of our sisters, Ann and Mouzetta, diverged from ours. Dad had become famous. He was in the news all the time, and had been pictured on the covers of *Time* and *Parade* magazines. There was also a big improvement in the family's material comfort. When Jim and I were young, we had really scraped along, but Ann and Mouzetta lived in luxury. Navy stewards waited on them and there were a number of other perks. Both Ann and Mouzetta were young and impressionable. I was afraid at times that they were adapting to this life a little too well. Every once in a while, Jim and I tried to bring them back to earth.

ANN ZUMWALT COPPOLA:

When Dad became CNO, Mouzetta was twelve and I was sixteen, and although I cringe about it now, I think we took advantage of Dad's new status.

At home, we ordered food over the intercom and the Navy stewards brought it to us. Elmo is eight years older than I am, and twelve years older than Mouzetta. When he thought we were getting spoiled, he and Jimmy once did this special routine to make their point. Jimmy pretended to be one of us girls, and Elmo played the steward. Jimmy ordered a bowl of ice cream, and Elmo did this pantomime of carrying it up three flights of stairs. Then Jimmy said in a high feminine voice, "It could use a touch more chocolate sauce," and Elmo bowed down and said, "Yes, Missy," and he went through the stair-climbing routine once more, huffing and puffing with every step. Then he brought Jimmy the ice cream again, and asked, "Is this enough chocolate sauce, Missy?"

Mouzetta and I laughed at the time. Even though it was a caricature, the experience proved painful. Elmo was letting us know he didn't want us to take advantage of our status, and knowing Elmo as I do now, I also realize he didn't think it was good for us.

DR. JAMES CALDWELL:

When Elmo was still in Vietnam, he wrote to ask if I would write a letter of recommendation for his law school applications, which I did happily. A while later, I received a call from Bud in Vietnam while he was still the naval commander. He asked if I knew the status of Elmo's law school application to the University of North Carolina. I told him I didn't, but I said I would call Dixon Phillips, the law school dean, who is an old friend of mine.

Dixon told me that Elmo's application had been rejected, but that the letter had not yet gone out to him. Dixon said because of Elmo's mediocre grades and poor test scores, he did not meet the admissions criteria for out-of-state students. Dixon knew that Bud was to be the new CNO, and he asked me if the university would be embarrassed if Elmo were not admitted. I said no, that Bud Zumwalt has as much integrity as anybody I know, and would not bear a grudge or in any way try to embarrass the university.

Then Dixon thought for a couple of minutes and said Elmo did qualify for acceptance under the less stringent in-state requirements. Because the Zumwalts had not really had a permanent home, and had spent as many years living in North Carolina as anywhere else, he said he would admit Elmo as an in-state student. "But," he said, "he won't make it."

I told Dixon, "Elmo will make it. He's bright, and he's one of the most determined young people I have ever known."

Of course Elmo did make it, but not without a lot of agonizing about whether he could or not. In the end, he had far better grades in law school than he had as an undergraduate, and Dixon Phillips, who had come to like and admire Elmo, strongly recommended him to his old law firm of McCoy, Weaver, Wiggins, Cleveland & Raper in Fayetteville, North Carolina, where Elmo was hired.

ADMIRAL:

By late 1974 and early 1975, President Nixon's self-inflicted wounds made any further large-scale U.S. involvement in Vietnam impossible. Politically crippled by his own venality in Watergate, he could not deliver on his secret promises to replace military equipment for South Vietnam and to retaliate vigorously by air in the event of North Vietnamese truce violations. Through VC agents, the Soviets had penetrated the South Vietnamese government and were aware of these secret promises. Quite certain that Nixon would be unable to keep them, they urged the North Vietnamese to violate the truce and test us with a few incursions. When we did not respond, the North Vietnamese geared up for a full-scale invasion. For many months, the South Vietnamese military held together despite a drumbeat of media reports that the United States had abandoned them. Congress, responsive to public pressures and unopposed by a weakened presidency, made the loss of South Vietnam inevitable.

As the fall of Saigon grew more imminent in the early spring of 1975, I returned to the Pentagon, now as a civilian after thirty-five years in the Navy. I wanted to telephone my old friend Admiral

Chon. We had met the previous June at the Naval Academy's commencement ceremonies, when one of his sons graduated from the Academy as part of a program to train South Vietnamese naval officers. Speaking at that ceremony turned out to be one of my last official acts as CNO because I retired from the Navy just a few days later, on June 30, 1974.

The Pentagon spliced my call through to Admiral Chon, who also had recently retired from the South Vietnamese Navy. I pleaded with him to leave South Vietnam with his family while he still could. I assured him I would give them a place to live and a start in this country. He said he deeply appreciated my offer, but he did not wish to leave. He said his parents were too old to travel and he did not want to abandon them in Vietnam. I told him I was certain there would be reprisals against him and other South Vietnamese military and political leaders when the North Vietnamese took over. He realized that, but he expected at most they would put him in prison for a year or so.

I called him two more times as Saigon was falling, but I still could not persuade him to leave the country he deeply loved. After Saigon fell on April 30, Admiral Chon's prediction proved tragically wrong. He was imprisoned in North Vietnam, where he remains to this day. I have tried in different ways and at different times to gain his freedom, but the Vietnamese authorities will not release him.

His friend Admiral Cang had become his successor as the Navy chief of staff and he did escape aboard a flotilla of twenty-four ships as the country collapsed. Although we have been left with the image of Vietnamese trying to flee their country on helicopters as the North Vietnamese moved toward Saigon, the Vietnamese Navy, which had become a cohesive fighting force, wanted to fight on.

Just days before Saigon fell, Admiral Cang approached General "Big" Minh, who had assumed leadership in Vietnam after General Thieu had been forced out. Admiral Cang said he wanted to take all available naval ships to Can Tho in the delta, where the Mekong River could act as a natural defense perimeter, and take a stand. When he asked Big Minh for orders, Minh, who in my view had become a quisling, answered, "I have no orders." Cang then offered to bring the ships to Phu Quoc Island in the Gulf of Siam to establish a Formosa-type government-in-exile. Not surprisingly, Big Minh did not support that plan either. He remained in Saigon to surrender, and was not imprisoned.

Admiral Cang then ordered the twenty-four seaworthy ships of the Vietnamese Navy, all of which had been supplied by our Navy, to sail as a task force from South Vietnam to the U.S. naval base at Subic Bay in the Philippines. On board were several thousand naval personnel and ten thousand civilians who were members of their families. In a ceremony at sea near Subic Bay, they returned the ships to our Navy. In our understandable wish to rid ourselves of that war, I think we overlooked some of these examples of steadfastness and leadership the South Vietnamese exhibited in the face of disaster, which went unreported by the media.

Admiral Cang was later sent to Guam, and then to a relocation center in Pennsylvania, which is when I first heard about him. Although I didn't know him, I realized that because he held such a high rank it would be difficult for him to find a U.S. sponsor, given the country's attitude toward the war, so Mouza and I offered to take him and his family of ten. They moved into our home in Virginia until they could be resettled. Elmo and Kathy also took a Vietnamese family into their home in Fayetteville.

From Admiral Cang, whom I grew to like and admire, I learned other details about the war's end. He reported that the People's Republic of China secretly offered to help establish a coalition government in South Vietnam in which Thieu would remain president. This was the same Chinese government that had wholeheartedly devoted itself to our—and Thieu's—defeat in South Vietnam for the past several years. Their offer made sense because they were concerned about the control and influence the Soviet Union had gained in North Vietnam. They hoped to prevent the Soviets from expanding their influence as North Vietnam was poised to overrun the South Vietnamese. The coalition government never was created, of course, but the Chinese concerns have proved to be valid because Vietnam has become a client of the Soviet Union.

Admiral Cang and his family lived with us for a few months. Mouza gave them great support. She took them all around to find jobs. She went up and down the area, walking into virtually every business she could find. One store owner told her that he wanted to hire "Americans" first. She looked around the store and told him, "I don't see any Indians here. They're the only real Americans." She managed to get them all jobs, and they didn't disappoint their employers. They worked hard on the job and in school. All three of Admiral Cang's children, as well as his three nieces and nephews, have either graduated from college, or are now attending college.

Vietnam will always be a focal point for debate in this country. I can look at it as a career military man and say with certainty that we did not lose on the battlefield. In fact, there was not one major battle in which the U.S. forces lost militarily. I think we had edged much closer to a Korean-type, two-Vietnam solution than this country will ever realize.

Regarding the consequences of being unable to win the war, I think many are already evident. Pol Pot was enabled to seize power in Cambodia, resulting in the wholesale slaughter of an estimated two million Cambodians. With the active support of the Soviet Union, Vietnam has now conquered both Laos and Cambodia. In light of these events, a two-Vietnam solution would have been a marked improvement over the situation that exists today in Southeast Asia.

There is no question that the communist regime in Vietnam is brutal and violates basic human rights as a matter of course. The government is vastly more repressive than any of the South Vietnamese governments at their worst. Doan Van Toai, a former member of the student opposition to the Thieu government and a supporter of the National Liberation Front during the Vietnam War, left his country in 1978, calling it a "giant prison camp."

Toai's opinion is shared by many South Vietnamese who fought against the American presence. They believe their victory has been betrayed by the government of the north, which controlled the war from the beginning.

Another result of our loss of the war is that the Soviets have established strategically important military bases in what used to be South Vietnam, allowing them to outflank our Philippines bases. The war has had one other cost: It has caused the American public, and our political leaders, to shrink away from a military presence in many places in the world where it is needed to protect U.S. interests. This has accelerated the rate at which the Soviet Union has obtained some of its goals in its long-stated objective to gain world domination.

For me personally, our defeat in Vietnam fills me with a terrible sense of loss for all those who were killed and wounded, whether the wound was physical or emotional. It is especially painful because we failed to win that war, so their losses are more difficult to accept. With the wisdom of hindsight, I have second-guessed myself many times. I realize that the Navy men killed in the river war meant a proportionately greater saving of lives for the Army and the accelerated pacification of the delta. But all that was accomplished for nothing, so all these soldiers and sailors died in vain.

In the final analysis, I believe our effort in Vietnam was worse than futile. We would have been far better off in every way never taking that stand. What has since happened to Elmo and his young son Russell—my first grandson—as a result of that war, has only made that feeling stronger.

NINE

★

ELMO:

When our son, Elmo Russell Zumwalt IV, was born on March 12, 1977, he was a beautiful, healthy-looking baby. Elmo had never been Kathy's favorite name, so we called him Russell. He appeared to be happy, responsive, and normal at first, but within two or three months Kathy became suspicious that something was wrong. Our daughter Maya had been born two years earlier so we knew when to expect certain changes in Russell.

Kathy realized that Russell was slower in his early phases of development. He was slow to lift his head, crawl, sit up, and walk. I realized that all of the Zumwalt men had developed slowly. Even though Dad had become the youngest Chief of Naval Operations in history, he had had some difficulties in his early years. So had I. Dad's younger brother, Jim, who had also been a top student, and his son, Jim, now a successful foreign service officer, had also developed slowly in early childhood.

I tried to reassure Kathy that Russell was going to be fine, but her intuition that he had problems was strong. She took Russell to a pediatric neurologist in Fayetteville who gave him a complete examination. He could find nothing wrong with Russell as far as his reactions to stimuli were concerned. I was somewhat relieved and again tried to reassure Kathy that Russell would be all right. She said the neurologist's opinion did make her feel better about Russell. But deep down she still felt something was wrong with our son.

Since my arrival four years earlier in 1973, I had busied myself with my law practice at McCoy, Weaver, the largest law firm in Fayetteville, a city of about 80,000 in the southern part of North Carolina. My law school dean, Dixon Phillips, had recommended me to the firm. Although Kathy and I had some concerns about moving to a small city, we quickly found that we liked Fayetteville very much. We bought an old home in a part of the city that had been allowed to decline over the years but was now beginning to be revitalized. Our next-door neighbors, Robert and Sandy Quinn, became very close friends, which added to our enjoyment of the area.

My sister Mouzetta, who is twelve years younger than I, had left Villanova University after two and a half years. She worked for a while, then decided to return to college. She didn't want to return to Villanova because her class had already graduated so I investigated a school in Fayetteville called Methodist College. It was a good school and I thought it offered the courses Mouzetta was looking for. Dad, Mouzetta, and I talked it over and in the fall of 1980 she enrolled.

Because of our age difference, I had only known Mouzetta as a little girl. But when she moved to Fayetteville I saw her for the beautiful young woman she had become. She visited our home often and she and Kathy became close friends. Mouzetta developed a special relationship with Maya and Russell. I also realized for the first time how much the Vietnam War had affected her.

Living at Clark Air Base in the Philippines, she had seen the most seriously wounded soldiers airlifted to the hospital there almost daily. These young men had suffered terrible wounds; some were paralyzed, or had lost a limb. She had seen families pack their belongings and leave because the father had been killed in the war. That whole experience forced her to acknowledge death and dying at a very young age, and it had had a powerful effect on her. She still has great difficulty talking about it. In some ways, I felt like a parent to my younger sisters and I was glad that I could be around Mouzetta during this time of her life. We became very close.

MOUZETTA ZUMWALT WEATHERS:

Elmo is so much older than me that I had always looked up to him as a child looks up to an adult, so besides loving him, I had a feeling of awe about him. I remember him as always serious and intense, and very determined. He could be hard on Ann and me sometimes. He got on us about studying harder. He was also adamant that we realize there were a lot of people in the world who did not have our privileges and that we should be sensitive to them.

He felt keenly that Ann and I were growing up with material comforts he and Jimmy never had, and that we should not take them for granted. That was his lesson in the ice-cream-and-chocolate-sauce routine he and Jimmy had put on at the CNO's residence. I think Dad was away so much that Elmo really felt that he should fill in for him. But he also teased us a lot, just like all big brothers do with their little sisters. I always felt he was looking out for our best interests and that there was never any meanness in it.

Our family talks to one another all the time on the telephone so we all know what each one is up to. I had realized Elmo was very concerned that I had dropped out of college and I knew he wanted me to finish. That kind of protective instinct for his family is typical of Elmo. After he had investigated Methodist College, I didn't need to be convinced to go there because I really wanted to get to know Elmo as an adult. It was very important to me to do that because he had been such an important person in my life, and I had only known him as a little sister knows her big brother.

During those years I saw a side of Elmo I had not seen before. I had thought he was so driven that he had no capacity to enjoy life, but I found out he really did. He loved simple pleasures, like a good meal with his family or a roaring fire in the fireplace. He was still very protective of me, but we related to one another as adults and I grew closer to him than I ever had before, and I have remained close to him. In retrospect, going to Fayetteville, and getting to know Elmo and his family, was one of the best things I have ever done.

ELMO:

I spent long hours at the law firm, but compared to my father, who once said, "My work is my fun," and routinely put in fifteen hours a day, seven days a week, I didn't consider myself a workaholic. I maintained a general law practice that included everything from making out wills to trying malpractice cases.

In many ways, Dad and I grew closer during the years after he left the Navy. Although he still worked hard, he was not as consumed with his job as he had been in the Navy. In his entire life, Dad had never thought much at all about money. Acquiring money or luxuries simply wasn't important to him. So after he left the Navy, about all he had was his retirement pay. Over the years, a number of business opportunities came his way and I tried to give him advice on which ones to take, and how to invest his money, so we talked on the phone at least once a day.

As an outgrowth of my youth when Mom and Dad had so little money, I was extremely careful with money. It even reached the point of absurdity, I'm afraid. One time when Kathy brought Maya and Russell to Washington to visit my parents and her parents, I took the opportunity to see just how cheaply I could live. It was during the winter, so I ate eggs and hot dogs and turned our thermostat down into the 50s. In the morning, I would go down to the basement and read the newspaper by the furnace, wrapped up in my robe. The rest of the time I would wear a thick woolen sweater.

When Kathy returned home with the children, I kept the thermostat turned down and she complained that the house had become too cold. I told her she would grow used to it, but she didn't. She would turn the heat up during the day when I went to work, but when I came home for lunch, which I usually did, I would turn it down again. Kathy tried everything she could to make me realize the house was too cold and when she couldn't, she finally called Dad to get him to convince me to turn the heat up. I knew Dad was going to side with Kathy, and for the first and only time in my life I would not take his calls. But the fact that Kathy took the extreme step of calling my father about the heat made me realize that I had probably gone too far, so I turned it back up. A little later when I talked about it with Kathy's father, Dr. Counselman, he said, "You know, Elmo, one of these days men in white coats may come after you with a net."

Dad and I have agreed about most things in life, but one of our major disagreements occurred when Dad was deciding whether to seek the U.S. Senate seat from Virginia in 1976. He planned to run as a Democrat against Senator Harry Byrd, a Virginia institution. Dad realized he did not have a strong chance of beating him, but he felt compelled to bring the issues he cared about before the American public. He had been appalled by the Nixon administration, and had said publicly and privately that the final Nixon years were as close as this country has ever come to a fascist dictatorship. He also took strong issue with Henry Kissinger, both as a person and as a policy maker. He thought Kissinger had given up on this country in the face of the Soviet threat, a position Dad found impossible to accept.

Despite his reasons for running, I was against it and told him so. I had always thought he would make an ideal university president, and at one point he was seriously considered for the presidency of the University of California. I thought politics was a dirty business and I did not want to see Dad mixed up in it.

He decided to run anyway, and soon after he started campaigning my fears seemed to be confirmed. I began receiving mysterious telephone calls at my office from a woman who said she must talk with Dad. I asked her what she wanted, and she would only say it was an extremely important matter. She gave her name but I did not recognize it. I tried to ignore her but her calls became more and more insistent. She began demanding to talk with Dad and hinted at dark things in his past.

After a few weeks I finally confronted Dad and asked if there was anything in his past that he had not told me about. He assured me there was not, and when I told him about the calls he seemed as perplexed as I was. Finally she called one time and demanded to know Dad's whereabouts. She hinted at dire consequences if I did not put him in touch with her. I told her I did not know where Dad was and I was sick and tired of her telephone calls.

Then I heard Dad's distinctive voice on the phone say, "I'm right here, Elmo." Next I heard Mouzetta's laugh, and I knew I had fallen victim to another Zumwalt joke. Mouzetta has always been clever at disguising her voice, and she had fooled me completely. She had not let Dad in on the joke at first, so she had gotten us both. After I muttered a few curses, I laughed along with them.

Although Dad found many things about politics personally uncomfortable, he made a respectable showing against Byrd. The campaign also permitted Dad to speak out on issues that concerned him. He delivered the defense speech at the 1976 Democratic National Convention, and Ronald Reagan quoted him at the Republican convention that same year. It also enabled Dad to get politics out of his blood once and for all. He had other offers to run after that, but he refused them.

When Russell turned four, Kathy and I enrolled him in nursery school. Russell was not a problem at home, and I thought at the time that he would adjust well in school. He was, and is, a very loving child, and although he and Maya fought at times, their fights were nothing more than normal sibling rivalry. Maya is an intelligent little girl who does well in school, and with so few children in our neighborhood, they often played together.

Not long after Russell began nursery school, his teacher called me to say she wanted to have a meeting. I asked why, and she said she thought Russell might have a problem. When I told Kathy she became deeply upset. She had grown more convinced that Russell's problem was serious and she felt, more acutely than I, that it would be a very painful encounter for us.

The teacher acted pleasantly, but the news she gave us was discouraging. She said Russell could not concentrate and he did not appear to learn what she taught. Kathy and I had realized that Russell couldn't learn colors. His teacher had also noticed that failing. She suggested that he be evaluated by a child psychologist. At that point I became convinced that Russell's problems were far more severe than any problems my family had experienced before.

The child psychologist put Russell through a series of tests and it became painfully clear he had not progressed as a normal four-year-old should, but the source of his problem remained uncertain. He did not seem to understand many simple things he saw or heard. At an age when other children are learning the alphabet sequence and how words are formed, Russell could not even recognize one letter.

He did not have the classic symptoms of mental retardation, yet he did not learn. His speech also had not developed as well as it should have for a boy his age, but the speech pathologists who examined him did not think Russell had a classic speech problem. Despite his speech difficulties, Russell could make himself understood and Kathy and I knew he was keenly aware of his environment. He had a good sense of humor and he played with toys so we believed he possessed a well-functioning brain, but for some unknown reason he was not able to use it as he should.

At one point, Russell had an electroencephalograph (EEG) study, commonly known as a brain wave examination. The results turned out normal. Although a normal EEG does not always mean normal intelligence, there is a high correlation. A brain scan also proved normal.

When Russell turned five, we placed him in a regular kindergarten where he got along well with the other children. But we realized Russell would not be able to function in a regular first grade, so the next year he was placed in a special education class in his elementary school.

At about this time, Kathy and I became aware through press and television accounts that many Vietnam veterans whose children had been born with serious defects believed their exposure to Agent Orange might be responsible. Kathy asked me if I had been exposed, and I told her I had. But the link between my exposure and Russell's learning difficulties seemed vague and I did not make a connection at that time. We continued to seek answers to our son's problem.

In 1982, Kathy and I, along with four close friends and members of my family, purchased a cottage in Pinehurst, North Carolina, a beautiful area about an hour's drive from Fayetteville. We went to Pinehurst on weekends and vacations, and during Christmas of 1982, we held a Zumwalt family gathering there. Besides my own family, Mom and Dad had come down from their home in Arlington, Virginia, and my brother Jim and his beautiful wife Lisa had travelled from Herndon, Virginia. Jimmy had left the military service and he too had become a lawyer. Both Ann and Mouzetta joined us.

I had not been able to shake a dry, hacking cough that I had had for a while. Kathy, along with Mom and Dad, insisted that I see a doctor when I returned to Fayetteville. At the time, I was thirty-six years old and I had not visited a physician in years. Even though I was convinced an earlier cold had caused the cough, I promised everyone I would visit a doctor because I thought it was time to establish a doctor-patient relationship.

From my malpractice experience, I knew a number of doctors in Fayetteville I had employed as expert witnesses. One surgeon suggested Dr. Douglas Henley, a young family practitioner. I made an appointment in early January. I found Dr. Henley to be very friendly and competent. He took my medical history, which was rather involved, and began his examination. He diagnosed my cough as post nasal drip, and then had me lie down on his examination table. He moved his hand back and forth over my abdomen, as if he were measuring something. I could tell by the concerned expression on his face that something wasn't quite right. He asked me if I had been feeling tired, and I told him I had, but I attributed my fatigue to an exhausting malpractice case I had recently finished. He lifted his hands from my abdomen and asked his partner to examine me. Within a few moments they agreed that my spleen had become enlarged.

I possessed enough medical knowledge to know it could mean cancer, and I asked if that was a possibility. He said yes, but I should not jump to conclusions because an enlarged spleen could mean many things. He recommended an outstanding local surgeon, Dr. Franklin Clark, to do a biopsy. Dr. Clark happened to be a friend of mine. He removed two of my lymph nodes and sent them to a pathologist for study while I waited it out.

I normally came home from my office at 1 PM to have lunch with Kathy. A couple of days after my biopsy the telephone rang while I lunched at home. It was Dr. Henley. "I'm afraid I have some bad news for you," he said. Just at that moment someone in his office fainted and he had to hang up.

I had a pretty good idea what the bad news was by the time he called back a few minutes later. He said my biopsy confirmed that I had lymphoma, a cancer of the lymphatic system. He said my specific type was called Nodular Poorly Differentiated Lymphoma (NPDL), a very slow-moving form of the disease. We talked about different options for a couple of minutes before I hung up. I turned to Kathy, who was standing right next to me, and wrapped my arms around her and we both cried.

That same day, I called Dad at his Arlington, Virginia, office. I told him I had gotten the results of my biopsy back and that I had cancer. We Zumwalts play a lot of jokes on one another, and they can get a little rough sometimes, so Dad laughed and said, "You're kidding me."

I said I wished I were, but I wasn't. It was the only time I ever remember Dad at a total loss for words. After a long pause he spoke in a soft voice. "Elmo, I just don't know what to say."

I told Dad I had a lot to decide in the next few days. He said he

knew there were many things to be done, an[d]
in every way he could.

"I want to be your partner in this," he told
had to take care of Maya and Russell, and giv
lems, that was already a full-time job. I thanked
I knew he would be there when I needed him.

I spoke with Mom that same day. She cried and told me how
unfair she thought it was. Dad had expressed the same feeling to
me. I didn't feel any sense of unfairness or anger over my cancer. I
realized I had a problem to deal with, and I had better get on with
it.

Dad had called my brother and sisters to tell them about my
cancer. I also called them. I spoke at length with Ann's husband,
Dr. Mike Coppola. I had liked Mike when I first met him, and
had grown closer to him since he and Ann had married. I also
trusted his medical judgment. He confirmed what I knew from my
malpractice experience: I needed a number of medical opinions.
He said there were many different ways to treat cancer, and that I
should hear from as many experts as I could. I knew I would have
to make the final decision about which treatment to choose, and
which doctor would do it.

Dad and I began a flurry of activity to learn as much as we
could. We telephoned cancer specialists around the country and
when we weren't calling them, we were talking to one another to
compare what we had learned. I had hoped to be treated near
home, and Mom, Dad, Kathy, and Mouzetta accompanied me to
the University of North Carolina, where I consulted with an
oncologist. He recommended immediate chemotherapy. I then
went to Washington to consult with another specialist at Georgetown University Hospital who recommended the same course of
treatment.

We then visited the National Cancer Institute (NCI), which is
part of the National Institutes of Health in Bethesda, Maryland.
There we met Dr. Paul Bunn, an oncologist at the NCI and one of
the most thoughtful and informed physicians I have ever encountered. Besides his widely recognized expertise in cancer, especially

...homa, Dr. Bunn was extremely conscientious about educating ...oth Dad and me about the disease.

After I went through a series of tests, I learned that my cancer had spread throughout my lymphatic system, and had invaded my spleen, bone marrow, and probably my liver. That was devastating to hear, but Dr. Bunn offered some good news about my cancer. He said because it moves so slowly, the median survival time even when my disease had reached this stage is eight years. That gave Dad and me a big lift because I thought I might be facing a much shorter time. But, as Dr. Bunn explained, that good news also had a dark side to it: My type of lymphoma was always fatal.

"Every time?" I asked him.

He nodded his head and said, "Yes."

Because my type of cancer moves so slowly there is a long median survival time, but it also meant certain mortality. Both chemotherapy and radiation therapy work most effectively against the most rapidly dividing cells. Malignant cells divide rapidly, which is why these treatments can be useful against them. But in the case of NPDL, the cancerous cells divide so slowly that neither radiation nor chemotherapy effectively kills them all.

Dr. Bunn offered some hope. He said Stanford University reported the cure of one NPDL patient very recently. The cure resulted from an experimental technique called monoclonal antibodies. This technique relied on modifying the body's own immune defense system so it would attack the malignant cells and rid the body of the cancer. Dr. Bunn said it had been successful in only one case, and none of the subsequent experiments on NPDL patients had succeeded. He suggested that I at least investigate monoclonal antibodies in the hope that when I needed them, I might be a candidate for the treatment.

In the meantime, he said I could begin chemotherapy immediately, or I could go on a "watch and wait" protocol. He said a ten-year retrospective study had shown that NPDL patients who received immediate treatment—whether it was chemotherapy, or chemotherapy plus radiation—did not have longer survival times than those who waited until the disease became more active. I asked Dr. Bunn what he would do if he were me. He said if I could psychologically deal with the fact that I had cancer and was not being treated for it, he would recommend the watch and wait.

I thought Dr. Bunn's advice over for a few days and in February of 1983, a month after my initial diagnosis by Dr. Henley, I decided on the watch-and-wait approach. The idea of having cancer and not treating it ordinarily would have been difficult, but I believed the information he gave me was excellent. In addition, I read articles given to me by Dr. Bunn written by Dr. Carol Portlock at Yale University, the researcher who had carried out the lymphoma study, and she confirmed what Dr. Bunn had told me. The watch-and-wait protocol had the advantage of delaying my treatment and its unpleasant side effects, while not placing me in any greater jeopardy.

I also made a decision to volunteer for a research protocol in order to have the progress of my disease monitored at the NCI, and when the time came to be treated as well. It would have been far more convenient to do it closer to home, but I wanted to be in an institution at the cutting edge of research and treatment. Also, besides Mom and Dad, my brother Jim and his wife Lisa lived in the Washington area, and my sister Ann and her husband Mike Coppola were moving back to the area because Mike had been offered a fellowship in pulmonary medicine at Georgetown University.

Dr. Bunn recommended that I become involved in the NCI monoclonal antibody program. It was a long shot, but when you don't have any shots at all, you take it. The NCI monoclonal antibody program was then under the direction of Dr. Kenneth Foon. They attempted to isolate one of my antibodies to determine if I might be a candidate for one of their experiments, but they were technically unable to do so. I turned out to be the only person from whom they were unable to obtain enough surface immunoglobulin to develop the monoclonal antibody. No one knew why, but one of the NCI chemists speculated that it might be because I had a cancer that was in some form of evolution.

I decided to go to Stanford to see if their researchers could develop my monoclonal antibody. They were pioneers in the process and I hoped they might have better luck. Dad was unable to go so Mom accompanied me there, but they ran into the same problem isolating my antibodies as had the researchers at the NCI. It dimmed my chances for this potentially life-saving experiment, but I thought if I were fortunate enough to live for a few years before my cancer became critical, it might be enough time to solve the problem they were having with my immunoglobulin.

The thought that Agent Orange might be connected with my cancer more than crossed my mind, especially in light of Russell's learning problems, but I did not research the subject at this time. I brought it up once with Dr. Bunn. He told me a number of Vietnam veterans had come to the NCI with lymphoma, but he drew no scientific conclusions from that small sample of patients.

Recent reports from Vietnamese medical authorities, including Ho Chi Minh's former personal physician, reported high rates of birth defects and illness in areas where Agent Orange had been heavily sprayed. At first I had dismissed these reports as propaganda, but with our own Vietnam veterans now claiming a link, coupled with experiences in my own family, they looked more plausible to me.

I became so immersed in my family's concerns at this time that it consumed virtually all of my time. Those concerns increased dramatically two months after my diagnosis when Dr. Counselman, Kathy's father, died suddenly of a heart attack. He was only sixty years old.

We went to the Washington area for his funeral and remained there for several days to put his estate in order. Dr. Counselman was a warm, gracious man who tended not to pay too much attention to paperwork, so Kathy, her brother Francis, my sister Mouzetta, Mrs. Counselman, and I spent days dealing with the details of his dental practice.

He had been a tail gunner during World War II and his plane had been shot down over the English Channel. He was picked up by a German U-Boat and became a prisoner of war. His harsh treatment as a POW caused lasting health problems for him. He suffered an early heart attack while attending dental school, and as a result he could not obtain much life insurance, so we worked long and hard to sell his practice. I think it was a testament to Dr. Counselman's high standing among his peers that many of them volunteered their time to keep his practice going so that we were in a better position to sell it.

Kathy had been extremely close to her father and his death came as a shattering blow to her. Together with my illness, I knew she felt desolated, and in some ways abandoned. I tried to give her comfort, but I knew that the only real comfort would come if I became well again, and I could not give her that.

KATHY COUNSELMAN ZUMWALT:

When I learned Elmo had cancer, I could not believe it, and I know a part of me refused to believe it. I was standing right next to Elmo when Dr. Henley broke the news, and I put my arms around Elmo and did not let go. I just wanted to keep hanging on to him.

A little while later my dad came down to see me. I have always been close to my dad, as close as Elmo is to his dad. He still called me every morning from his office, and his nurse and Mom both told me that Dad always said talking to me made him feel good. His pet name for me was Koo. When Dad visited me in Fayetteville he said I should begin working full-time because I might have to support my family.

I knew Dad was right to suggest I work, and within a few weeks I found a job with Intra Design in Fayetteville. I had done the interior design for our own home and the homes of some friends, and felt I would like the work. The night before I was to begin Mom called me with news of Dad's death.

Dad had taken Elmo's illness very hard. Mom said he had always returned from his visits to Fayetteville with a sparkle in his eye, but the time he returned after Elmo's diagnosis he appeared depressed. When Mom asked him what was wrong, he would not say. But she and I knew he felt bad because of Elmo.

It may be my own rationalization for Dad's death, but in some ways it may have been a blessing, because Elmo's illness would have been very hard on him. He really loved Elmo.

Because of the love I had for Dad, it is still difficult for me to talk about his death. Coming as it did so close to the news about Elmo, it made me feel as if I had lost everything. But it also made me realize that I had to survive, and that I would have to do whatever it took to keep myself and my family going. There is a saying that goes, "What does not break you makes you stronger." There is a lot of truth to that. I feel I did become stronger through adversity.

ADMIRAL:

Of all the crises Elmo and I had been through together, his cancer was the toughest. I wanted to be his partner so I could remove as much of the burden from him, and his family, as possible. Elmo had endured so much medically, first with his polio, and later with his heart surgery, I could not comprehend why he now had to endure cancer. It seemed so damned unfair to me. But in all the times I talked to Elmo about his illness, he never expressed the least bit of anger. He accepted Dr. Bunn's verdict that he had a fatal disease and although he maintained hope, he did not delude himself into believing that he was going to be cured.

I think Elmo and I have many similarities, but we approach life with a fundamental difference: I am an optimist and Elmo, by nature, is more of a pessimist. I continued to hold out some hope. I called doctors and looked into a number of possible cancer treatments, some of which were not widely accepted. I hoped for a long shot that might allow him to survive long enough for a cure to be developed. Elmo didn't see it that way. He believed he had a fatal disease and the best he hoped for was to live as long and as well as he could. He would fight with everything he had, but he thought if he entertained too much hope it would only cause deeper disappointment down the road.

It also seemed to me that he felt his own medical condition was secondary to his family's financial condition. He was deeply worried, almost to the point of obsession, with their welfare if he did not survive very long. He once said to me, "Dad, you were always overinsured and I've always been underinsured, so it looks like we both guessed wrong." He worried about how Kathy could keep going financially, and how Maya would do without her father, but he was most troubled by Russell's future. I do not think a day went by when Elmo wasn't trying in some way to broaden his knowledge about Russell's problems.

We investigated a number of ways to get more life insurance. Elmo found one small policy available to all alumni of the University of North Carolina with no physical examination needed, and he persuaded his law office to increase their group policy. With great effort and many phone calls, we also found two insurance companies that offered coverage to cancer patients, provided that Elmo was alive three years after the policies went into effect. The premiums on these policies were more than $500 a month, which placed a heavy burden on his finances.

After I had run for the U.S. Senate, I accepted a number of offers to serve on many corporate boards. With the help of retired Admiral Worth Bagley, I also write a syndicated newspaper column on defense and national security issues. I became a board member in 1977 of American Medical Building, a medical building company based in Milwaukee. I also served as that company's chief executive officer between 1977 and 1980, and again for twenty-five months from 1983 to 1985. I operate my own consulting firm, Admiral Zumwalt Associates, in which Elmo is a vice president. I had also inherited some money from my stepmother, which she had inherited from my dad, who had died in 1973. I placed that in a trust fund for Russell because I knew Russell's future was so much on Elmo's mind. I promised Elmo I would continue to contribute to that trust so that if the worst happened, Russell would have enough money to subsist in adulthood even if he were unable to hold well-paying work.

I had not become extremely wealthy, but I was happy that I was in a far better position to help Elmo than I would have been if I were still in the Navy. Elmo and I also made some joint real estate investments in Fayetteville that I hoped would add to his family's security, and Elmo's peace of mind. Despite his circumstances, Elmo maintained his instinctive sense of fairness. One time when I called him and told him that I was planning to stipulate that on my death the proceeds of one of my pension funds would go to Russell's trust fund, Elmo said no, that it would be unfair to the other grandchildren, especially if Russell turned out to be better off than we now thought he would.

The effect Elmo's illness had, and continues to have, on me runs very deep. As he became an adult, and then a lawyer, I found myself relying more and more on his advice and judgment. We had a daily association on the telephone. Every time we talked on the phone we laughed over something, even after he knew he had cancer. Elmo loves to laugh and always has something funny to say. He has a number of voices and has an ability to crack jokes even in the grimmest circumstances. He said it was part of his defense mechanism, but I saw it as a way of relieving stress. He has great mental discipline and is able to keep unwanted thoughts out of his mind. He said it was not difficult for him to deal with the emotional effects of his illness. He said he knew death was out there waiting, but he felt well, and said it seemed to be a long way off. He wondered how he would feel when it became more imminent, and I told him that knowing him as I did, I did not think he would change one bit. He said he hoped that was so, but he was not sure.

More than a year after Elmo's initial diagnosis, I invited my two sons, and my son-in-law, Mike Coppola, to the annual Alfalfa Club dinner at the Statler Hilton in Washington. This is an annual all-male black-tie affair attended by political, business, and military leaders. Usually the president and vice president attend, and this year was no exception. The Marine Corps Band played John Philip Sousa marches. I introduced Elmo, Jim, and Mike to Vice President Bush, and I also met my old nemesis, Henry Kissinger, but we managed to avoid saying anything to antagonize one another.

Long after the dinner and the speeches had ended, Mike, Elmo,

Jim, and I were at the bar drinking. A fair amount of wine had already been consumed. Elmo became emotional as he talked with Mike. I could see tears welling up in his eyes. He spoke of death and dying. Mike volunteered to be the one to make the final decision to turn off his respirator if and when that time came. Elmo agreed, saying he did not want Kathy to have to make that decision and have that kind of responsibility. He thought it would be an unfair burden to place on her.

But he insisted if it were close enough to the time when his two insurance policies vested, he did not care how badly off he was, he wanted Mike to keep him alive if it were humanly possible. It became a tearful exchange for all of us. As I thought about it later, I realized it was so typical of Elmo. Even facing the prospect of his own death, he considered the feelings and needs of the people he loves.

KATHY COUNSELMAN ZUMWALT:

Elmo and I have always been completely open with one another, and when he returned from the Alfalfa Club dinner in Washington he said, "Kathy, I know you're not going to want to hear this, but I've made a decision and I want to know if you agree."

He then told me about the conversation he had with Mike Coppola about terminating treatment. I wasn't shocked or horrified. I realized the kind of stakes that were involved in Elmo's illness, and I knew such a decision might have to be made at some point.

I respected Mike's medical judgment and I knew I could trust what he told me, if and when the time came to turn off Elmo's respirator. I did not know if I could ever make that decision, but I appreciated the fact that Elmo wanted to spare me any agony or feelings of guilt. But our conversation did cause me to focus on thoughts of losing him, filling me with an indescribable sadness.

TEN

★

One of Russell's speech teachers had attended a seminar at which Dr. Salvatore DeMarco of East Carolina University spoke on sensory integration problems among children. As she listened to him, she suspected that he might be talking about Russell's problem. She recommended that we contact Dr. DeMarco.

At the time, Russell was nearly seven and we still had no clue as to his specific type of problem. Kathy and I realized he became deeply frustrated. At times, he bit his hand or smacked it against something, occasionally Maya's head. But these outbursts proved relatively rare. He remained affectionate, even to his sister. One time after he and Maya fought, he asked her to pass the butter at dinner. When she did, he leaned over and kissed her.

Russell enjoyed "cooking" in the kitchen. After these sessions, he left a stack of dirty dishes and pots and pans. Kathy never stopped him from working in the kitchen. She recognized it was a creative outlet for him, and we even thought he might be a chef one day.

Right after Russell's teacher told us about Dr. DeMarco, we made an appointment. Kathy, Russell, and I drove over to Greenville, North Carolina, a two-and-a-half-hour drive from our home.

Dr. DeMarco is a friendly man about my age. He quickly gave Kathy and me a sense of confidence. He is a member of the speech, auditory, and language pathology department at East Carolina, and has a special interest in Russell's type of problem. We related Russell's medical history, and he asked us a number of questions about Russell's development. He then brought Russell to a soundproof testing laboratory. Kathy and I were allowed to watch through a one-way mirror. We listened on an audio headset. For the first hour, an autism specialist tested Russell, and then Dr. DeMarco performed a number of tests.

It pained Kathy and me to watch. At times Kathy turned away in tears at seeing the incredible level of frustration Russell suffered trying to perform the simplest tasks. He was unable to concentrate for all but the shortest periods. Dr. DeMarco opened a booklet that portrayed simple visual concepts, such as the picture of a bicycle or a car. Russell struggled to identify them. Dr. DeMarco showed him a picture of four people, one of whom held something, and asked him to identify that person. Russell would not even look. He simply could not pay attention. For Kathy and me, these tests were an undeniable realization of just how far from normal Russell was.

I had tried to look at Russell's problem as something we had to learn about so we could begin to solve it. But when I watched him in that testing room I realized just how profound his problems were. It only deepened my anxiety over not being around to take care of him.

That initial testing took a full day, and over the next three or four weeks Dr. DeMarco tested Russell several more times. In one session, an occupational therapist performed a number of exercises with Russell, such as rolling and unrolling him in a mat. That had a calming influence on him and enabled him to answer the questions much better.

After completing his tests, Dr. DeMarco told us that Russell suffers from sensory integration dysfunction. In some ways it relieved us to finally understand what Russell's problem is, but we were discouraged to fully understand the dimensions of it. Dr. DeMarco said the problem originates in the brain, but its specific cause is uncertain. The symptoms are an inability to discriminate sounds and sights and an inability to concentrate. For Russell, it meant the Sunday funny pages became a blur of colors instead of the individual cartoons. In a room with different noises coming from different sources, it becomes very difficult for Russell to concentrate on any one sound. It was hard for him to hear his teacher, for instance, because of the other noises in the classroom.

Dr. DeMarco said Russell's audio perceptions were only a year or two behind what they should have been for his age, but his visual perceptions he estimated to be only those of a three-year-old. At first he had thought that Russell had a mild to moderate dysfunction, but further tests convinced him that it was moderate to severe.

A consultation with a pediatric neurologist recommended by Dr. DeMarco appeared to confirm that Russell has a normal intelligence, but because of his sensory and attention problems he is unable to express it. In a sense, they felt Russell's mind was trapped inside him. That was probably the major source of his frustrations. But realizing the level of frustration Russell has to endure, I now marvel all the more that he is such an affectionate, loving little boy who conducts himself in a very calm way under the circumstances. I am very proud of Russell.

There is no surgery that would improve Russell. Drugs improve some children with Russell's condition, but they did not help him. Dr. DeMarco told us that in many cases when children reach eleven or twelve they begin to outgrow these problems to some extent. But given the level of Russell's dysfunction, he did not think he would ever completely overcome it. Dr. DeMarco wanted to see Russell on a continuing basis. He also gave us a series of physical therapy exercises, such as rolling him back and forth on a big ball, or holding him in the air on his stomach. Normally, most children would get excited with these exercises, but they have a calming effect on Russell.

★

In February of 1985, two years after my initial diagnosis of lymphoma, I flew to San Diego in my continuing pursuit of the monoclonal antibody. I had befriended a physician who also had lymphoma, and he told me of Dr. Ira Royston at the University of California at San Diego. Dr. Royston is a leading researcher in monoclonal antibodies and I went there with the hope of inspiring his competitive instincts. I had told him Stanford and the National Cancer Institute had both been unable to develop a monoclonal antibody for me and he remarked that it would really be something if he could do it.

While I was out there I stayed with Uncle Jim, Dad's younger brother, and my Aunt Gretlie. I also saw their daughter Frances, who is several years younger than me and, like her father, a schoolteacher. Uncle Jim has taught high school history and civics in El Cajon, California, for thirty years. Although he and Dad have some similarities, they have very different political views, and Dad kiddingly calls Jim "my radical-liberal brother." I know Dad has always felt bad that the death of their mother in 1939 was much harder on Jim. He was only fourteen at the time, and was with her during her final days.

Dr. Royston's group performed what was then my ninth lymph node biopsy in order to develop a monoclonal antibody. They told me it would be a few days before the results were known. Soon after I had arrived back in Fayetteville, I called Dr. Royston in San Diego for the results. He said he had encountered something totally unexpected. Instead of finding non-Hodgkin's lymphoma in the biopsy, they had found evidence of Hodgkin's disease. Although Hodgkin's disease is a form of lymphoma, it is a completely different type from non-Hodgkin's, and it is believed that the two are unrelated. Dr. Royston said the findings were preliminary, and shocking.

Dr. Elaine Jaffe, one of the world's most noted pathologists, had performed the original pathology studies at the National Cancer Institute and it was hard to believe she could have made such a mistake. Cells from these two cancers are very different from one another. He told me he would call me back when they completed their pathology studies. I had always told Kathy everything, but in this case I thought I had better hold off. I did not want to upset her unnecessarily until I learned the final test results.

Two days later, Dr. Royston called back and said as incredible as it seemed, I had Hodgkin's disease as well as non-Hodgkin's lymphoma. Unless I had experienced it myself, I would have thought that having one cancer on top of another would make little difference. But the news had a big impact on me. I knew that besides the slow-moving non-Hodgkin's cancer, I had a fast-moving, aggressive form of the disease as well. I realized I could no longer remain on watch-and-wait, that I needed to be re-evaluated at the NCI quickly.

KATHY COUNSELMAN ZUMWALT:

For a couple of days I could sense something was bothering Elmo. He was quieter than usual and sometimes I would catch him with his eyes a little misty.

I really knew something was up when his secretary, Lynda Miller, walked into our house with Elmo one afternoon. Elmo had planned to pick up some tickets at the travel agency, but he said to me, "Kathy, I want you to come with me to the travel agency. Lynda is going to babysit."

I had not even combed my hair but Elmo said not to bother and there was real urgency in his voice. As we were walking to the car in the driveway he broke it to me. "I've just learned I've got a second cancer," he said. I was stunned. I said it couldn't be possible. People don't get two cancers at the same time. He said he knew it was unusual, but he really did have two of them. After we parked, I put my arms around him and just held on. Then Elmo went into the travel agency and I stayed in the car alone. I began screaming and crying and pounding the car in a blind rage. I was filled with so much anger I couldn't believe myself. For a while I almost thought I was losing my mind.

ELMO:

I had returned to the NCI about once a month since my initial diagnosis in early 1983. In February 1985, NCI doctors confirmed what Dr. Royston had found: I now had two completely different cancers. When they biopsied a lymph node from under my arm, they found NPDL. When they biopsied a node from my groin area, it revealed Hodgkin's disease. Dr. Bunn had never seen a case like mine. Initially it had appeared that my Hodgkin's disease was in stage one, the least invasive stage of the disease. But further tests revealed it was in stage two, which is one step more invasive. It appeared that my Hodgkin's disease had developed exceedingly fast.

There are about one dozen cases reported in the world medical literature of people who had my two cancers simultaneously, but I was the only one who first had a non-Hodgkin's lymphoma and later developed Hodgkin's disease. In these other cases of dual cancers, the Hodgkin's disease had first been treated by drugs or radiation, or both, and doctors believed that the treatment of the initial cancer caused cellular changes that resulted in the second cancer. My cancer had never been treated with anything. It was not comforting to realize I was a statistic of one.

I consulted with Dr. Bunn and he seemed perplexed by the turn of events. "Elmo, we're at the outer edge of medical knowledge with you. We can't even intelligently estimate your survival odds because we don't really know what is happening. Anything we say is a guess."

Watch and wait was over, and with it my hope that I could continue indefinitely with a good quality of life before treatment. One internal lymph node had already grown so big it impinged on my bladder, and was moving toward my ureter and kidney. Because my cancers appeared in so many areas of my body, radiation would not be effective, nor of course would surgery. The only potentially useful treatment was chemotherapy. But there were many different choices. The chemotherapy used for non-Hodgkin's lymphoma was not the same as that used for Hodgkin's disease. Hodgkin's disease has a high cure rate, but the fact that I had another cancer would complicate treatment.

The physicians consulted with Dr. Vincent DeVita, the director of the NCI, a well-known expert in lymphoma and Hodgkin's treatment. They could either try to knock out the Hodgkin's, because that posed the most immediate threat, or try a drug regimen that might prove effective against both cancers.

But there were also dangers. The chemotherapy might cause the now-indolent non-Hodgkin's lymphoma to turn more aggressive. After considerable weighing of the options, Drs. DeVita and Bunn, and the other NCI doctors, recommended PROMACE-MOPP, an eight-drug chemotherapy regimen that included methotraxate, prednisone, nitrogen mustard, and other anticancer drugs.

I would be treated at the Bethesda Naval Hospital, which is directly across the street from the National Cancer Institute, as part of a combined Navy-NCI cancer research protocol. Like all NCI patients, my treatment would be free and they would pay my travel expenses from Fayetteville to Washington. I would receive chemotherapy three Mondays a month for a period of six months. After that, they would restage me, meaning they would give me tests to determine the extent of my disease. That would determine the next step. The hope going in was that the Hodgkin's disease would at least be put into remission, perhaps even cured, by this regimen, and the non-Hodgkin's lymphoma be put temporarily into remission, with the enlarged lymph nodes returned to normal size.

Dr. Bunn had accepted a faculty appointment at the University of Colorado School of Medicine so I had to be assigned a new physician. I knew I would miss the clear-headed advice I had received from Dr. Bunn, but he assured me that any time I had any questions I could call him.

I met a young Navy lieutenant commander named Dr. John Nanfro in the course of my visits to the NCI. He practiced in the oncology department at the Bethesda Naval Hospital and was on the staff at NCI. Besides having excellent medical credentials, I had found him cheerful and upbeat whenever he examined me. He also took a lot of care to explain things to me. I was asked if I would like him to be my physician, and I agreed. I could not have made a better choice.

In my own mind at this time, I strongly believed that my cancers were directly linked to my Agent Orange exposure. It wasn't just the fact that my case was so rare, but a number of other factors entered into my thinking.

Because of Dad's fame, news of my illness had become public knowledge. I had been asked by a lawyer to be one of five representative plaintiffs in the class action lawsuit brought on behalf of Vietnam veterans against several manufacturers involved in the production of Agent Orange. He made a Herculean effort to convince me that I could benefit the cause because of my name, my experience as a lawyer, and my illness. I knew he was right. I wanted to join the cause not for myself, but for all the Vietnam veterans who suffered from their exposure to Agent Orange. At the time, I thought the case would drag on for months, if not years, requiring much of my time to prepare for depositions and court testimony. I did not know how long I would live, but I knew I wanted to spend as much time as I could with my family. I weighed the choices carefully and made a very hard decision: I chose not to join the suit.

A short while later, the suit was settled without trial for $180,000,000. I called the plaintiff attorney and said, "I guess you didn't need me after all."

He said, "Since you've raised it, I would say someone with your name, and with your set of problems, probably could have driven the settlement price up."

That may have been exaggerated, but it made me feel bad that I had not joined the suit. Had I known it would be settled that quickly, I would have joined.

My experience with this lawsuit, as peripheral as it was, opened my eyes even further to the scope of problems linked with Agent Orange exposure. Veterans from all over the country reported medical illnesses that included nervous disorders, cancers, and skin problems. Many also reported their children were born with serious birth defects, some similar to Russell's. In October 1984, I wrote an article about my illness, and the plight of Vietnam veterans, for *Parade Magazine*. I received many letters from veterans' families telling me of the medical problems other veterans suffered.

I realize there are a number of different medical problems veterans now claim are linked to Agent Orange, but that is not unusual. Consider the range of dangerous side effects associated with cigarette smoking: some people get lung cancer, others get tongue, throat, esophagus, mouth, or bladder cancer. Others suffer heart attacks, emphysema, or chronic bronchitis, and smoking mothers have babies of lower birth weight. The specific health effect of a toxic substance, whether it is Agent Orange or tobacco, depends on each individual's susceptibilities. As one of my doctors explained to me, Agent Orange may have been one of the sequence of events that initiated my cancers.

I am a lawyer and I do not think I could prove in court, by the weight of the existing scientific evidence, that Agent Orange is the cause of all these medical problems. But I am convinced that it is. I believe Agent Orange is responsible for my cancers, for Russell's learning disorder, and for illnesses suffered by many Vietnam veterans.

Agent Orange is so potent a herbicide that one scientist said it is as devastating to foliage as DDT is to insects. As is the case with DDT, I believe Agent Orange has a number of hazardous side effects. The chemical itself is a fifty-fifty mixture of two herbicides, 2,4-D and 2,4,5-T. A third element, dioxin, which is an extremely toxic chemical, was found as a contaminant in Agent Orange, apparently as a result of the production process itself. In some instances, unusually high levels of dioxin were found in Agent Orange. Although there were other defoliants used in Vietnam, such as Agent Purple and Agent White, Agent Orange was by far the most widely used. Eleven chemical companies were involved in defoliant production, including some major ones such as Monsanto, Dow, Diamond Shamrock, Hercules, and North American Phillips.

Soon after the onset of my second cancer, Dad and I visited the Pentagon and examined a map showing the areas of heaviest spraying in Vietnam. About 5 to 15 percent of the country was sprayed with Agent Orange, and I had spent much of my time in two of them, Da Nang and Sea Float. But in virtually every combat area I patrolled in Vietnam, there was evidence of defoliation.

In 1966 the U.S. State Department had issued a report that herbicides used in Vietnam "are nontoxic and not dangerous to man or animal life." I think the State Department was acting on the best evidence it had. However, later investigations have revealed that some of the chemical companies knew at the time of the State Department's report that evidence existed indicating 2,4,5-T caused birth defects in animals. And when evidence was later published suggesting there were potentially serious health hazards with this chemical, the companies denied it.

They argued that reports of birth defects were the result of small levels of dioxin contamination in the 2,4,5-T. If this reasoning was true, it suggested that dioxin is one of the most potent causes of birth defects known. As one Food and Drug Administration researcher reported, dioxin would be as potent a cause of birth defects as thalidomide. It is also worth remembering that the first evidence of thalidomide's dangers came from animal studies. Casting it in the best possible light, I find the attitude of these chemical companies in this regard to be the height of capitalistic arrogance.

Controlled studies found rats that ingested dioxin had abnormally high rates of malignancies, those ingesting lesser amounts had fewer malignancies, and those that ingested no dioxin had no cancers.

As reports about Agent Orange's potential hazards mounted, and congressional hearings brought additional presure to bear, this country discontinued spraying Agent Orange in Vietnam in April

1970. This was little more than a month before my tour ended. I had been there during the heaviest spraying.

More recently, new studies have given added evidence of Agent Orange's hazards. In 1980, Dr. Lennart Hardell published a Swedish study in *The British Journal of Cancer.* It described workers who were exposed to the two major chemicals in Agent Orange. I will quote from his summary: "As regards the present investigation, it suggests, in summary, that exposure to organic solvents, chlorophenols and/or phenoxy acids (2,4,5-T) constituted a risk factor for the incidence of malignant lymphoma." In that same study, which was confirmed in a reinvestigation, 2,4-D, which is the other major chemical component of Agent Orange, was also implicated as an initiator of lymphoma. Dr. Hardell stated he was uncertain how these chemicals led to lymphomas—including Hodgkin's disease—but suggested they might depress the immune system, thus permitting the cancers to develop. There is now also evidence that dioxin does depress the immune systems of humans.

I realize the scientific evidence linking Agent Orange to human illness is disputed, and in some cases apparently contradicted. The Defense Department sponsored a study of 1,200 U.S. Air Force pilots and crew who flew the planes that sprayed Agent Orange and found they did not have higher rates of disease than the rest of the population. I realize these men probably were exposed to Agent Orange, but they sprayed it *out* of planes and after they flew their missions they returned to their bases where they could shower and wash themselves. Those of us out in the field had Agent Orange dropped on us, and had to live with this chemical on our clothes and skin for days at a time. I also think 1,200 people with such limited exposure is too small a number for a conclusive statistical analysis of this kind. One major population study linking cancer and cigarette smoking involved one million people.

I believe the Reagan administration has made a good-faith effort with regard to helping veterans exposed to Agent Orange. An Agent Orange office has been established in the Pentagon, and is helping collect data that the Center for Disease Control in Atlanta will use to investigate the relationship between Agent Orange exposure and the health effects on veterans. The CDC is looking at ground troops to determine if there is any such association, and their report is due in 1987. I am not certain what the CDC will conclude. It may be the case that they cannot scientifically prove or disprove anything because of the difficulties in determining the levels of Agent Orange exposure among different ground troops.

I think over the next several years the full story of Agent Orange's health hazards will emerge. It may be too early for definitive answers, since latency periods for a disease like cancer can be twenty to thirty years. This may be one case in which the layman is ahead of the scientist. Perhaps the Agent Orange issue was best expressed by Paul Reutershan, who formed an organization called Agent Orange Victims International in 1978. Paul was only twenty-eight at the time he learned he had terminal stomach cancer. He had been a helicopter pilot in Vietnam and often flew through the Agent Orange mists sprayed by the C-123s. Paul said: "I got killed in Vietnam. I just didn't know it at the time."

I realize what I am saying may imply that my father is responsible for my illness and Russell's disability. But I do not second-guess the decisions Dad made in Vietnam, nor do I doubt for a minute that the saving of human life was always his first priority in his conduct of the war. I have the greatest love and admiration for him as a man, and the deepest respect for him as a military leader. Certainly thousands, including me, are alive today because of his decision to use Agent Orange. I do not hold him responsible for what has happened to Russell and me. And knowing what I now know, and facing what I now face, I cannot say I am sorry, or feel any bitterness, for volunteering to go to Vietnam. I made the choice and created my own destiny.

I know what Dad is going through for me right now is extremely hard on him. Throughout my life, he has always been there when I needed him, and he is with me now. I have always felt we were in this together.

ADMIRAL:

I too am convinced, based on what I have read, and conversations with people, that Agent Orange can cause cancer and birth defects, and in the case of many Vietnam veterans has done precisely that. I realize the final scientific word is not in yet, but I think that because of all the veterans Elmo and I contacted, and all the illness and medical problems they told us about, we are ahead of the scientific evidence.

Because of the orders I gave to step up defoliation in the Ca Mau Peninsula around Sea Float, there is no question in my mind that, indirectly at least, I was responsible for Elmo's heavy exposure to Agent Orange, which makes me an instrument in his tragedy.

Elmo and I know each other so well that I never thought he would hold me responsible, nor did he think I would feel guilty. He made his decision to go to Vietnam, and I made decisions on how to conduct the war based on the best information I had at the time. But what has happened to Russell and Elmo deepens my own sense of futility about the Vietnam War, and makes its memory all the more painful for me. I regard Elmo and Russell as casualties of that war.

I also realize that had I not used Agent Orange, many more lives would have been lost in combat, perhaps even Elmo's. And knowing what I now know, I still would have ordered the defoliation to achieve the objectives it did. But that does not ease the sorrow I feel for Elmo, or the anguish his illness, and Russell's disability, give me. It is the first thing I think of when I awake in the morning, and the last thing I remember when I go to sleep at night.

In March of 1985, Elmo began commuting from Fayetteville to Washington three Mondays a month for his chemotherapy treatment at the Bethesda Naval Hospital. He received different anticancer drugs on succeeding Mondays. A member of our family was with him every time.

For the first few weeks, Ann, who is a registered nurse, picked Elmo up at National Airport and they made the thirty-minute drive to the hospital together. Ann lived in nearby Alexandria, Virginia, and has a baby daughter, Lauren. She arranged babysitters on Monday mornings so she could be with Elmo. It was their first opportunity to get to know one another as adults.

In many ways, Elmo had been hardest on Ann when they were growing up. I think it was probably because they are so similar. Elmo and Ann are much more talkative than Jim or Mouzetta, and have quicker tempers. What gratified Mouza and me as parents was that all four of our children had become very close to one another, and all the sibling rivalries they had had as children have evaporated into loving relationships not only among themselves but among their spouses as well. Mouzetta was the last to be married. She lived in Raleigh, North Carolina, with her husband, Ron Weathers, a project management analyst with the Carolina Power and Light Company.

ANN ZUMWALT COPPOLA:

When I was an adolescent, Elmo always wanted me to remember that I had it much better than most of the people in the world, and at times he pressed that point so hard that it brought me to tears. But he was also my advocate, and I never felt he did not love me.

I think Mom and Dad raised Mouzetta and me differently from the way they raised Elmo and Jimmy. They wanted to hang on to us more, and I remember Elmo arguing with them that I should go away to college, and not attend one nearby. He thought it would be good for me. So did I. Eventually we won, and I did go away to school in Washington State, which turned out to be a good experience for me.

Later on Elmo and I developed an adult relationship and we

grew very close to one another. I could relate to him as an adult.
We share a deep love for one another.

I really cherished those Mondays when he came up to the
Bethesda Naval Hospital to receive chemotherapy. It was my time
to be with him and for us to deepen our relationship. We talked
about our children, our family, childhood memories—just about
everything. I consciously tried to make him laugh at times because
I thought that could help his mood. Elmo always enjoyed a good
laugh.

I also have absolutely no doubt that if our situations were re-
versed, Elmo would be there for me. I am sure he would have
done as much research for me, or for any of our family, as he did
for himself, because that's the way Elmo is.

ADMIRAL:

I also spent several Mondays at the hospital with Elmo, as did
Mouza and Jim. We could see the toll the chemotherapy exacted as
the weeks passed. He became paler—because the drugs destroy
healthy blood cells—and he began to lose weight. Elmo has always been slender, so a five- to ten-pound weight loss made him
appear quite thin. By late April his hair loss became noticeable. He
never lost all his hair, but it became very wispy. He said vanity was
the least of his concerns, so he had no interest in a wig.

He tolerated chemotherapy well enough to keep up his law
practice full-time, and he busied himself with renovating a rental
property he had bought to provide Kathy and his children a better
income. His doctors were amazed at the amount of energy he had.

Mustard nitrate, a drug similar to the mustard gas used in
World War I, was the only one that truly did him in. He became
nauseated by it almost as soon as they gave it to him, and he stayed
sick for hours. Every time he received it he could not return to
Fayetteville the same day, as he did with all the other drugs. He
stayed overnight with Mouza and me, Ann and Mike, or Jim and
Lisa.

In the early summer Ann and Mike moved to Springfield, Massachusetts, where Mike had joined a private group practice. He is an internist with a special interest in pulmonary medicine. Before she left, Ann, who was really Elmo's major support during those first weeks of chemotherapy, wrote a detailed account of all the things that needed to be done for Elmo when he came to the hospital. It was a great help to the rest of us. Each Monday travel arrangements had to be made, vouchers had to be obtained, prescriptions had to be filled out. It would have been difficult for Elmo to have done all that and cope with the effects of his treatment at the same time.

When Elmo was not busy with his law practice or renovating his rental property, he spent time teaching Kathy to manage their family finances. That had always been Elmo's responsibility and he wanted to make sure Kathy knew all of those details. It was very difficult for Kathy to do it, not because what Elmo told her was so hard to understand, but because she realized he was teaching her because he would not be around too much longer. Elmo also encouraged Kathy to learn more about business so she would be better able financially—and emotionally—to deal with his death. Kathy was becoming a capable real estate manager, and had established a reputation as a superb interior designer.

He talked openly to her about the prospect of remarriage, and he told her he hoped she would remarry. That was very difficult for Kathy to deal with, but Elmo honestly thought she should remarry because she was still a young woman, and he wanted to ease any feelings of guilt she might someday have about it.

I continued to feel optimistic that somehow, someway, Elmo would beat the cancers. That is part of my nature. I spoke with researchers and some people in the forefront of biotechnical research who thought there might be a breakthrough in lymphoma treatment in the near future. I hoped Elmo would at least beat the Hodgkin's disease, and then have a long remission with the non-Hodgkin's lymphoma. By that time, I hoped the breakthrough might have arrived.

Beginning in August 1983, I had begun commuting to Milwaukee every week because the board of the American Medical Build-

ing Company had fired the chief executive officer in a major
shakeup and asked me to once again assume that position, and I
agreed to accept an interim appointment. As soon as Elmo developed Hodgkin's disease, I accelerated my plans to terminate my
appointment. I wanted to spend more time with Elmo both on his
trips to Washington, and on weekends at Pinehurst, and I felt it
was time to relinquish that time-consuming job. I resigned in June
1985 but remained as chairman of the board, which required
much less of my time. I also gave up a few other positions but
maintained the most financially lucrative ones. Although I wanted
to spend more time with Elmo, I also wanted to earn as much as I
could to help his family should the worst happen.

Elmo's basic attitude about his illness remained the same as it
had been from the beginning. He knew he had a fatal disease, and
he intended to live as well as he could for as long as possible, but
he would not allow himself to hope for a cure. That did not mean
he would not fight. He fought like hell. But he believes what will
be, will be. I think in part this attitude comes from his mother.
Mouza is a great believer in fate. But I also think Elmo's childhood experiences were part of it. From the time he was old
enough to think, his heart condition forced him to confront the
possibility of death. He had developed a truly a remarkable attitude. It is one thing to say you will accept what life gives you, and
quite another to live it.

Elmo made an extraordinary study of his own disease and became conversant in a number of technical details about it. He read
widely and talked with physicians all the time, and he knew all
about treatment alternatives, the different probabilities of success,
and what each medication did. He was totally comfortable talking
about his cancer, even the possibility of dying from it. It was the
unblinking way he faced the prospect of death that so impressed
me. In the military, I had run into courage in many areas, and I
think Elmo's courage is the most impressive example I have ever
seen.

Elmo disputed his own courage. He contended no one could
really say who was courageous and who was not. It all depended

on the circumstances he or she was in, and just because someone performed well in one circumstance, did not mean he would perform well in another. He simply thought of himself as someone who had been thrust into difficult circumstances and was trying to do the best he could. But to my mind, his service in Vietnam had measured up to the very best I had seen in battle in three wars. And before that, the way he dealt with his polio, then his heart surgery, and now cancer, demonstrated a depth of courage I had never before known.

Through everything—his hair loss, increasing weakness, weight loss, and frequent nausea—he maintained his sense of humor. He kidded with the nurses on the oncology ward, and with everyone else. Sometimes it had the ring of gallows humor. When someone commented that his medical file was pretty thick, he answered, "Yeah. And I hope it gets a lot thicker."

I remember one Monday at the hospital when Jim and I were there with Elmo. Jim had an important business meeting in downtown Washington after Elmo's treatment. He wore a brand-new suit. Elmo was lying down on an outpatient hospital bed as he received his intravenous chemotherapy, a process that normally took two to three hours. As usual, he was a little groggy from the tranquilizer and the antinausea medication Dr. Nanfro had prescribed.

Jim and I were giving him our usual hard time, kidding him that he was lying down on the job. Elmo just lay there with his eyes closed and never said a word. When his chemotherapy was completed, the nurse unhooked the intravenous line and Elmo draped his legs over the side of the bed and put on his shoes, still not saying a word. Then he stood up and started walking toward the bathroom, but he suddenly became very wobbly. He lurched for Jim and grabbed his shoulders. Then Elmo opened his mouth and made a noise like he was going to vomit. Poor Jim had this stricken look on his face. He knew if he tried to pull back Elmo would fall to the floor, and if he stood there Elmo would vomit all over him. Just at that moment, Elmo cracked a smile and laughed, "Worried about the suit, Jim?"

One of the oncology nurses once said she always knew when Elmo was around because it was so unusual to hear laughter there.

MOUZETTA ZUMWALT WEATHERS:

I kept in close touch with Elmo and Dad by telephone, and frequently saw them in Washington and at Pinehurst. I think of all of us in the family, Dad has been hardest hit by Elmo's illness, besides Elmo's own family. I really think he feels Elmo's pain. He told me that he wished it could have been him instead of Elmo.

I have seen Dad age tremendously since Elmo became ill, and at times I wondered because of the terrible toll it takes on him if he is almost too involved in the illness. He seems obsessed with the idea that he may outlive Elmo. He wants to be there all the time for Elmo and take away as much of his pain as he can. You know, Dad has been so successful at solving problems in life, that he is now facing the one problem he wishes he could solve, but he cannot. I think it depresses him more than anything else in his life.

I think Dad feels deeply responsible for the role Agent Orange may have played in Elmo's illness. He recognizes the extreme rareness of Elmo's condition, and Russell's learning disability. Dad's belief that their problems may stem from his orders in Vietnam is very hard on him.

I do not think that Dad is helping Elmo because he feels responsible for what has happened. He would do it anyway because that is just the way Dad is. But this sense of responsibility wears on him a lot. I realize how emotionally hard this is on Elmo, but in some ways I think it is harder on Dad. Elmo talks openly about his emotions, but Dad keeps his pain inside.

ELEVEN

★

KATHY COUNSELMAN ZUMWALT:

I had a very tough time when Elmo tried to talk to me about finances and tell me I should do this or that after he died. I am not superstitious, but I had the feeling if we talked about it enough it was going to happen. So when he brought the subject up I tried to change it, or I just walked out of the room. But I realized it was very important to Elmo because he worried about taking care of us far more than his own illness, so I made myself listen.

I could see the physical changes in Elmo caused by the chemotherapy, but he did not become depressed or morose, and I really could not see a big difference in the amount of energy he had, except for those times when he was nauseated from the drugs. But he did have some changes in attitudes. Elmo has always been tight with money and concerned about security. He never allowed himself any extravagances. But the summer after he learned about his first cancer, he and I took a two-week vacation in England. I am not sure he would have taken that trip before he learned he had cancer.

This past Christmas he surprised me again. A couple of weeks before Christmas his secretary called me and said Elmo had to attend a meeting that night and would be home late. Well, when he arrived home his eyes were so bloodshot he looked like he had had ten drinks. I said, "You must have had a good time," and he sort of ignored me. Then for the next couple of nights he could not sleep. I asked him what was bothering him and he said it was nothing.

We spent the Christmas holidays at Pinehurst, and every day before Christmas Elmo began disappearing. When I asked him where he went, he would say, "I just went for a little walk." On Christmas morning he gave me a bottle of Jean Naté bubble bath and I laughed. An attached card said something about an English racer. He took me by the hand and led me out toward the garage. I thought why in the world did he keep a bicycle out here? He opened the garage doors and there was a beautiful yellow Triumph TR-6 sports car.

I asked him if he had rented it. He laughed and said no, it was mine. I could not believe it. I had always wanted a sports car but I never imagined Elmo would buy one. He told me on that night two weeks earlier when he had come home so late, he had picked up the car from the previous owner. He then drove it over to Pinehurst and from there he drove back home. He said he had been disappearing the last few days to polish it. He wanted it to be perfect. That's the little boy in Elmo.

Later he laughed and told me, "You know, Kathy, I never lost a night's sleep over having cancer, but I did after I spent that money on your sports car."

His willingness to spend money was not the only change I saw in Elmo. He also was not as obsessive about his law practice. He still worked hard at it, but it did not consume him as it had before. He has always been very loving to our children, but he had not spent a lot of time with them. Now he did.

He usually helped Russell with his physical therapy, and they worked on the alphabet together. He took Maya and Russell for long walks and drove them around in the sports car. He talked to Maya more and took her and Russell out to Saturday morning breakfast, and became far more interested in their lives. He said this was one of the benefits of a terminal illness, but he could not understand why he had to have a terminal illness to realize what was important in his life.

I felt a great sense of sadness. I had imagined living my entire life with Elmo, of us growing old together. He is so full of vitality and humor that it is impossible for me to think of living without him. He is very strong and has an unbelievable amount of determination. I am pretty strong-willed myself, so we have had our share of fights over the years. But there were many more good times, and I cannot imagine that anybody else's good times were ever better.

More than for myself, it is sad to see the effects on Maya and Russell. Maya is a very mature, sensitive little girl, and she understands the seriousness of Elmo's illness. She worries about him and she always reminds him to take his medication. She also writes him little love notes. Once, after some people were at our home and Elmo talked to them about his illness, he went into the kitchen where Maya had left a note saying, "Daddy, I love you very much and you will survive the cancer. Don't worry that you cannot have chocolate or beer . . . you will survive."

Elmo is always honest with both of them. Once Maya asked if he could die from his cancer. He told her he could, but he said he could die from many things. I know the thought of Elmo's illness is on her mind all the time. Elmo's immunity dropped because of the chemotherapy, and one night Maya had a dream that she had a cold and could not go to his bedroom to see him. Russell does not have as deep an understanding of Elmo's illness, but he realizes something is terribly wrong. Several times when I have been with him alone, he has started to cry and when I asked him why, he answers, "Daddy."

ELMO:

I understood the sadness and helplessness Kathy felt about my illness because a few years earlier I had experienced the same thing with her. Kathy had had an inner ear problem and she was given a diagnostic brain scan. Her doctors found a dark spot deep within her brain. They were not sure what it was, but if it was a tumor they could not remove it because of its location. I remember how frantic and helpless I felt at the time.

Neither I nor her doctors told Kathy that if it was a tumor, it would be inoperable. Over the next several months she had follow-up scans and the dark area did not change, meaning it was *not* a tumor. The relief I felt when the doctors told me was immeasurable.

Kathy had fallen off a horse when she was young and had been knocked unconscious, and her doctor thought that might have been the reason for that dark area. I finally told Kathy about the scan when I knew she was depressed about my condition. I said it made me realize that as difficult as my circumstances were, I thought hers were probably tougher. I could not imagine anything more difficult than loving someone who faced a terminal illness.

Before every Monday chemotherapy session at the Bethesda Naval Hospital, I met with Dr. Nanfro in an examining room in the oncology ward. He gave me a thorough physical exam and the lab did my blood studies. He palpated my lymph nodes and found they were shrinking, but one of them in my left groin area remained enlarged. He thought the cause might have been scar tissue from the effects of chemotherapy. I received a full cycle of chemotherapy every month, and ideally the first full cycle or two would shrink all my nodes back to normal size. But because of the rareness of my case, nothing was really normal.

As a consequence of chemotherapy, my white blood counts were dropping, which made me susceptible to infection. I lived in dread of catching a cold. My red cell count also was down and because red cells carry oxygen to the tissues, I felt more tired than usual. By the end of April my red cell count had dropped so low that I had to be given two bags of packed red cells. Within twenty-four hours I could feel my energy returning.

Another side effect of the chemotherapy was mouth sores. They were so bad at one point I could not even eat ice cream. But basically I felt reasonably well while on chemotherapy. New medications helped ease the nausea, and while I did not like the thought of these drugs going into my body, I thought of them as helping cure my disease.

Kathy prepared nutritious meals and I took a prenatal vitamin every day to try to keep the rest of me as healthy as I could. Soon after my initial diagnosis, I had considered taking very large doses of vitamin C after I spoke with Dr. Linus Pauling, twice a Nobel laureate and one of the major proponents of vitamin C's power to cure cancer. I met Dr. Pauling at the graduation of Kathy's brother, Dr. Francis Counselman, from the Eastern Virginia School of Medicine. Dr. Pauling was the commencement speaker, and after the ceremony I approached him and told him I had cancer. He was very gracious to me, and recommended I take 10,000 milligrams of vitamin C a day, which was more than ten times the amount I was taking at the time.

I spoke to Dr. Bunn about it and he said there was no hard evidence that vitamin C was effective against cancer, according to the most recent experimental trials. I realized that Dr. Pauling claimed these experiments had not been done properly, but after giving the issue a lot of thought, I decided against taking large doses of vitamins and I stuck with that decision.

In June, halfway through my six-month chemotherapy regimen, I had another CAT scan to determine the extent of the existing disease. The CAT scan gives a detailed, cross-sectional X-ray picture that is far superior to standard X rays. It showed the nodes in my abdomen that had been impinging on my bladder were both completely gone, but two other areas indicated slightly abnormal nodes. I was neither encouraged nor discouraged. I kept pointing toward September. That would mark the end of my six months of chemotherapy, and if all went well, the beginning of a long remission.

A doctor once said to me all of life is a terminal illness, but most of us don't do much thinking about it. Because of the situations I had found myself in before, I had thought about death in the past but I had not dwelled on it. I did not dwell on it now, but I had to accept the fact that it did not appear as if I were going to live a long life. The more I thought about it, the more I became convinced that the age of dying probably is not all that important in one's attitude toward it. I suspect that individuals who are sixty or seventy years old find it just as difficult as a thirty-nine-year-old to face the fact they are dying.

I did not feel anger, with one exception. That happened when Kathy and I drove Russell to Greenville for his appointment with Dr. DeMarco. I was not feeling well when we left Fayetteville, and by the time we arrived in Greenville I had a fever and chills. Kathy drove me to the emergency room of a local hospital. I knew my blood counts were low, and I realized a lot of people die from infection during chemotherapy. I did not feel ill enough to be dying, but I knew enough to realize it could happen and I wondered if it could be the beginning of the end. I was mad as hell. I said to myself, *I damned well better not die now.* It turned out to be a virus and I was able to throw it off, but I had a few anxious hours.

I guess we all wonder how we will react when we realize our time is short. For me, there is value in having a terminal illness rather than dying suddenly. It has allowed me to prepare for my family's future, and it focused my mind on the important things in life, such as spending time with the people I love. I do not lie awake at night fearful of dying. I feel the worst thing I could do would be to dwell on thoughts of death and be miserable every day until that happened. I have tried to mentally shut out depressing thoughts and live every day as valuably as I could.

Thanks to my law partners, my legal caseload was reduced. I handled a few routine matters because they knew I could not carry a heavy load. Kathy and I spent many weekends at Pinehurst. Our neighbors the Quinns and Whiting Shuford from my swift boat crew also were there often. Whiting ran a family hosiery business in Hickory, North Carolina, and he and I had kept in touch over the years, and had become very close friends. He was one of our partners in the Pinehurst cottage. Whiting and his wife Denise paid Kathy and me the high honor of asking us to become godparents for their baby daughter Adrienne. Whiting also paid me the dubious compliment of naming his English sheepdog after me.

Whiting had kept in closest touch with members of our swift boat crew. He and Harvey Miller, who was a food plant foreman in Baltimore, talked on the phone often and exchanged visits. He also kept in contact with Billy Nairmore, now a draftsman for a power company in Alabama. Nobody knew where Geoff Martin had gone until my *Parade Magazine* article was published and he called me up. He was living in the Los Angeles area, where he worked for an export company. It had been fifteen years since we all had last been aboard the PCF 35, and Whiting and I thought it was time for a reunion. As it turned out we had two in 1985. The first was in the spring at Pinehurst, and the second a few months later in Baltimore, for Harvey Miller's August wedding. Dad, who knew all four of them, joined us.

A long time had separated us, but when I first set eyes on my old crew at Pinehurst, it felt as if we had only been apart for a few minutes. We had shared such an intense experience together that I was permanently bonded to all these men. We embraced one another and I felt as if they were all members of my family. Under the worst conditions imaginable, they had proved not only good and courageous fighters, but we had been able to live harmoniously. The love we have for one another is deep and permanent.

Billy Nairmore brought his family, including his beautiful daughter Tara, fifteen, who was born while Billy was in Vietnam. His wife Alice had remained the strong, loving woman I had remembered from the lecture she had given me in San Diego before we left for Vietnam. Billy and I were the only members of our crew who were still married to the same women from our time in Vietnam. Whiting had divorced once, as had Harvey, and Geoff had been divorced twice. I wondered if the war might have been part of the reason.

All of us still had powerful memories of our time together. They are a permanent part of all of us. Whiting said two weeks did not pass when he did not wake up at night from a dream about the war. Geoff said for the first two years he would wake up at night screaming, "Go for the guns, go for the guns." Both Whiting and Geoff, who manned the 50 caliber machine guns, had suffered substantial hearing loss as a result of firing those weapons. They also had concerns. Whiting said he worried every day of his wife's pregnancy, fearful that his Agent Orange exposure might cause a birth defect. All of them were worried about cancer, and they wanted to know about mine.

We also relived some of the laughs we had. They referred to themselves as the "little fucks," and at Harvey's wedding, Whiting ordered shirts made up for each one of us. Theirs said, "The Little F's" and mine said, "The Big F." Geoff, who is the best storyteller among us, related something they had never told me in Vietnam for fear I would have been angry at him.

He said one night he and Whiting were drinking with several other enlisted men in Ha Tien when he and a petty officer got into an argument. According to Geoff, the petty officer suddenly flew at him and took a swing, and Geoff swung back. Whiting intervened and calmed Geoff down, and they walked back to the swift boat. I was not around. They ran into another swift boat sailor named Greg Rose. Rose asked what happened and Geoff told him. Rose said, "I'll fix that son of a bitch."

Rose found my officer's shirt on the boat. It had bars on the shoulders and a Zumwalt name tag. Rose put my uniform on and marched over to the chief, who immediately stood at attention. Rose moved right in front of him and wagged his finger in his face and started screaming: "My men are fighting a war! I don't want any crap from you, and I don't want you to touch my men! Do you understand?"

According to Geoff, the only thing the petty officer said was "Yes, sir" about a dozen times.

I laughed as hard as everybody else, but I told Geoff I would not have laughed at the time. He said, "That's why I waited fifteen years to tell you."

At our Pinehurst reunion, all of us, including our families, slept in the cottage. Late one night I went down to the kitchen and found Billy Nairmore and Whiting at the kitchen table. Billy, who is a giant of a man but as gentle a person as there is, was sobbing. Whiting had his arm around his shoulder, trying to console him. I did not intrude, and later Whiting told me, "Billy was crying about you."

ELMO'S CREW:

BILLY NAIRMORE:

Elmo changed me from a boy to a man, and I am not saying that now because he is ill. I am saying it because it is true and I have told the same thing to my wife dozens of times. He made me feel that if I had to depend on myself, I could do it. He gave what we did in Vietnam a sense of purpose and a sense of mission and we all felt as if we counted. Elmo has meant a lot to me, and his illness hit me very hard. It hit the whole crew hard. He is like a brother. At our reunion in Pinehurst, I told Kathy I wish there were some way the crew could share what he has, because we would. I love the man.

WHITING SHUFORD:

The second time the crew met in August for Harvey Miller's wedding. Harvey, Geoff, Billy, and I drove over to Washington to visit the Vietnam Memorial. Just getting close to that wall was overwhelming. The emotion was so strong I could not talk, and neither could the other guys. The wall is shiny black, so when you look at it you see your own reflection. It's like looking at a year of your life. I thought of the problems all of us from the PCF 35 have faced, such as our divorces. We saw the name of Lieutenant Ken Norton, and our memories of him came flooding back. But what really hit me hard was thinking of Elmo's illness. It struck us all. I have no doubt that what has happened to him is a result of the war.

Since Vietnam, Elmo and I have become very close, and my respect and affection for him have only increased. I feel we all owe a lot to him. I am certain I would not be alive today if it were not for him. I am also certain he is going to beat this cancer. He has too much guts and determination not to.

GEOFF MARTIN:

I can see now that the way Elmo pushed us in Vietnam was something he had to do because it was part of who and what he is. It was hard to take over there, especially in the beginning, but now as I look back on it I would not have traded that year with him for anything because of the pride I have in the job we did, and the love I have for Elmo and that great crew.

I have such confidence in them that if a mission came up now to go into Southeast Asia to rescue some MIAs, I would say, give me back the old crew and Elmo, and let's go. I would do it in a minute.

It was a hard awakening when I returned home. I was in a bar in San Francisco when someone called me a baby killer. I swung as hard at him as I ever had at anything or anyone in my life. I hit him too, and got out of that bar fast. I think all of us closed the door on Vietnam. I know I did. I did not talk about it and I wanted it out of my life.

But when the four of us went to the Vietnam Memorial, something blew the hinges off that door. I could not say a word for an hour and a half. I felt things I had not felt in years, and it hurt. There was so much that was painful: memories of the war, the people we knew whose names were on the wall, and bitterness at the way this country treated us when we returned home. And of course there is Elmo. I think all of us feel Elmo is a casualty of the war, and that makes me sad and angry.

HARVEY MILLER:

When we were on the boat we had arguments and disagreements like you do with your wife, but you still love her and that's the way we felt about Elmo. He was loyal to us and we were loyal to him. There's a bond between all of us that is indescribable, and knowing Elmo is sick is like knowing my brother or father is sick.

ADMIRAL:

The week after Harvey Miller's wedding reception, the doctors scheduled Elmo for a series of tests at the Bethesda Naval Hospital. He had completed his six months of chemotherapy. These tests would now determine the success of his treatment. Based on the expectations of Elmo's physicians, I felt the test results would show he had been cured of Hodgkin's disease, which usually responds well to chemotherapy. I also hoped his non-Hodgkin's lymphoma, which I knew could not be cured with chemotherapy, would be in remission.

With these tests hanging over him, I marvelled at how relaxed Elmo acted at the wedding reception. Dr. Nanfro had lifted Elmo's beer drinking restriction, so for the first time in more than six months he was able to enjoy a couple of beers. The camaraderie among Elmo and his crew was heartening for me to see. I realized how deeply they cared for him. Elmo later told me his crew gave him too much credit for bringing them all out of Vietnam alive. He said the fact that they had survived made him appear larger in their eyes than he really was. I did not buy that explanation. Other officers had brought their crews safely through combat and did not enjoy the love and respect Elmo's crew had shown for him.

In early September, Elmo and I went to the Bethesda Naval Hospital together where he went through the series of restaging tests. The doctors again gave him computerized tomography (CAT) scans, and inserted a needle into his hip to remove a bone marrow sample for study. Elmo also went through yet another lymph node biopsy in the groin area. He was hospitalized overnight as a precautionary measure. Elmo loves ice cream as much as I do, so I made sure he had a good supply by making ice cream runs to the hospital cafeteria.

The analyses would be performed by pathologists at the Bethesda Naval Hospital, as well as by Dr. Elaine Jaffe at the

National Cancer Institute. The results were to be ready in three days. Elmo returned to Fayetteville and Mouza and I left for Seattle, Washington, where we were to attend a reunion of the *Robinson* crew. I had been on the *Robinson* forty years earlier when Mouza and I had first met in Shanghai. Crew members had formed an honor guard at our wedding.

Our flight landed briefly in Kansas City, where I called Elmo from the airport because I knew his test results were imminent. When I reached him he told me he had talked directly with Dr. Jaffe, who reported that the cells she had examined from his bone marrow were not malignant. Moreover, he said the preliminary pathology reports on his lymph nodes, where Hodgkin's disease had first shown up, were negative.

The CAT scans were also very encouraging. Although there appeared to be some enlarged nodes, it was thought they resulted from scarring caused by the chemotherapy. He said there was no evidence at this time of either Hodgkin's disease or non-Hodgkin's lymphoma. It was the best possible news we could have hoped for. Elmo's voice was so enthusiastic he sounded as though he could not believe what he was saying.

"I've grown so accustomed to bad news that I don't know what to do when I get good news," he said.

I shouted with joy. I told him if anyone deserved a break, he did, and it was about time that one had gone his way.

I immediately told Mouza, who was equally overjoyed at the news. When we arrived in Seattle, I also told two business associates and some members of the *Robinson* crew who were at the airport to meet us. There was a press conference about our reunion that same day, and I was still so elated that I announced it publicly. I wanted the world to share our good fortune.

Later that afternoon, I called my son Jim. His wife Lisa answered. I asked if she had heard Elmo's good news. She said she had, but her voice was not very enthusiastic. I did not know what to make of that. I then called my daughter Ann in Springfield, Massachusetts, and asked her if she had heard from Elmo. Ann said she had, but also did not sound very happy. I was unable to reach Mouzetta.

I then called Elmo and learned why Lisa and Ann had been so subdued. Elmo said he had broken the news to Ann and Jim earlier, and had asked them not to tell me because he thought I should hear it from him. He said he had misunderstood Dr. Jaffe when she told him the results of her tests. She apparently had said that the bone marrow cells she examined were "not inconsistent" with non-Hodgkin's lymphoma, and he had heard her to say they were "not consistent" with his disease.

It was a small difference in words, but a huge difference for Elmo's prospects. He had discovered his error when he spoke to Dr. Nanfro, soon after he and I had talked during my Kansas City stopover. There was one other piece of terrible news. The final pathology report on Elmo's lymph node biopsy corrected the preliminary finding, and now said there were Hodgkin's disease cells present. In the space of a few hours, the news had gone from the best we could have expected to the worst.

Elmo apologized for giving me false hope. "I don't know how I could have made such a stupid mistake. I guess some wishful thinking got in the way."

His voice was completely under control. He sounded as if he were just giving me a rundown of the day's events. He said Kathy had become distraught and could not understand how he remained so calm in the face of the news he had heard. I thought Elmo's reaction was typical of him. He had always had a tendency to become frustrated and upset over little problems, but he had always shown great courage in the face of the really tough ones.

When I told Mouza Elmo's news she broke down and cried, and cursed Elmo's fate. A terrible gloom set in and turned what was to be a happy reunion into a solemn occasion for me. Having heard the good news first made the bad news all that much worse. I had to face the hard truth that after six months of taking our best shot at Elmo's two cancers, neither one had been halted.

We had made some progress in helping to take financial care of Kathy, Maya, and Russell if the worst did happen. Kathy now managed eighteen apartment units I owned in Fayetteville, and was maintaining her full-time job as an interior designer. She was able to schedule her hours so she would be home when Maya and Russell returned from school. I had transferred my share of three houses that Elmo and I had jointly owned in Fayetteville. I wanted to do all I could to ease his worry about his family's future, now that the prospect of living long enough for his two large insurance policies to vest seemed dimmer.

Elmo was uncertain what the next medical step would be. Initially, his doctors had said that as a general practice, they did not extend PROMACE-MOPP chemotherapy beyond six months. In light of Elmo's test results, Dr. Nanfro had scheduled a meeting with several cancer specialists from the Bethesda Naval Hospital and the National Cancer Institute to discuss Elmo's case. In a few days, we would know their recommendation.

As devastating as the news had been, I continued to hope. I thought there was something indestructible about Elmo, and that the next months would produce the miracle we all needed.

ELMO:

Even the pessimism I maintained about my illness in order to protect myself from deeper disappointments was not enough to prepare me for the devastating pathology reports I had received. In my own mind, the worst case I had imagined was that the non-Hodgkin's lymphoma would still be in my bone marrow. I did not think that I would still have evidence of Hodgkin's disease. Neither did Dr. Nanfro.

It was now September 1985, still more than a year before my two big life insurance policies would kick in and provide Kathy with enough money to maintain a good standard of living for our children. Thinking about Maya and Russell was the hardest part for me. After I broke the bad news of my test results, Maya asked me if I wanted to die to get rid of my cancer. I told her I would rather be on earth with her.

Because of Kathy's Catholicism, Maya attends Catholic school. I think Maya believes that if I die I will be in heaven, looking down on her. I know she includes me in her nightly prayers, and at times I have been near her bedroom at night and heard her sobbing. I have gone in there and put my arms around her to try to comfort her. It was becoming more difficult to give her comfort because of the hard reality of my medical condition.

Russell did not understand the full implications of everything that had happened, but I think he has always had a deep sense of my problem. I think my passing will be most devastating to him.

I have seen the worry and hurt in Kathy's eyes. She had quit smoking for eight years, but the stress had driven her back to cigarettes. I told her there should be one parent without cancer so she promised to quit.

I suspect religious faith can be helpful in situations like mine. My legal secretary, Lynda Miller, is a religious person and has tried many times to help me see the light. I think she feels I am a lost soul, but my agnosticism is too deeply rooted for me to change.

Soon after my first cancer diagnosis, I visited a client in the hospital. He was a brilliant college professor at North Carolina State University in Raleigh who originally had been misdiagnosed and later found to have terminal cancer. I had represented him in a medical malpractice case. I told him that I also had terminal cancer and asked him how it affected his mind.

"Elmo, it destroys the mind," he answered.

I have always been determined not to let my disease destroy my mind. I fought to keep thoughts of my disease, and death, from dominating my consciousness. When these thoughts occurred, I forced them out by concentrating on other things. But after I had learned about the test results, I found myself dwelling on dark thoughts more and more, especially when I was alone. I wondered what death would be like, and how I would feel when it approached. I really had to work on myself mentally to avoid sadness and depression, and gain a small fragment of hope that I might live for another year or two. I kept waging an internal struggle to keep myself from dwelling on these thoughts.

I began to see my illness as a process of diminishing expectations and choices. When I had first learned in early 1983 that I had non-Hodgkin's lymphoma, I hoped that I would at least live the median survival time of eight years and, if I were lucky, perhaps I would live a few years longer than that. My choice then was treatment or no treatment. I chose no treatment. When my Hodgkin's disease was discovered two years later, I no longer had a choice to be treated or not treated, but had to choose among many treatments. Now my choices were narrowing even more.

In early September I spoke with Dr. Nanfro by phone after he had presented my case at a meeting of physicians. He said they reached a consensus that I should take three more months of PROMACE-MOPP chemotherapy.

He explained when patients with lymphoma do not respond to the first six months of this type of chemotherapy, the likelihood of their responding to an additional three months is diminished, but it was the only reasonable alternative I had right now. This additional chemotherapy presented new risks.

In August, just at the end of my first six months of chemotherapy, I began to feel terrible, as if I were pulling a 500-pound weight around with me. When I awoke one morning with a fever of 102 degrees, I realized I had an infection, probably caused by dropping blood counts. On Dr. Nanfro's instructions, I immediately checked into a hospital in Fayetteville where tests revealed my white blood count was perilously low. Neutrophils are components of white blood cells that fight infection. Normally, neutrophil counts are 2,000. Mine had dropped to 75 because of my chemotherapy. I had virtually no bacterial immunity.

I had some very tense moments in the hospital. I felt caught in the grip of something over which I had no control. In chemotherapy there is a fine line between overtreatment and undertreatment. If you undertreat, you run the risk of not killing off all the cancer cells. If you overtreat, you run the risk of killing too many healthy blood cells, and opening up the possibility of a potentially fatal infection.

A friend visited me and said he did not understand how someone with my temperament could stay confined in a hospital room day after day. I told him I felt lucky to still be in the hospital room.

Gradually my blood counts went up and my fever went down. I apparently had a virus of some kind. I remained in the hospital for nine days and managed to avoid anything more serious.

This time around, the chemotherapy would assault my already depressed blood counts again, exposing me to a greater risk of infection. In mid-September, with my options running out, I went back to the Bethesda Naval Hospital where I would begin three more months of PROMACE-MOPP chemotherapy.

I continued to learn about my diseases. I knew there was one remaining treatment possibility, a bone marrow transplant. This is an experimental procedure in which I would be given total body radiation, coupled with high levels of chemotherapy, in order to rid my body of cancer. The treatment is so powerful, it completely destroys the bone marrow, the substance inside the bones that manufactures blood cells. No one can live without it, as the world has learned from the Chernobyl disaster. The bone marrow is destroyed because its cells divide very rapidly, and both radiation and chemotherapy are most destructive to rapidly dividing cells.

After the radiation and chemotherapy, bone marrow must be transplanted into the patient. It was a long shot, but I knew it was attempted on patients with Hodgkin's disease and non-Hodgkin's lymphoma, as well as those with leukemia and aplastic anemia.

There are different types of bone marrow transplants. One is autologous, meaning I would have some of my own marrow stored and it would be put back into me after the radiation and chemotherapy treatments. Because my non-Hodgkin's lymphoma had already invaded my bone marrow, that method would reintroduce cancer back into my system. There were some experimental programs that used monoclonal antibodies to remove the cancerous cells from the extracted marrow, but Dr. Nanfro thought this procedure had not been sufficiently tested.

The second type of bone marrow transplant is called allogenaic. In this procedure bone marrow would be transplanted to me from a genetically matched sibling. With two sisters and one brother, there was a 25 percent chance one would match.

Dr. Nanfro had prior experience with bone marrow transplants while he was in San Diego, and he warned me that it is the most excruciating medical procedure he knew. "Your system is brutalized by drugs and radiation," he told me. "If you combined your polio, heart surgery, Vietnam experience, cancer, and chemotherapy all together, the bone marrow would still be a worse experience. It is unbelievably difficult and the risks are very high."

A bone marrow transplant represented the medicine of last resort, but if my next three months of chemotherapy were not successful, I would need a last resort.

A bone marrow transplant required a donor who had a perfect tissue match with me. Tissue-typing is a far more complicated process than blood-typing. First, it had to be determined if any of my siblings had human leukocyte antigens (HLA) that matched mine. These antigens are found in white blood cells and are that part of the immune system involved in recognizing and attacking foreign tissue. Under normal circumstances they attack and destroy bacteria and viruses that invade the body. In organ transplants they attack the transplanted organ, a process called rejection.

The specific gene responsible for determining these antigens is situated on the sixth pair of chromosomes. Because my brother, sisters, and I inherited our forty-six chromosomes from the same parents, there was a chance that one of my siblings had a set of antigens identical to mine.

For most organ transplants a precise tissue match is not required, but for bone marrow transplantation there usually has to be a complete match of all leukocyte antigens to succeed.

In October, one month after I renewed my chemotherapy regimen, Jim, Ann, and Mouzetta had their blood drawn for tissue typing. Jim had it done at the Bethesda Naval Hospital, as did Mouzetta when she came to Washington to visit my parents. Ann had her sample sent down from her home in Springfield. I also had a blood sample taken, and all the samples were sent to the tissue-typing laboratory at Bethesda to see if one of my siblings could be my bone marrow donor.

ADMIRAL:

At about the same time Elmo began his new round of chemotherapy, Walter Anderson, the editor of *Parade Magazine,* called to tell me that the New York Vietnam Veterans Leadership Program had voted to present their first annual Vietnam Veteran Leadership Award to Elmo.

Walter and Elmo had become friends ever since Elmo had written his *Parade* article in October of 1984. Walter is a wonderful example of talent and character arising from adversity. He is a Marine Corps veteran of Vietnam and a member of the Leadership Program's board of directors. He told me the board created the award for Vietnam veterans who had demonstrated courage and leadership not only in Vietnam, but also at the present time. He said the board selected Elmo because they wanted to set a high standard for all future awards. He also wanted the award to be a surprise for Elmo.

Originally, Walter wanted Vice President Bush to present the award, but the Vice President was unable to do it. Walter then asked James Webb, a highly decorated Vietnam veteran who is an assistant secretary of defense. The ceremony was to be held at 4 PM on November 13 in Webb's Pentagon office. Elmo would be in Washington that day anyway to receive chemotherapy.

To surprise Elmo, I told him that I was receiving an award and I hoped he could attend the ceremony. I said I would also like Kathy to attend. I later called Kathy and explained why. Besides members of our family, I invited Elmo's third-grade teacher, Dona Weakley, her husband, Harry, and Elmo's swift boat crewmate, Harvey Miller, from Baltimore.

Harvey said he would attend with his dad, William Miller, who served as a Navy chief petty officer during World War II, and for whom I had developed affection and respect. In fact Bill Miller and I had both joined the Navy in 1939. Eugene Gitelson, president of the Leadership Program, also attended. A military photographer was also present.

At the ceremony Walter spoke first. He smiled at Elmo and said he hoped Elmo would forgive the ruse we used to get him here, but the award was really for him. Elmo looked over at me with arched eyebrows and smiled. Walter said the award was an important symbol for Vietnam veterans, and when Elmo's name was mentioned as a possible recipient, it was met with unanimous agreement. James Webb made the formal award presentation, and handed Elmo a beautiful glass vase on a lighted stand.

Elmo spoke. He said the award was a surprise to him, and he felt humbled accepting it. He said he also felt deeply honored because the award was presented by Walter Anderson and James Webb, two people who had exemplary war records in Vietnam. He said he accepted the award on behalf of all Vietnam veterans, and he hoped it would help bring further recognition for their service to their country. Elmo was genuinely moved and gratified by the award, and by the thoughtfulness of Walter Anderson and the others who presented it to him.

The inscription on the vase read: "The Vietnam Veterans' Leadership Award 1985. Presented by the New York Vietnam Veterans Leadership Program to Elmo R. Zumwalt III for Perseverance and Courage in the Face of Adversity—Then and Now."

Elmo appeared in excellent health at the award ceremony, even though it was his eighth month on a very powerful chemotherapy regimen. He had not had any worrisome episodes of fever or severe weakness, although his blood counts had dropped quite low on at least one occasion.

To minimize his chances of becoming infected, he tried to avoid large groups of people and had requested continuances for his district court cases for that reason. With the consent of Dr. Nanfro, Elmo's Fayetteville physician, Dr. Henley, gave Elmo a flu shot to better protect him against the flu. Elmo even considered wearing a surgical mask but he learned viruses penetrate right through them, so he gave up that idea.

Despite his long siege of chemotherapy, Elmo never completely lost his hair. In fact, some hair was growing back. He had had a full head of dark hair, but it was now short and gun-metal gray in color. To someone who had not seen his hair before, it looked normal, and except for looking a bit pale, he did not give the appearance of being ill. I doubt anyone would have concluded he was sick just on the basis of his appearance.

Elmo's sense of humor had not deserted him. As we were served coffee and dessert at the end of the awards ceremony, Elmo said he wished the award were made of something other than glass because with his deserved reputation for clumsiness, he was afraid he would drop it. I offered to carry it for him, but he laughed and said, "No, I'm afraid you'll keep it."

To the astonishment of everyone, Elmo continued to work full-time in his law practice. He was representing a personal friend in a large settlement, and he worked as hard on that case as he had on any other. He also had remodeled a duplex home he bought so it could be rented at a higher price, and provide more income for Kathy and the children in the future.

When I looked back over the past year, I realized that my whole life had been recast because of Elmo's illness. I had long maintained a strong interest in national security affairs, but it requires a lot of time to keep abreast of developments. Because of the attention I gave to Elmo I could not keep up with new events and information. I no longer gave lectures on national security issues, and I also stopped working on the Committee on the Present Danger in order to have more time to devote to Elmo. I found I did not miss it, and I continued to concentrate my business activities only on the most profitable ventures.

Most recently, I had been on the telephone to people knowledgeable about bone marrow transplants to find out as much as I could. Elmo also actively investigated this procedure. He had not given up on the idea that this final round of chemotherapy would be successful, but considering everything that had happened to him in the past year, he did not see great reason for optimism. But we approached the possibility of a bone marrow transplant with caution. Everyone familiar with the procedure told us it is very high risk, and only attempted in terminal situations. They also said the center where it would be done must be chosen with great care.

I have always believed in the basic goodness of most people, and that was demonstrated amply by the loving support Elmo and I received from our friends. It is something I shall never forget. Two gestures especially linger in my memory.

At Elmo's award ceremony, Elmo and I had brought Harvey and Bill Miller up to date on Elmo's medical condition. I told them that Elmo would be restaged in one month, and that would determine the next step medically. I said if his cancer was not in remission, the only alternative appeared to be a bone marrow transplant.

Both Elmo and I were deeply touched a few days later when we received a letter from Bill Miller. He told us that on the ride home to Baltimore, he and Harvey had decided if it were at all possible, they would like to be bone marrow donors for Elmo. Because of the importance of tissue matching in bone marrow transplants, I was quite certain that was not possible, but I sent the letter on to Dr. Nanfro, and wrote Bill our warmest and most heartfelt thanks for their thoughtful and courageous gesture.

The second act of kindness was extended by Deborah Szekely, the owner of a health spa called Rancho La Puerta in Tacate, Mexico. Through the intercession of a mutual friend, Mouza, Elmo, and I were invited to meet Deborah when Elmo was in Washington. A few years earlier, Deborah's college-age son, Alex, had been stricken with Hodgkin's disease. In addition to his conventional treatment, Deborah, a widely recognized health expert, had devised a nutrition, exercise, and vitamin supplement regimen to maintain Alex's strength, and return him to health. Not only did she share all her knowledge with us, but she also invited Elmo and Kathy to be her guests for one week at Rancho La Puerta during the month of November. They went during Elmo's "off week" in chemotherapy, and agreed it was the nearest thing to heaven on earth. It gave them both a respite from the rigors of Elmo's illness. Inspired by the vigorous atmosphere of "The Ranch," Elmo began exercising more when he returned.

I am also happy to report that Alex Szekely is free of all disease, and manages the Rancho La Puerta, as well as his family's other spa, The Golden Door. Meanwhile, Deborah heads the Inter-American Foundation in Washington, D.C., an organization that funds innovative projects to improve economic conditions for people in South and Central America.

Toward the end of November, we received both bad news and good news about Elmo. The bad news happened the day before Thanksgiving, while Elmo was flying home after his chemotherapy treatment. In the space of only an hour or so, he went from feeling relatively healthy to running a fever and suffering chills. He even became a little disoriented. He was coherent enough to explain his problem to the flight attendant, and the pilot wisely radioed ahead for an ambulance. Elmo was taken off the plane and rushed to the hospital.

Elmo asked someone to get word to Kathy, who was at the airport to meet him. In a short while, Kathy met Elmo at the hospital. He did not look well, but she was thankful he was still alive.

Elmo's white blood counts were again perilously low. The suddenness of the drop was another reminder, when none was needed, of how chancy his condition could be. Elmo remained in the hospital over the Thanksgiving holidays, and his condition gradually improved.

Mouzetta provided the good news. She turned out to be an identical tissue match with Elmo, and therefore could be his bone marrow donor if Elmo's situation required it. When I found that out, I immediately thought back nearly thirty years. Two years after the birth of our third child, Ann, Mouza suffered a miscarriage and her doctors had some doubt about whether she could bear any more children. Three years later, Mouzetta was born.

Mouzetta Zumwalt Weathers:

I knew Elmo and Dad were talking about the possibilities of a bone marrow transplant, and in October Dad had called me to ask if I would give a blood sample for tissue-typing.

It was at least a month before we learned if any of us would match, and Jim, Ann, and I talked on the phone a number of times, wondering who it might be. Elmo kidded Jim and said he wanted it to be him because he wanted Jim to suffer a little bit too. I know Elmo really did hope it was going to be Jim because Jim is a very strong guy and would be able to withstand it more easily. Also, because they are only two years apart, and played together when they were young, and stuck up for one another when one of them was threatened, I think they had developed a special closeness that made it seem right for Jimmy to be the donor.

I secretly hoped that I would be the match because I felt it would be my way of making a contribution to Elmo. Ann and Jim had been with Elmo many times at the Bethesda Naval Hospital and had really done a lot for him, but I had not. I also look up to Elmo, and if I could give him this gift, he would look up to me as well. I think that was part of still being his little sister, but it meant a great deal to me.

My husband Ron and I were not home when Dad called with the news. He left a message on our answering machine and I could tell that his voice was happy. He congratulated me and said that I was the only one who matched with Elmo. I felt excited and gratified to hear that news.

I also knew if Elmo ever had a bone marrow transplant he might need me to be with him for two or three months. It was not just a question of donating bone marrow, but of giving him blood and blood platelets throughout the procedure. I knew a long separation would be hard on Ron and me. We had only been married a year, and I had just arrived at the point in my real estate career where things were picking up. But I knew that was a trivial concern compared to what Elmo was going through, so I really did not consider it to be a sacrifice.

Elmo began kidding me after he found out he and I matched. He called to tell me to drive carefully because both of our lives might depend on it. He also told me to eat well and take care of myself because if he needed a transplant, he wanted the very best bone marrow.

TWELVE

───────── ★ ─────────

ELMO:

Less than two weeks after my final chemotherapy treatment, and only five days before returning to Bethesda Naval Hospital to restage my cancers, I was taking my morning shower at home when I felt an enlarged lymph node in my left groin area. This is the same area where Hodgkin's disease had appeared before, and I was certain the moment I felt the node that it was Hodgkin's disease.

I felt a knot in my stomach. This was the worst possible sign. Hodgkin's disease was the more aggressive of my two cancers and, for that reason, was the primary concern of my doctors. I could not believe it had appeared so quickly in the face of nine months of potent anticancer drugs. If it were Hodgkin's, I knew my time could be very short, and hard decisions had to be made quickly.

Despite my desire to tell Kathy everything, I did not want to tell her this news, not yet anyway. I needed to confirm my own suspicions. I made an appointment that morning with Doug Henley, the same physician who had first diagnosed my cancer nearly three years earlier. I had kept in regular contact with him throughout my treatment, and had seen him just a few days earlier at the hospital when my white blood cell count had dropped.

He examined the area and confirmed it was an enlarged lymph node. He said it was about a centimeter in size.

"I'm positive it's Hodgkin's," I said.

He told me not to jump to conclusions, and that I needed a biopsy first.

I called Dr. Nanfro at the Bethesda Naval Hospital from my office later that same morning.

"I'm afraid I have some ominous news to report. I have a one-centimeter lymph node in my left groin area and I'm sure it's Hodgkin's."

Dr. Nanfro was taken aback with that news. He paused for a moment and agreed it did sound ominous, but he said that if the node proved malignant, it would probably be the non-Hodgkin's lymphoma, a far more cheerful possibility than Hodgkin's disease.

Dr. Nanfro reasoned that Hodgkin's disease should be in remission after all the chemotherapy I had received, but the non-Hodgkin's lymphoma probably was not because it is so resistant to chemotherapy. Based on logic and medical experience, he should have been right. I hoped he was, but I had a strong feeling he was not.

I discovered the node on a Wednesday and was scheduled to be at Bethesda Naval Hospital the following Tuesday. Dr. Nanfro said he would make time for me a day earlier. I called Dad to break the news. Forever optimistic, Dad said I had to at least give myself the benefit of the doubt because it might not be Hodgkin's disease.

I told him I did not want to tell Kathy at this time, but I was also concerned because I did not want her ever to think that I withheld information from her. Dad agreed I should wait a few days until I had definitive word on the node.

"If it is positive, she'll worry anyway, but if it turns out to be negative, she'll worry unnecessarily for the next few days," he reasoned.

That made sense to me, but it did not completely erase a nagging feeling that I was not being open with Kathy.

When I arrived at the third-floor oncology ward at Bethesda

Naval Hospital on Monday, Dr. Nanfro ushered me right into an examining room and palpated the node. It was rock hard, an almost certain sign of malignancy. He still thought it would prove to be the slower-moving non-Hodgkin's lymphoma instead of Hodgkin's disease. He scheduled me for a biopsy the next day.

Dad and I were alone in my hospital room the next morning before I was taken to surgery for what was to be my fourteenth lymph node biopsy. Dr. Bimal C. Ghosh, the head of surgical oncology at the hospital, and an extremely skilled surgeon in whom I placed great trust, would again perform my biopsy.

Neither Dad nor I openly express our emotions often, but there were some things I felt very deeply and wanted to express to him that morning. I said he had done more for me than any father could possibly do for his son. His absolute, steadfast determination to help in whatever way possible had sustained me in countless ways. He had lifted so many burdens off me that I said I could never adequately express my gratitude.

I told him I had absolutely no doubt that when the end came for me, he would do all he could to make certain Kathy and my children had as good a life as possible, and that realization gave me great peace of mind.

Dad put his arms around me and told me how glad he was that he was able to help, and what I meant to him as a son. Neither one of us could talk for a while after that.

I returned home to Fayetteville Wednesday, and on Thursday the pathology report on my lymph node was complete. The worst had happened. It was Hodgkin's disease.

ADMIRAL:

I had always let myself have hope, but that hope was shattered when Elmo called to tell me the results of the pathology report. Before, I had tried to help Elmo see the optimistic possibilities, but now I could not.

We both realized we would have to move quickly to investigate the possibility of a bone marrow transplant, but that prospect filled me with more fear than hope. The Bethesda Naval Hospital did not have a bone marrow transplant program, nor did the National Cancer Institute. The two programs that Elmo had researched and wished to visit were the Dana Farber Cancer Institute in Boston, which is a part of Harvard University, and the Fred Hutchinson Cancer Research Center in Seattle. I told Elmo I wanted to accompany him when he visited these centers. He already had a long-standing appointment at Dana Farber, and had just gotten one at Seattle. Both were before Christmas.

Elmo wanted Kathy to come with us because he did not want her ever to feel she was left out of this decision. He thought if he did try the bone marrow transplant, and died as a result, it might leave her feeling bitter. I agreed with him. However, I did not think Mouza should join us because I realized Elmo's illness was becoming more and more emotionally difficult for her. Listening to doctors tell us the hard realities of a bone marrow transplant would only increase her anxiety.

Over the next few days, I found myself thinking back on the three years since Elmo first found out he had cancer. There were many bright spots amid the darkness. There were Elmo's courage, the support and love of many friends, the closeness of his brother and sisters and their willingness to rearrange their lives to help Elmo. All that was deeply gratifying to me.

But I could not escape the sadness I felt at the prospect of facing life without Elmo. I always had felt like a father to Jim, Ann, and Mouzette, but I had not really had a father-son relationship with Elmo since he was a little boy. He is more than a son to me, he is also my partner, my brother, someone in whom I have absolute trust and confidence.

I have always consulted with him on everything in my life, going way back to his teens. He has always given good, tough-minded advice. He sees through my weaknesses, such as my willingness to be too trusting. I have come to count on his advice. I knew that life would never be the same without him. It would never have the zest and fun that Elmo puts into it.

I think I have helped Elmo go beyond some of the insecurities he felt about academics. I have also tried to help him when he had become so personally involved in some of his law cases that he lost his perspective. He had put his heart and soul into one medical malpractice case and eventually lost it. He was devastated, not so much for his own loss, but because he lost for a client he cared for personally, and whom Elmo was convinced had been a victim of medical malpractice. I talked to Elmo often during that period to help him regain his perspective, to recognize that although defeat is difficult to accept, he had done all that could be asked of him.

Elmo is a giving person, and by all odds he has given me more than I have given him. He is a shining example to me, and to our whole family. He is just one hell of a man.

KATHY COUNSELMAN ZUMWALT:

I knew at some time we would face a crossroads with Elmo's illness, but I had never thought it would happen so soon. When Elmo told me that his lymph node was Hodgkin's disease, I knew enough about his condition to realize it was about the worst thing that could have happened.

I knew he and his dad were talking about a bone marrow transplant, but I really had no idea what it was. After he learned the biopsy results, Elmo felt great urgency about investigating a transplant. He realized because his Hodgkin's disease appeared less than two weeks after his chemotherapy ended, it could spread very quickly.

In both Boston and Seattle I was overwhelmed when the doctors explained what a bone marrow transplant involved. When they said Elmo would be hospitalized for at least a month, be an outpatient for three more months, and would need a year's leave of absence from his law practice to recover, the full impact of its severity hit me. With his one-in-five chance of dying during the procedure, I also realized they offered no guarantees of success, or of Elmo's survival.

Elmo had travelled many roads with this illness, and we all

knew this was the final one. That scared me. We were really at the point where life and death hung in the balance.

Elmo, his dad, and I were very impressed by the Fred Hutchinson Cancer Research Center bone marrow transplant program. It is the most experienced bone marrow transplant center in the country. They had performed three thousand transplants since the late 1960s. Moreover, the physicians we visited, Donnall Thomas, the program director, and Fred Appelbaum, one of the attending physicians, gave us thorough and honest answers to all our questions. Elmo left there feeling he had all the information we needed to make a decision.

There was an extremely heavy fog in Seattle so we drove our rental car to Vancouver in order to get a flight back home. During the two-hour drive, the three of us discussed the choices. I could tell by the way Elmo talked that he leaned toward the transplant, but he first wanted to meet with Dr. Eli Gladstein at the National Cancer Institute, to discuss other options.

Elmo asked me what I thought he should do, but I did not give him my opinion. Truthfully, I was not sure what I wanted him to do. I told him I would support whatever he decided, but I did not want to influence him in any way. His dad gave him the same answer for the same reason. This was such a momentous undertaking that we both felt if Elmo wanted to do it, it should be his decision alone.

ELMO:

I was faced with the hardest decision of my life. I understood the odds. I had a one-in-five chance of dying during the procedure. The potential causes were bacterial, viral, and yeast infections, the failure of Mouzetta's bone marrow to "take" in my body, and graft-versus-host disease. The latter complication is similar to the rejection seen in organ transplant patients. However, instead of rejecting Mouzetta's transplanted marrow, her marrow would in effect reject me because it would produce lymphocytes, the white blood cells of the immune system. These cells would recognize my body as foreign tissue, and attack it, specifically my liver, skin, lungs, and gut. If graft-versus-host disease could not be controlled by immune-suppression drugs, that disease itself would prove fatal.

Eighty percent of the patients who undergo a bone marrow transplant survive the procedure. Of that number, one-half are cured of their disease. Based on those percentages, that meant I had a 40 percent chance of a cure. But my odds might be less than that because I have two cancers. No one was certain how these two cancers affected my chances.

There were other factors to consider. I was thirty-nine, which is young by most standards, but old for bone marrow transplants. People my age did not do as well as people in their teens and twenties. Also, some studies suggest there are additional complications when the transplanted marrow is from a donor of the opposite sex.

In my favor was the fact that I was in good health, and that after nine months of chemotherapy, I had low tumor mass. The transplant is less successful when there is a large tumor mass in the body. That was why I discarded the possibility of waiting until my cancer was in a more advanced stage before attempting the transplant.

After a brief Christmas Eve reunion with Maya and Russell in Pinehurst, on Christmas day I returned to Washington. I had appointments with Dr. Eli Gladstein, a radiation oncologist at the National Cancer Institute, and Dr. Nanfro.

Dr. Gladstein is internationally recognized for his brilliance in his field. He was very candid with me.

"Elmo," he said in a very somber voice, "face the fact that you have two terminal illnesses. Why don't you just treat your Hodgkin's disease with local radiation and try to buy as much time as you can?"

I realized Dr. Gladstein was speaking in my best interests. He understood the risks and limitations involved in bone marrow transplants, and he thought he could buy me another year of good quality of life with local radiation. I also realized the truth of what Dr. Appelbaum had told me in Seattle. In the final analysis, my decision about a bone marrow transplant would be philosophical, not medical.

Dr. Gladstein is a bachelor. I think someone who is single and has no children looks at life differently than does someone like me. I also had become very skeptical about how long I could live by treating the Hodgkin's disease with local radiation. Every optimistic prediction about my cancers had turned out wrong.

I looked into myself as deeply as I could. I consider myself an active person, not a passive one. I have fought for things in my life. Although my chances for a total cure were not great, and the transplant procedure would be brutally difficult, I thought I would be better off psychologically and emotionally in that situation. If I only took local radiation to buy more time, I would leave myself without hope. I would feel more and more trapped as my days grew short, and I would regret passing up my only chance at a cure. I did not want to put myself in that position. I knew it was a gamble between two unknowns, but I was willing to risk the last year of my life for the chance at winning an additional two or three years, or perhaps even a cure.

It was really a decision based on my personal values. In the end, I decided on the bone marrow transplant because I love Kathy, Maya, Russell, my family, and life, and I wanted to do the one thing that would give me a chance at being with them for a long time.

I wanted to have the transplant in Seattle and the doctors strongly encourage families to move there to support the patients emotionally. I knew this would be a big disruption for my family since we would be in Seattle for at least three months.

It was also a major disruption for Mouzetta. She would have to remain in Seattle with me for at least one month, but more likely two or three months, in order to give me continuing blood and blood platelet support. The platelets are what cause blood to clot, and sometimes are not produced by the transplanted marrow.

Mouzetta and her husband Ron did not yet have children, but they recently had bought a home and I knew her absence from work would pose a financial hardship for them. Mouzetta knew how much of her time would be involved in the transplant when she first learned that she and I were a tissue match, and yet she had no second thoughts now that I decided to do it.

I telephoned Seattle and made arrangements to be there at the end of January. They helped us locate a two-bedroom apartment for rent near the hospital.

Before I went to Seattle, I took local radiation treatments five days a week for the next four weeks at the National Cancer Institute to hit the area where an enlarged lymph node in my groin area had been surgically removed.

When I told Kathy and Dad of my decision a couple of days after Christmas, they both said they already knew I would choose the bone marrow transplant.

"I'll be there with you," Dad said.

Kathy Counselman Zumwalt:

After Elmo decided on the bone marrow transplant, I had about five weeks to prepare to move to Seattle. We drew up a list of things that had to be done and there were two hundred items on it, everything from cancelling the newspaper delivery to packing clothes. Elmo's dad is a great organizer, so we were able to get a handle on all of this. He has a very calm, rational approach to everything, and it was a great comfort to me that he would be in Seattle to help us over the rough spots.

Maya's and Russell's teachers were a great help. They outlined the schoolwork they had to do over the next few months. Russell's teacher copied all of his worksheets and wrote out instructions on each one telling where we needed to help him.

Because of the danger of infection from other children, and the risks that might pose for Elmo, the doctors did not want Russell, who was eight, or Maya, eleven, to attend a regular school class-room. We had to arrange special teachers for Russell, and a tutor for Maya. I worried about Russell. After a lot of trial and error, he was now in an ideal school situation and he was responding very well. His speech had improved dramatically, and his attention span

had also increased. In most every way, Russell was d[...]
better than Elmo and I had dared hope just a few mont[...]
But he had never been able to handle change very we[...]
hoped the move to Seattle would not prove a major set[...] for
him.

The most difficult part about leaving home was losing contact
with all my friends. They had been a great support for me during
the past three years. I was also in the middle of a big design project
and I had to break that off. Betty McDonald, the owner of Intra
Design, could not have been more understanding. Besides being
my boss, she had become a close friend.

The mother of one of Maya's classmates was also undergoing a
bone marrow transplant at another medical center in Fayetteville,
so Maya had an idea of what it meant. She asked Elmo if the
transplant was a situation in which you either made it or died.
Elmo was truthful with her and said that was the case, but he was
going to do everything he could to make it.

Late one night Elmo and I talked for a long time. I told him I
was worried about myself. I said I was not sure if I would hold up
emotionally during the bone marrow transplant. I did not want to
become a burden to him when things got rough. Elmo put his
arms around me and said he had no doubt at all that I would come
through it and be a great support for him. He said he had always
known I had strengths I did not realize. I hoped he was right. I
wanted to be there when he needed me.

As we were about to leave for Seattle, I felt as though we were
going off to a strange, faraway place. I had no idea if I would
come back alone. I told one of my friends before we left that if
Elmo had to die, I had always hoped he would die at home. I did
not want him to die in Seattle.

ADMIRAL:

The fact that Elmo chose to attempt the bone marrow transplant was completely in character for him. He said if it were just
for himself, he probably would not do it. But he wanted to do it

for Kathy and for his children. I felt he had made the right decision, and after my despair of December, I began to have a glimmer of hope again.

Dr. Nanfro had once made an analogy between baseball players and cancer patients. He said when some baseball players come to bat with two out in the bottom of the ninth inning, and way behind in the score, they just go through the motions and strike out. He said Elmo is different. He would try to hit a home run.

Six of us arrived in Seattle on January 30, 1986, hoping to hit that home run. Kathy, Mouzetta, Maya, Russell, Elmo, and I took up residence in a small apartment that was a brief walk from the Fred Hutchinson Cancer Research Center, which is where Elmo was to receive his bone marrow transplant. Mouza did not accompany us. Witnessing firsthand the devastating effects this transplant procedure would have on Elmo would have been extremely difficult for her. I would keep in daily telephone contact with her.

A wonderful friend of mine in Seattle, Bob Bateman, had arranged for me to use one of the spare offices in the law firm of Ferguson & Burdell so I could continue to conduct business. I planned to stay in Seattle for three months. I wanted to take as much of the burden off everyone as I could.

For the first few days of February, Elmo and Mouzetta went through a series of tests as outpatients. They were tissue-typed again to reconfirm their match. We also received our first encouraging news. Both Elmo and Mouzetta were found not to have cytomegalovirus (CMV), a type of virus that is present in one-half of the population. This virus could have turned into lethal pneumonia when Elmo's immunity was destroyed by the transplant procedure.

The weekend before Elmo entered the hospital, we all drove over to nearby Indianola where my dad had lived twenty-five years earlier. We found his old house and Elmo proudly pointed out that it still had the same coat of paint he and his brother Jim gave it the summer they spent with my dad after Elmo's junior year in high school.

On Tuesday, February 11, Elmo was admitted as an inpatient.

We felt fortunate that Dr. Donnall Thomas, who had performed the first bone marrow transplant in this country in the 1960s, was scheduled to be the chief attending physician for the early stages of Elmo's transplant. He directed the bone marrow transplant program, and had struck me as a man of wisdom and compassion.

Elmo lived in a sterile environment to lessen the chances of infection. His living space was an eight-by-ten-foot cubicle partitioned off from the rest of his hospital room by a nylon curtain. Attached to the curtain were two plastic arms with rubber gloves through which Elmo could be touched. There was a small open doorway through the curtain so the nurses and doctors, suited in sterile gowns, boots, gloves, and caps, could enter and exit. His cubicle was kept under positive air pressure to prevent any infectious organisms from entering through that opening. New sterile air was constantly pumped into his cubicle.

I brought a calendar for Elmo's wall so he could mark off the days. I thought marking off each day would give him a psychological lift. It would remind him how far he had come. Elmo tacked up pictures of Kathy, Maya, and Russell on the far wall of his room so he could see them from his bed.

He told me, "I want to keep pictures of the people I'm doing this for right in front of me all the time."

Wednesday, February 12, was day one, the beginning of the bone marrow transplant process. As the time approached, it reminded me of the tension I used to feel just before the kickoff when I played high school football. Outwardly, Elmo remained quite calm about everything.

"I'm just going to hunker down and get through this somehow, no matter how bad it gets," he said.

On Wednesday and Thursday the doctors gave Elmo massive doses of chemotherapy, and on Wednesday and Friday they injected him with two spinal injections of chemotherapy as well. Beginning Saturday, he was given six full days of full-body radiation. These treatments were designed to kill every last cancer cell in his body.

Elmo experienced some nausea and fatigue that first week. He talked to family and friends on the telephone and he remained his usual upbeat self when we visited him. He had an exercycle in his room and the doctors asked him to ride it regularly. He also was given a device to blow into several times a day. Both of these exercises were designed to build up his lung capacity. Elmo pumped away on that cycle for the equivalent of two miles a day. As we expressed our astonishment at how well Elmo appeared, Dr. Thomas warned us that the full effects of the chemotherapy and radiation had yet to hit Elmo.

On Thursday, February 20, one week to the day after Elmo's first treatment, Mouzetta was admitted to Swedish Hospital directly across the street from the Hutchinson Center where surgeons removed some of her bone marrow.

Mouzetta is rather small, and her bones proved hard, so the doctors really had to work to pull out 1,000 cubic centimeters of her marrow. Mouzetta's marrow, which is a slightly viscous material, was rushed to Elmo's bedside where it was put into Elmo through an intravenous catheter, much like a blood transfusion.

If successful, Mouzetta's bone marrow cells would settle in Elmo's bones, where they would begin to manufacture blood cells. In two weeks, doctors would take their first bone marrow aspiration from Elmo to determine if Mouzetta's marrow was working.

Mouzetta paid a price. She bled so profusely from all the marrow punctures she required two blood transfusions. And for at least three weeks she felt as if her hips were arthritic. She developed what the doctors and nurses call the "Hutch shuffle," a slow, painful walk.

MOUZETTA ZUMWALT WEATHERS:

I had some fears as the bone marrow transplant approached. I worried about the risks of general anesthesia, and about how I would feel after the procedure. But I mostly worried about my marrow not working in Elmo. I tried to tell myself that if it did not take, I should not blame myself.

I did not know if mental attitude could influence my body, but in the days before the transplant I began thinking of my bone marrow and telling myself that it was a good, healing marrow for Elmo. I felt those kinds of thoughts could not hurt.

The Sunday before the Thursday transplant, I suddenly had an overwhelming sense that something from me could actually save my brother's life. It was almost a spiritual feeling and I was surprised at how powerfully I felt it. I have never given birth, so donating marrow brought me as close as I have ever come to feeling I could give life to someone.

The day of the transplant, I remember being back in my room after surgery, still groggy from anesthesia. Dad was there with me and he handed me the telephone. Elmo had called.

"Mouzetta, I want to thank you and tell you how much I appreciate what you have done. I am lying here in my bed watching your beautiful red healthy bone marrow coming into my body."

ADMIRAL:

Just as the doctors had predicted, over the next several days Elmo's condition steadily worsened. He began having esophagus pain and spasms, as well as almost constant hiccups. His skin turned so red from the full-body radiation that he looked as if he had spent a day at the beach. The radiation had damaged his salivary glands, so Elmo had an excess of mucus. With no immune system to protect him, he developed mouth, throat, and esophagus sores so severe he said it felt like someone was inside his mouth with a branding iron.

He could not take too much morphine because it would impair his kidney function. Several nights he paced until dawn because of the pain. Then he could not even do that because one of the drugs he took caused the bottoms of his feet to hurt so much he could hardly stand on them. His face puffed out and in a single hour he lost all his hair. He began to bear a striking resemblance to my father.

Sometimes he was in such agony that he snapped at us. Then he would call us later on the phone to apologize. We told him no apology was needed, just get well.

He tried to help himself. He peddled his exercycle every day until he was too weak and in too much pain to do it. But no matter how bad he felt, he found a way to stagger over to the calendar and cross off another day.

The previous Christmas, Mouzetta had given Elmo a folder of pictures she had taken of him and his family, and friends, at Pinehurst. In Seattle, I continued to take my early morning jog, and always came to Elmo's room at about 6:30 AM just to check up on him. Several times I found him looking through those pictures.

Six days after the transplant, Mouzetta and I stopped by early one morning to see him. He was too groggy from fatigue and morphine to respond to us. At noon, Mouzetta and I attended a luncheon held by my company, American Medical Building. The luncheon was held for the local American Stock Exchange club. During the lunch I received an urgent telephone call from Elmo.

"Dad, maybe it's just the drugs or maybe it's psychological, but I am really feeling deeply distressed and hurt that you and Mouzetta went off to lunch and out of contact while I was suffering."

His voice sounded broken and plaintive. "Elmo, I'll be right over," I told him.

At that point, Elmo broke out laughing, having successfully pulled my leg.

ELMO:

I felt anticipation, not dread, going in for the bone marrow transplant. I kept telling myself I would fight through it as best I could. But when the side effects hit me, I realized why this procedure has been called the most punishing medical treatment known.

I have never experienced such physical agony. The way I felt shifted dramatically from minute to minute. The number of physical changes and symptoms defied imagination.

Vomiting when you have a bone marrow transplant becomes as routine as coughing when you have a cold. I constantly gargled with a medicated mouthwash to rid my mouth of bacteria. I took countless medications. I tried to urinate in the commode next to my bed one night and became dizzy and fell, gashing my head. I coughed up blood of just about every color from cherry red to black. At times, my skin itched so badly that I scratched myself until I bled. Pain was the only constant.

Vietnam was psychologically tougher because you feared for your life month after month. But throughout my time in Vietnam, I never allowed myself to think I would not survive. I never allowed myself to think I would not survive with the bone marrow transplant either. When thoughts of death crept in, or when I felt so bad that I asked myself if this is how I was supposed to feel before I died, I fought off those thoughts.

"I'm only thinking this way because of the morphine," I would tell myself.

Dad came by every morning, but sometimes I felt so terrible I did not say a word to him. He would always try to cheer me up, and tell me he loved me.

I thought of things and people I loved in life—weekends at Pinehurst, my family. I thought of what I wanted to do when I left the hospital. I thought Kathy and I would take a trip down the Pacific coast when I got out, and perhaps stay in Coronado, California, for a few weeks.

My beautiful Kathy went through the hardest part of the transplant with me. I felt her there. I could see her almost physically flinch at some of the things I suffered. I know it caused her almost as much pain as it did me. I could see her force herself not to flinch and tell herself she had to be a part of this transplant with me.

I began to fully appreciate why the doctors had said patients' families should accompany them to Seattle. You begin to feel so isolated, so much in pain, and so emotionally stressed that your family is your only link to what is real and what is worth fighting for. Seeing Kathy, Maya, and Russell were constant reminders to me of why I wanted to live.

I had established a ground rule that no one in my family could visit me unless I called them first. One night I ran a high fever. I felt a strong need to see Kathy, but I did not call her. Suddenly, she just appeared in my room. I was so happy to see her. She reached in through the plastic arms and massaged my head, neck, and shoulders and I began to relax and feel better. She asked me if I wanted her to stay the night. I said I did. She sat on the lounge chair in my room and it gave me great comfort to know she was there.

KATHY COUNSELMAN ZUMWALT:

We had had a nice dinner back at our apartment, and Elmo's dad took everyone over to Baskin-Robbins for ice cream. I do not eat ice cream, so I stayed behind. Then I began to have this feeling that Elmo needed me. I did not even bother to call him on the phone, I just walked over to the hospital, and when he saw me I could tell by the look in his eyes that he wanted me there.

I felt so happy that Elmo wanted me to stay with him that night. Elmo always tried to make things easy on us, no matter how hard it got for him. But that night he was running a fever of 105 degrees, and it gave me a great feeling to know I could help him.

I thought a lot that night, about how sad this all was, and how incredibly difficult the bone marrow transplant was on Elmo. No matter how thoroughly the doctors had prepared us, to actually see what it did to Elmo was unbelievable. His entire appearance changed. He looked like an old man, as if he had aged thirty years in the space of three or four days. It was wrenching to look at him.

I also thought how brave Elmo was, and I came to realize I never could endure a bone marrow transplant. An occasional bone marrow transplant patient has to be strapped in his bed because of thrashing so wildly in pain. I know Elmo experienced terrible pain too. He kept telling himself that he just had to take it for a while until it subsided. Compared to what some patients put their families through, Elmo was a blessing to us.

He told me that I was very strong, just like he always knew I was. I feel I am a strong person, but I also feel I drew much of my strength from Elmo. If you see someone as strong as he is, it inspires strength in you.

Maya and Russell suffered seeing Elmo go through the transplant. Maya attended the hospital school established for the children of bone marrow patients. Sister Cele, a wonderful Catholic nun, tutored Maya, but for the first time in her life, Maya, who has always been an excellent student, showed no interest in her studies. She cried often, which is unlike her. Elmo had a long talk with her and told her that he knew it was a difficult situation for her, but she still had to keep up with her schoolwork. Over the next several days, Maya began to concentrate more on her schoolwork, but I knew she still felt a lot of sadness.

Maya suffered another terrible blow when the father of a young girl with whom she had become close died from complications during his bone marrow transplant. That brought the idea of death much closer to home, and she became even sadder.

We were fortunate that Dr. Bob LaGarde of the Washington State education system had helped us find excellent special education, occupational therapy, and speech teachers for Russell at Children's Orthopedic Hospital in Seattle. But Russell went through changes that I know were caused by Elmo's situation. He began clinging to me more, and he felt threatened if I even spoke nicely to another child. I am not sure why he reacted this way, but I suspect it was caused by his fears of losing Elmo. He may have felt he could lose everyone he loved. I had no doubt that Russell realized that Elmo could die.

When Maya's friend's father died, Mouzetta and I were talking about his death in Russell's presence, and he asked us to stop. The thought of death disturbed him deeply.

When we visited Elmo at his worst, Russell would only stay in his hospital room for a couple of minutes. Then he would run out and lie down on a bench outside Elmo's room and fall asleep immediately.

I tried to find ways to cheer up Russell. His ninth birthday came while Elmo was in the hospital, and I made it a special occasion. I decorated the apartment and invited some children of friends to come. I think it made Russell feel special, but it could not erase the fears he felt.

MAYA ZUMWALT:

I felt scared that my dad might die, and worried that he was sick and in a lot of pain. That was the hardest part for me. When he was real sick, Dad didn't want us to visit him, but that was only for a couple of days. The other times I visited him a lot; many times I came alone. My school was nearby and I went to his room after classes. I would put my arms into the plastic sleeves and give him a big hug around his chest, and he held my hand. I always asked him how he felt, and I told him I wanted him to come home real soon. He would say he couldn't wait to get out of the hospital. I always told him I loved him, and he said he loved me.

My dad always kids a lot. I remember I came up to see him once after he had lost his hair. He was totally bald. I was real shocked because he had his hair when I had seen him earlier that day. Dad smiled at me and said, "How do you like my new haircut?"

I missed my school and my friends in Fayetteville, but I wanted to be with my dad more than I wanted to be back home.

ADMIRAL:

On February 26, two weeks after receiving Mouzetta's bone marrow, the doctors drew out bone marrow from Elmo for analysis. The laboratory results the next day indicated that Mouzetta's marrow was producing both red and white blood cells. It was our first positive indication that Mouzetta's bone marrow was working in Elmo's body. We were all jubilant. A major hurdle had been surmounted.

Over the next several days Elmo's daily blood analyses showed remarkable leaps in his white and red blood cell counts. His white cell count was of special interest because it meant he was producing cells for his immune system. One day his white count was 300, the next 750, and on the twenty-first day post-transplant, his white count reached 3,750. A normal white count ranges from 5,000 to 10,000. Moreover, the specific white cells responsible for fighting infections were also rising steadily. Elmo now had a functioning immune system, which sharply reduced his risk of infection. He was taken off all antibiotics three weeks after the transplant.

We also learned more good news. Mouzetta earlier had donated platelets to Elmo so his blood could clot. In some instances, although transplanted bone marrow produces red and white cells, it does not produce platelets and the patient then must receive them for the rest of his life. But Elmo also showed strong evidence of producing his own platelets.

The physical changes in Elmo were as remarkable as his climbing blood counts. The mouth sores that had pained him so much began to clear. His persistent fever came down and his hiccups became only occasional. The swelling in his face subsided.

On Monday, March 24, we gave Russell the honor of walking first into Elmo's heretofore bacteria-free bubble. It was a symbol that Elmo's immune system could now tolerate normal air and contact with people. That same day, Elmo was discharged from the Hutchinson Center. It was a time of great emotion and joyous celebration for the entire Zumwalt family.

Elmo began a period of recuperation as an outpatient in our apartment in Seattle. Part of that recuperation meant intravenous feeding nightly through his Hickman catheter, still in his abdomen, which Kathy administered so that Elmo would maintain a high caloric intake. He still faced the ongoing threat of further complications, such as pneumonia and graft-versus-host disease, and had to continue on cyclosporine and methatrexate.

Every day Elmo gained strength, and his blood counts reached the normal range. He called his friends and family every day on the telephone and continued to take regular walks to build up his endurance. Before returning to Fayetteville, he and Kathy rented a home for two months in Coronado, California, near the amphibious base where Elmo entered swift boat training seventeen years earlier. His old crewmates visited him there.

As I write these final words, it has been three and a half years since Elmo was first diagnosed as having cancer. I think back on those times during the bone marrow transplant when Elmo was at his absolute worst, so fevered, pained, and weakened that it was hard for him even to lift his head. I remember him whispering to me, "Dad, it will have to get a hell of a lot worse than this before I give up."

I take one exception to what he said. Elmo will never give up.

Before he left for Seattle, Elmo wrote private letters to Kathy, Maya, Russell, his brother and sisters, Mouza, and me. He said they should only be read in the event of his death. He phoned the members of his swift boat crew and said if he did not make it back, he wanted them all to know he thought they were a great group of men. He called Jim and Betty Caldwell and other old friends to tell them how much their friendships had meant to him.

Elmo had told me one advantage of his situation was that it allowed him to tell all the people he loved just how deeply he cared about them.

Five weeks after Elmo's transplant, I could no longer fight the urge to read his letter to me. My hands trembled and I wept as I read what were intended to be his last words to his father.

Dear Dad,

I saw the tears in your eyes as you read the letters I left the family. I know that more than anything I wrote, it was the helpless desperation and agony as death approached someone you loved that caused those tears. I have felt those feelings when Kathy's X rays discovered a spot on her brain that was inoperable.

I also knew you continued to help us with your spirit for our sake. You made a difference. You lightened our burden.

Both in Vietnam and with my cancers, we fought battles and lost. Yet, we always knew even when the battle was clearly desperate, that our love could not be compromised, and that however bad the odds, we were incapable of ever giving up.

After my death, your strong burning torch of love, which only death extinguished from my being, will light in Maya, Russell, and Kathy. Then, once again, my strongest quality, the essence of my love and its incapacity to relent, will come alive once more in the family I left behind.

How I loved you. How I would have loved to have continued to fight the battles by your side. You always made a difference. You made my last battle, the journey to death, more gentle, more humane.

I love you,
Elmo

EPILOGUE

In the weeks after Elmo's transplant, he gradually gained strength. By June, five months after the transplant, he left Seattle and he, Kathy, and the children went to Coronado, California, where Elmo had trained for his swift boat command eighteen years earlier. One of the highlights of his stay in Coronado was another reunion with his old swift boat crew. He recuperated there all summer, and in August he and his family returned to their Fayetteville home. They had been away for more than seven months.

Elmo continued to suffer ups and downs, but each week he seemed a little stronger than the week before. One benefit of returning to the East Coast was to be reunited once again with Dr. John Nanfro at the Bethesda Naval Hospital, where he went periodically to be checked. In November Elmo felt well enough to return to his law practice on a part-time basis.

By early 1987 Elmo looked so well and began to feel so well that everyone who saw him began to assume that he had beaten the odds. But in early February, a year after the transplant, Elmo began to feel ill, with fever, weakness, and chills. At first he suspected he had a virus, and indeed he seemed to get over it. A short time later, however, the symptoms returned, and it was then that Elmo's Fayetteville physician, Dr. Douglas Henley, suggested Elmo go to the hospital for X rays. The X rays revealed lymph nodes two-and-a-half times normal size in his upper right chest. There remained the possibility that the enlarged nodes were caused by an infection, but the far likelier possibility was that one of his cancers had recurred.

Within a few days Elmo flew to Bethesda Naval Hospital, where Dr. Bimal C. Ghosh, the surgeon who had performed most of his previous biopsies, once again removed a wedge of tissue for biopsy. This surgical procedure proved especially difficult because the enlarged nodes were right near Elmo's upper right lung. The lab results confirmed everyone's worst fear: Elmo again had Hodgkin's disease, the faster moving of his two cancers. Elmo had tried to prepare himself for this kind of blow because despite how well he had begun to feel, he had never allowed himself to believe he had been cured. No amount of preparation, however, could lessen the devastation that he and the whole Zumwalt family felt when they heard the news.

Elmo's symptoms during this time worried everyone, especially when they suddenly grew far more severe as his cancer raced out of control. In the space of forty-eight hours Elmo went from running a fever to suffering shaking chills, night sweats, and excruciating back pain. He looked—and felt—gravely ill.

Dr. Nanfro realized that Elmo faced a medical emergency. They had to halt the spread of the cancer quickly, or his time would be very short. Nanfro recommended a new regimen, called ABVD, a combination of four anticancer drugs. Elmo, who was not about to quit fighting, agreed.

Although Elmo was nauseated for hours after the first round of ABVD therapy, within a short time his fever, chills, and pain went away and his strength gradually returned. Elmo had come back from the brink once again.

Because Elmo's Hodgkin's disease recurred despite nine previous months of chemotherapy plus a bone marrow transplant, he realized from the outset that there was little possibility that this latest drug treatment would cure him. He did gain considerable encouragement several weeks after he began treatment, however, when he learned that his enlarged lymph nodes had receded significantly. He also had been able to tolerate the chemotherapy quite well.

Elmo is continuing to investigate other potential treatments. Because he still has not fully recovered from his bone marrow transplant, Dr. Nanfro advised against attempting another one, as has been done in several cases. He feared it held the real possibility of immediately costing Elmo his life. Recently Stanford University researchers developed a new six-drug anticancer regimen that Elmo plans to try when he completes his present course of ABVD. These six drugs, which include cis-platinum, are very potent, and will have a number of unpleasant side effects. Normally they would be given only if the cancer recurred after the ABVD regimen ended, but due to the highly unusual nature of Elmo's case, he will begin taking them right after he completes ABVD. Elmo intends to try every possible means to save his life.

Because Dr. Nanfro left the Navy in June 1987 and moved to Rome, Georgia, to begin private practice, Elmo will travel to Rome, where Dr. Nanfro will adminster these new drugs. There remains the long-shot possibility that the Stanford regimen may successfully kill off the remaining cancer cells in Elmo's body.

Elmo is also reading and consulting with doctors on psychoim-munology, a method of treatment whereby he can use his mind to battle the cancer. He is also using relaxation techniques as well as visualization therapy—in which he imagines the cancer cells in his body being destroyed—to wage this battle. This psychological ap-proach to fighting disease is based on well-established links be-tween the mind and the immune system.

As of this writing, July 1987, Elmo continues to live as normally as possible under the circumstances. He works on law cases part-time from his home, and he and Kathy have been gratified with the signs of marked improvement their son has shown in the past months. Russell now speaks in complete sentences and is able to make verbal jokes—neither of which he was able to do until very recently. He also shows clear signs of conceptual thinking. Maya, now a seventh-grader, continues to be a top student and, as before,

watches out for her father. The extended Zumwalt family visits
Elmo quite often; they continue to marvel at Elmo's courage, at
his willingness to fight, his determination to succeed in his biggest
battle.

INDEX